How to Organize a Better Conference

How to Organize a Better Conference

KEN CLAYTON

Hutchinson Business
London Melbourne Sydney Auckland Johannesburg

Hutchinson Business

An imprint of Century-Hutchinson Limited

62–65 Chandos Place, London WC2N 4NW

Century Hutchinson Group (Australia) Pty Ltd
16–22 Church Street, Hawthorn, Melbourne, Victoria 3122

Century Hutchinson Group (NZ) Ltd
32–34 View Road, PO Box 40–086, Glenfield, Auckland 10

Century Hutchinson Group (SA) (Pty) Ltd
PO Box 337, Bergvlei 2012, South Africa

First published 1986

© Ken Clayton

Set in 11 on 13 point Times by
Mathematical Composition Setters Ltd, Salisbury, UK

Printed and bound in Great Britain by
Butler & Tanner Ltd, Frome and London

British Library Cataloguing in Publication Data

Clayton, Ken
   Organize a better conference.
   1. Congresses and conventions
   I. Title
   658.4′562   AS6

ISBN 0-09-164190-X

Contents

Part 2
Where to find the information

6

Dedication
To my wife Celia

Acknowledgements

Setting down the knowledge and experience accumulated during many years of organizing conferences was a big enough task in itself. To add to that the gathering together of names and addresses from all over the world in order to make this book as comprehensive a reference work as possible and the job becomes even more demanding. Fortunately, there were many people and organizations willing to help with information for the lists. To all of them, I offer my heartfelt thanks, but perhaps most important of all, I am grateful to the people for whom I worked at Austin Rover. They gave me the opportunity to learn about the fascinating business of conference organization. At the same time, thanks are due to the production companies with whom I worked, particularly Caribiner and Roundel. Their staff taught me a great deal about the business and managed to retain a sense of humour even when faced with impossible demands.

Introduction

Within companies all over the country there are people who, while normally performing a wide variety of other tasks, are occasionally asked to do one particular job — to organize a conference. Sometimes it seems that the average conference is organized by the person who was unfortunate enough to be standing in the wrong place when the sales director realized that it was almost time for the annual sales conference. He or she gets the job on the basis that it will be 'good experience'. Very often the truth is that no one else wants to do it.

Although a few books on conference organization have been published, none appears to have been aimed specifically at helping such individuals. This book has been written for the person who has to organize a company conference for thirty or more people. Each chapter covers one aspect of conference organization, and the listings in the second part of the book provide appropriate sources of information.

Although an organizer can learn the business of producing a conference by reading the book straight through, I know that many will need to consult certain sections in isolation at times. One of the consequences of this is that some subjects are covered in two places since there is inevitably a degree of overlap between chapters. The book has been written in this way to avoid a plethora of cross-references.

I have attempted to commit to paper the accumulated experience of eight years spent organizing around fifty conferences on the client side of the business. I hope you find it of use.

Ken Clayton
Tamworth, 1986

PART I
How to organize a conference

Why a conference?

The only certain thing about the conference business is that it represents different activities to different people. The task of defining a conference is further complicated by the fact that other words are often used to describe similar events. Conferences, conventions and presentations are all roughly the same thing – meetings at which information is communicated or views are expressed or exchanged. In itself that is a very broad definition, and so it is necessary to refine it.

In general terms the 'meetings' industry can be divided into two distinct areas. *Association meetings* involve gatherings of people who are members of a professional or social association, trade union or political party. The audiences can vary from a handful to several thousands. Sometimes the meetings are organized in order to impart information about new techniques or equipment, or other matters such as new legislation which affects the members of the audience. Other association meetings give the audience an opportunity to express views on specific topics. Some of these meetings are organized for profit, such as when surgeons or bankers gather together to learn about new developments in their fields. They pay to attend but, more important, there will usually be an exhibition attached to the conference. The exhibitors pay a considerable amount of money to have prime sales prospects delivered to them 'on a plate'.

Typically, an association meeting will involve a small stage with a table on it, behind which sit the members of the association council or governing body. Slides are sometimes used, but the speakers tend to deliver dissertations on their particular specialities. There is usually very little attention paid to the staging of the event in theatrical terms. Whether or not that is the case, they usually differ in their format from the other type of conference – the corporate meeting. It is the latter type of conference that is the concern of this book.

Corporate meetings today are one of many different forms of communication available to a company and, as a result, even in a commercial environment, the term 'conference' can have various meanings. In its broadest sense, a conference is simply a meeting where views are exchanged and matters of common interest are debated. This type of meeting happens every day in the average commercial organization and, so far as this book is concerned, it is not a conference.

What we *are* concerned with is the type of event that involves an audience of more than thirty people. These are organized for a variety of reasons, but they all have at least one feature in common: they are paid for by a commercial organization and usually involve the communication of information that the sponsoring company wants the audience to understand. The audience very rarely have the opportunity to express other views.

These corporate meetings fall into three categories. Straightforward business meetings will be called to communicate the company's future business plans. A new product launch will be held to introduce a new computer, car or other product or service to the sales force or the company's customers. The third type of conference will be organized as part of an incentive trip which the participants are given as a reward.

It is claimed that around 40 000 conferences are organized by companies every year in the UK alone. That means that over one hundred separate audiences are sitting down in darkened rooms somewhere in the country every day of the year. Those audiences may be the company's staff, customers, sales force, the press or, indeed, any group with whom the sponsoring company wishes to communicate.

That is the primary purpose of the conference – *to communicate*. No matter who the audience is, they are present because the organizer wants to tell them about some aspect of its operations.

Alternatives to conferences

Of course, conferences are not the only communications medium available. Any manager working within a company today has a wide range of communications techniques at his or her disposal. Printed brochures, films, video tapes, advertising, face-to-face meetings – all of these have a role to play in communicating a message. Nevertheless they all have to be used with care. None of them can be regarded as a universal panacea. Each has a particular role within the marketing mix, and so one of the first skills to be learned by anyone organizing a conference has to be the ability to decide when to use a conference. Equally, he or she has to be able to recognize when one of the other methods of communication would be more suited to the task.

Printed materials

A printed brochure is particularly well suited to communicating a complex message that involves a considerable amount of factual detail. A brochure has an advantage over a conference in that a conference audience is unlikely to be able to remember many of the facts contained within the conference. It is generally accepted that the average audience member will remember only four or five facts in addition to a series of general impressions. One other advantage that a printed brochure has is that it is permanent. Conferences, by their very nature, are a transient medium.

On the other hand, a busy sales executive may only skim the contents of a brochure. The temptation will always be to put the brochure on one side to be read properly later. Unfortunately, later sometimes never comes. At a conference the organizer has the undivided attention of the audience for a reasonable period of time, provided they are not bored into a comatose state.

Video and film

Video tapes and film are very good for demonstrating messages in a dynamic fashion, particularly if they relate to a subject that involves movement. In that respect, they have no advantage over a conference because video and film and, if necessary, live television can be used in a conference environment for the same purpose. Where a video or film will win, however, is in their ability to be re-run over and over again. Additionally, if the audience is spread over a wide geographical area, or if it is impracticable to bring them all together in one place, video and film can be used to take the message to them.

Even so, there are disadvantages. The organizer may have no control over the conditions under which films and video tapes are seen. Even if notes are provided for the person who is presenting the film or video, there is no guarantee that the material will be introduced in the right way. It will also be difficult, if not impossible, to arouse the sort of group feelings that can be generated within a good conference.

Advertising

Advertising is designed to reach an audience that may be measured in millions. The average conference venue cannot cope with more than, at most, a few thousand; but it can deal with the subject in greater depth than the average newspaper advertisement or television commercial. So a conference is best used to communicate with a clearly defined, relatively small audience.

The question of optimum audience size is difficult to define. There have been conferences with audiences of 10 000 and more. A major car launch may be seen by a total of 15 000 people over a period of time in several different venues. But, obviously, there will come a point where the conference is not the most efficient means of communicating the message because the audience is just too big.

One of the interesting contrasts between conferences and advertising is that expenditure on the latter is often subject to very close scrutiny by senior managers and directors. While this may not please the advertising staff or the agency, it does show that there is a recognition of the importance of good advertising. This is also often the reason why advertisers undertake extensive research into the effects of their advertisements. The same is not true of conferences. Research into the effectiveness of conferences is rare. Most companies seem content to continue to spend considerable amounts of money without knowing if it has been spent wisely. Indeed, decisions to stage a conference are often taken without proper consideration of the cost of the event.

It is also true that senior company people take an interest in advertising because they all seem to consider themselves experts in that field. In this respect advertising has much *in common* with the conference business. It is surprising how many people claim to know about the subject, particularly *after* the event when an organizer will be surrounded by people only too happy to tell where he or she went wrong.

Face-to-face meetings

A series of face-to-face meetings gives the opportunity for questions to be asked and for each individual's doubts to be dealt with in a positive fashion. Against this, if a company has limited resources and needs to reach a large audience, then to deal with several hundred people in this way will take an enormous amount of time and effort.

All of these techniques have a role to play in business and it is true that a complex conference may involve the use of all of them. The event will need to be advertised to the potential audience, usually by sending invitations to attend. A brochure may be needed to back up the message of the meeting and, on occasions, a film or video tape of the conference may be distributed after the event. During the conference there will be many opportunities for face-to-face discussion outside the formal sessions.

To summarize, a conference can be seen as being the best medium for communicating a message when:

a the audience numbers are relatively small and can be clearly defined;
b there is not a mass of complex facts to be absorbed;
c the objective can be achieved with one performance to each audience;
d there is no need for detailed, two-way discussion with everyone with whom the organizer wishes to communicate.

Costs

In deciding whether or not to hold a conference, the organizer must also take into account the thorny question of costs. There are, in fact, a variety of costs which have to be considered. Some of them, like catering, are relatively easy to define; others may never be added up on paper.

For example, it takes a considerable amount of management time to organize a conference, and by that is not meant only the time of the manager responsible for the organization. Most company conferences involve directors delivering scripts, and they will have to devote time to briefing scriptwriters or to writing the scripts themselves. It will be necessary to have meetings to discuss the sequence of speakers, the content of scripts, any film or audio-visual modules and speaker support slides. Time will also have to be devoted to rehearsing the speakers.

All of this time costs the employer money, but it is very rare for this to be totally considered.

Then there is the audience. If they are the company's sales force, they will be taken away from their prime task for a period. On the other hand, it if is decided to hold the event over a weekend, there will be an unquantifiable cost in terms of staff relations. Many people regard their weekends as sacrosanct and take a very dim view of having to give them up to go to a conference.

All relevant costs must be considered by the organizer in order to establish that a conference is the most effective way of achieving the objectives. It is obvious, then, that he or she has to establish those objectives at an early stage.

Objectives

The logical thing to do, of course, is to ask the person demanding a conference what the event is expected to do. Unfortunately, the manager demanding the conference will often not have actually considered the question.

One product manager working for a very large company said that he wanted a conference. He was asked what the objectives were for the event. 'What do you mean?' he demanded. 'Well', said the conference organizer, 'What do you expect to achieve by means of the conference?' 'Look, don't mess about', replied the product manager, 'Just organize the conference for me.' Such a short-sighted attitude may seem strange but, sadly, it does exist.

No matter how it is done, a set of objectives *must* be defined in order that a positive decision can be made to organize a conference because it is the best solution to a particular problem.

It is worth remembering, too, that a conference that is staged without clear objectives is likely to be short on content. The result is almost always the opposite of what was wanted. The audience will be left wondering what it was all about, instead of feeling well-informed and motivated.

If it is decided to hold a conference because it is the best way of communicating a particular message, there are other benefits that will go hand-in-hand with the event. For example, a national sales force can happily function for years without ever coming together in one place. As a result, it is quite possible that a sales executive working in County Durham will be grappling with a problem that has already been solved by a colleague in Cornwall. If the two never meet, they may never know that they have common problems.

Added to that, bringing together a group of people who have a common interest, whether it be that they all sell the products of one company or even that they all buy them, can bring benefits related to identifying with the company.

In this, it is necessary to recognize that there can be a valuable exchange of information in the bars and at the lunch table as well as in the conference room.

All of these factors can help to improve group identity and can rekindle feelings of corporate pride. In addition, every conference that is staged makes a statement about the sponsoring company. If it is organized well and has a professional appearance to the audience, their perception of the company will be improved. In this regard it is worth remembering that a conference is very much like a swan: cool and calm on the surface, with various people paddling like crazy out of sight. There is nothing wrong with that so long as the audience never see the paddlers. That is part of the theatrical aspect of the conference business. Any problems that the organizer has are less devastating if the audience are not aware of them.

So, while it is necessary to identify clearly the objectives and make a positive decision to meet those objectives by organizing a conference instead of, say, printing a brochure, it must be remembered that there are other benefits to be gained from a professionally staged event. Indeed, a conference may be necessary for just those reasons.

Recognition events

Conferences that are staged to recognize exceptional effort are fairly common today and often form a part of an overseas trip which is a prize within an incentive campaign. It must be said, however, that these conferences are sometimes staged because an overseas trip that involves *no* element of work is viewed by the Inland Revenue as a benefit in kind. That means that the participants may be landed with a tax bill which will be calculated on the value of the trip. Under these circumstances, a conference can be regarded as work and therefore can help to reduce or even avoid the possibility of income tax being demanded.

In fact, the Inland Revenue have fairly clear ideas on how much time an individual has to spend in a conference in order that an overseas trip of this nature can be deemed to be work. As with so many tax matters, the rules vary from one office to another, so it is worth checking.

There are two benefits to be derived from this type of event. The whole of the audience is motivated to do better in the future, and the individual being recognized receives a morale-boosting public pat on the back. While most of us like to see ourselves being congratulated in print, this is usually a poor substitute for the public appreciation of the managing director and the applause of the audience.

Product launches

A conference is also a very effective way of raising and harnessing strong emotions. A product launch, for example, often has two objectives among many others. One is to inform the audience, and the other is to motivate them either to sell the product effectively or to buy it. The conference therefore has to be designed to engender enthusiasm that will last until the audience get back to their places of work, and it must also persuade them to take action.

Sales conferences

The traditional annual sales conference may happen merely because it has happened every year for the last ten years. That is not sufficient reason for repeating the exercise. The conference has to be targeted to achieve something. The organizer may have difficulty in persuading others to accept that 'getting the lads together' is insufficient reason for a conference.

If that is the only purpose of the meeting, why not dispense with the cost of the conference altogether and simply organize a seminar followed by lunch? The seminar can be used as a refresher on selling techniques and this should be much cheaper than a full-blown conference. Just as important, it should avoid the annual procession of predictable company speakers who have been heard every year, saying the same things.

This is likely to bring the organizer into the difficult area of corporate politics. It is often felt that particular individuals ought to speak. The company chairman, for example, has to deliver a 'state of the nation' address. That may be necessary if the company has enjoyed particular success or is passing through troubled times; but not if the speech is merely a repetition of what the chairman has said before. A responsible organizer should try to persuade the chairman to be an observer and not speak, even if the organizer feels he or she is on a hiding to nothing in doing this. (Of course, it may be that the chairman only makes a speech because he or she feels it is expected, and will jump at the opportunity to drop out!)

The effective organizer

The talent that a successful organizer needs above all else is the ability to organize a complex series of events. This is more important even than creativity, and is just as necessary for the event that is to be produced by an outside production company. In fact, it is easy to buy creative services. It is much more difficult to bring in organizational talent if this does not already exist; and if it does not exist, then the conference is likely to be a shambles.

It helps, too, to have a sense of theatre. Many people have described conferences as 'industrial theatre' and, although this term is frowned on in some circles, it is accurate. A conference uses many of the techniques of theatre and an understanding of these will be of considerable help.

Finally, it is necessary to be able to think clearly, quickly and logically under pressure. If the organizer can do this, there will be times when he or she is the only one around who can. When the world appears to be falling in, it is also useful to be able to exert a calming influence on others. In this, an organizer will be greatly helped if the boss can be persuaded to keep others off the organizer's back while he or she sorts out the problems.

A footnote

So the organizer's task is to define the need for a conference, determine what sort of conference is required, and then to sit in the middle, holding various strings which are steadily pulled in until they all meet on the day when the audience comes into the auditorium. If that is done in the right way, there will be a successful conference.

An organizer will find the task less trying if he or she retains a sense of humour, and notes that the following six stages of conference development are likely to be experienced:

- *Stage 1* – Euphoria
- *Stage 2* – Confusion
- *Stage 3* – Disenchantment
- *Stage 4* – The Search for the Guilty
- *Stage 5* – Punishment of the Innocent
- *Stage 6* – Distinction for the Uninvolved

Anyone who has been responsible for a number of conferences will confirm that this sequence is all too familiar. But don't let it depress you too much. At the end of a successful event, all the blood, sweat and tears will fade from the memory.

• CHECKLIST •

- **Define the communications need**
  (What needs to be communicated?)

- **Define the objectives**
  (What is to be communicated?)

- **What budget is available?**

- **Compare available communications media and only choose a conference if:**
  a the audience numbers are relatively small and easily defined
  b there is not a complex mass of detail to be absorbed
  c the message can be communicated in one performance to each part of the audience
  d there is no need for two-way discussion

2

The conference budget

Over the years conference budgets have been treated in a fairly casual fashion, for many reasons. To begin with, it is unusual for a company to employ one person whose sole task is the organization of conferences, so when it comes to establishing budgets for any given year the requirement for conferences is often overlooked. As a result, the money to pay for a conference has to be taken from elsewhere, often from the advertising budget. Added to that, some clients have not been clear about how much a conference should cost, and so have not been able to calculate how much to allow in the annual company budget. To complicate the problem further, some conference production companies are aware that inexperienced clients may be persuaded to spend more than they first intend. Indeed, some production companies have succeeded in persuading even experienced clients to spend more than they intended.

In many companies these factors persist, but improvements are being made. The attitude of clients today is becoming more professional. This change of attitude is inevitable given the current business climate where every item of expenditure has to be fully justified.

No matter what the company's attitude, defining a realistic budget is one of the most important tasks facing a conference organizer. If the calculations are wrong, then there will inevitably be an overrun, with consequences that can be catastrophic.

Calculating the budget

Work on a conference budget happens in three stages. First, the organizer has to estimate how much the event will cost. This is very much a matter of educated guesswork and involves calculating the numbers of delegates and the likely costs of the services that will be provided for them, along with the costs of producing the event. Very often, the decision to stage a conference will be made on the basis of these estimates.

It is an unfortunate fact that there are so many areas within a budget that are difficult to forecast that the novice organizer has enormous scope for making mistakes.

The second stage is to discuss the job with the various suppliers and to get firm quotations. This will enable the organizer to refine the original budget into a working budget. In most cases some degree of adjustment will have to be made to the original budget, reducing the allowances for some elements to compensate for underestimating the costs of others. The budget will now become more reliable and can be used to keep a firm control on expenditure.

The third stage happens as work progresses. There will inevitably be budget changes as modifications are made to the event, and it is necessary to keep track of all of the changes.

Costs fall into the following broad categories:

1 Readily definable items, some of which are dependent upon the number of delegates. For example, the costs of travel, catering and bedrooms are relatively easy to calculate. Similarly, room hire for the conference venue will be reasonably easy to define.
2 Falling into the 'how long is a piece of string' category are the costs of producing the conference, and other items like the cabaret, if there is to be one.
3 Finally there are the costs that are often hidden, such as the expense account items charged by staff. One that is very rarely included is the cost of client staff time.

Stage One: The estimated budget

Food, drink and bedrooms
The first factor to define is the number of people who will have to be fed and accommodated. It is very easy to fix this as the number of delegates who are likely to accept an invitation. In fact, there are many others who may attend and therefore swell the numbers. Delegates' partners, company hosts, sales personnel and the conference crew can all add substantially to the total numbers of bodies at a conference.

Calculating the numbers of people who will attend will form the basis for calculating many parts of the budget, but it is also necessary to establish what the client is to pay for and what bills will be paid by the delegates and others at the conference.

If the client is going to pay for overnight accommodation for the delegates, then it is necessary to decide how many nights' accommodation is to be provided. With meals and drinks, which are more difficult items to forecast, the organizer has first to decide what is to be provided and then estimate the costs involved.

Once these factors are known, then rough estimates of the cost of individual elements can be multiplied by the number of people attending the event to obtain a total catering and accommodation budget.

For example, if 200 delegates are going to be accommodated for one night, then they will be likely to be given coffee on arrival, a cocktail party followed by dinner, overnight accommodation, breakfast, morning coffee and lunch, possibly again with drinks beforehand. Guide prices for food, beverage and bedrooms can be provided by the venue and these can then be multiplied by 200 in order to arrive at a total.

Some venues, of course, will quote a daily conference rate which includes coffee and all meals. If this is the case, then the type of menu being offered must be considered since the menus included in the conference rate may not be acceptable and changing them may affect the conference rate.

If a venue has not been selected, then the organizer has first to establish a guide price for each of the individual elements in the area that he is likely to go to.

It is also necessary to know how the costs incurred by company staff are going to be handled. If the cost of accommodation and catering is going to be cross-charged to other departments, then there will be no effect on the conference budget of having large numbers of staff in attendance. Of course, this is a fairly foolish exercise from the company's point of view because it means that the total cost of the event may never be known. Since the cost of taking staff to a conference has to be paid by the company, the real reason for this sort of cosmetic operation can only be to conceal the real costs of the conference.

The effect of Value Added Tax
It is worth remembering that, in the UK at least, most of these costs will be defined by the tax authorities as 'entertaining', and VAT must therefore be included since it will not be reclaimable. On the other

hand it is asserted by some people that outside contractors who are producing work to be used overseas do not need to charge VAT, even if the bill is being paid in the UK and the work is to be shown to a UK-based audience.

To a degree this is academic in most areas except those involving entertainment. However, as in most areas of taxation, this is potentially extremely difficult to clarify and so is probably best left to the finance staff to sort out. Where finance staff are not available to provide this service, the local Customs and Excise Office will give a ruling. As with everything concerning either Income Tax or VAT, different offices will give different rulings and so it is vital that the local office is asked for their views.

Travel costs
The costs of delegate travel are relatively easy to define on the same basis as catering and accommodation. If the organizing company is going to pay for delegates to fly to an overseas location, a guide price for flights can be defined and multiplied by the number of delegates.

In order to calculate an initial budget, the safest course is to take the price of a scheduled flight and use that as a basis for the travel element of the budget. It is true that an organizer who is taking significant numbers of people to an overseas destination will be able to negotiate a discounted price. It is also true that, if there are enough delegates to warrant a special charter, this will be cheaper than taking the same number of people on scheduled flights. However, until discussions are begun with airlines, scheduled prices will provide a degree of latitude to avoid seriously underestimating the cost.

Obviously, as work progresses, more accurate costings will be needed and these can be obtained from the airline or the travel agent.

Print budget
To some extent the cost of print can be added in fairly easily too, since most companies will have someone who can take an educated guess at the cost of the various items of printed material that will be needed.

It is necessary, again, to work out what printed items will be required in order that the calculation can be made. This is also an area in which some companies unwittingly hide costs if all print is paid for out of the print buyer's budget.

If the organizer does not have the services of a print buyer available, then he or she must talk to a printer in order to get a guide on the costs of the various items needed. The most likely items are dealt with in Chapter 7.

Production costs

All of the above is reasonably straightforward. Estimating the costs of conference production is an altogether more complex matter.

There is really no simple formula for this since there are so many different variables. The type of venue to be used is a major factor. A 'black box' environment like an exhibition hall, for example, will be more expensive than a traditional theatre style venue. This is because everything has to be brought in. Stage, sound, lighting, seats, walls for the conference auditorium area, carpeting and all the other items that already exist in a theatre will have to be paid for separately. Against that, the 'black box' does give more flexibility. Overseas venues will affect production costs, too, although occasionally that effect will be beneficial because some towns overseas do not charge for the use of conference rooms.

The balance between film, video, audio-visual and live speakers will also dramatically affect the costs. Once again, it is difficult to give even rule-of-thumb guidelines for these since prices will vary, depending on where the work is done and who does it. For example, some film production companies will say that, for budgeting purposes, 16 mm film will cost in the region of £2500 for each projected minute. Others will quote more, some will quote less and, if the film is to require overseas locations or extensive special effects, it will be more expensive still.

Audio-visual modules are just as difficult to cost out in the early stages of budgeting. Again, some companies will advise allowing £1500 for each minute of time on screen. Others will advise less or more. There is no fixed price. In addition, if it is envisaged that there will be a significant amount of computer graphics, for example, then the budget needs to be substantially higher.

The cost of speaker support slides is equally difficult to calculate. Some companies will quote an average of £25 to £30 per slide. Others will be substantially cheaper and, to complicate matters still further, some production companies will suggest more slides for a ten-minute script than others. The same applies when a production is being handled in-house, because some speakers will want more slides than others. In either case, it is worth calculating that the budget will allow, say, twenty-five slides for a ten-minute script and then stick to that. One of the phrases that any conference organizer has to learn and repeat is: 'We can't afford any more.'

So, it can be seen that it is very difficult to calculate the cost of all the production elements within a conference. While it may be possible to say that there will be two films, each of ten minutes duration, along with three speakers, each of whom is going to be on his feet for ten minutes, and calculate the rough cost of that, the extra costs of set building, sound, light, projection and any staging tricks will be much more difficult to estimate. Once again, there is no guide that can be given for calculating these parts of the event. What it comes down to is that the organizer must ask what figure would represent a reasonable maximum acceptable cost. For example, if the conference is being staged to launch a new product that has cost millions of pounds in research and development, then the production budget may well run into six figures on the basis that such expenditure can be justified in order to give the product a good sales start.

Nevertheless there is one way of estimating the production cost. This relates to the numbers in the audience. For example, the total production costs for a business conference for 100 people can be cheaper than one with an audience of 1500. The reason for this is that everything for the larger audience needs to be bigger. The auditorium has to be larger and so the stage is likely to be bigger. That will usually mean that a bigger set has to be built to fill it. More lights will be needed and a more powerful sound system will have to be installed. As a result, the total budget has to be increased. However, if that budget is expressed as a cost per head of audience, it may well be that the *unit cost* of the bigger conference is lower then for the smaller event. It is impossible to give cost per head guidelines; but, instead of calculating the total budget first, an organizer may find it easier to establish how much he or she thinks is reasonable to pay to make sure that each delegate gets the message. That sum is then multiplied by the numbers of people attending in order to establish a rough production budget.

Thus, if it is decided that it is worth spending £75 per person on the production of a conference for 200, the rough budget would be £15 000.

Cabaret costs

The other major variable cost will be the cabaret, if there is to be one. These are becoming much more common features of the company conference and the likely cost has to be calculated at an early stage. It is a question of deciding what sort of cabaret is wanted. If the client wants the delegates to go home having been entertained by several big television names, then higher prices must be expected. Internationally known cabaret 'artistes' tend to command fees that look like telephone numbers.

It is worth remembering that some agents tend to inflate prices when a well-known industrial name is behind the booking. One way to find out how much an act is worth is to get to know someone who works in light entertainment, who may be prepared to divulge prices paid elsewhere. However, in order to find out how much it will cost to stage a cabaret, it is necessary to decide how much the company is prepared to spend on entertaining each delegate in this way. As a rough guide, it may be that the company is prepared to pay the equivalent of the cost of a good seat to see a West End show; but this price will not buy a cabaret made up of well-known television names — for that, the price per seat has to be lifted by perhaps as much as 50 per cent.

If money is limited it is worth remembering that a good after-dinner speaker may be more effective than a 'cheap' cabaret. The aim must be to send the delegates away feeling that they have been well-entertained, whichever route is chosen.

Contingencies

Generally speaking, at least 10 per cent of the budget should be defined as a contingency to cope with the almost inevitable unexpected costs. If the finance department of the client company is short-sighted enough to refuse to allow a contingency, then it must be built in by some other means. In other words, the sums allowed for each part of the budget must be inflated by 10 per cent. The organizer should also know how the finance people will react to his budget. In many companies there is a well-defined process of asking for 15 per cent more money than will be required in the certain knowledge that the budget allowed will be 15 per cent less than the sum demanded. This is a matter of local conditions which each organizer will have to determine.

Hidden costs

Every conference involves hidden costs. These will include the cost of time spent on the organization of the conference, along with the expense account items that employees charge as a result of attending. The way in which these are to be handled depends entirely on the company policy. It may be that they choose to ignore them. While this makes life easy, it means that the true cost of the event can never be seen. The advantage of the client understanding the real cost of a conference is that it may instil a more professional approach to the subject, and that has to be an advantage.

The effect of outside organizations
Inevitably, outside organizations will become involved at some stage, even if the conference is organized in-house. Their impact on the budget should be calculated too.

For example, if the conference is to be staged overseas, a ground agent will help to smooth over some of the myriad problems that will occur. The agent's costs have to be included; and they can be quite substantial, particularly if there is some form of orientation tour included in the programme. These costs are often quoted as a cost per delegate. As a result, even if a ground agent only charges £10 per delegate for a conference for 200, the bill will be quite substantial.

If a UK travel agent is used to arrange flights for the delegates, then the fee will usually come as a commission from the airline; but there may be some extra costs, depending on what the agent is asked to organize. In fact, if the first estimated budget for travel is calculated on the basis of scheduled fares, there should be sufficient leeway to allow for most of the extra items that a travel agent may be asked to provide.

Forgettable costs
In compiling this first budget, it is very easy to overlook some items. For example, the cost of hiring the conference room, for installing the show as well as running it, transporting the set and equipment to the venue, transporting, accomodating and feeding the crew, travelling to the venue for site surveys and the cost of electrical power are all among the budget costs that are easy to forget.

Transport
If the event is to be staged any distance from the base at which it is created, then transport can be a significant factor. It is also one of the areas in which the client often feels tempted to cut costs by using his own transport. This is a subject that must be approached with extreme care.

While it is true that the average client company probably does transport goods around the country – and may even export them – taking a conference to any venue is a specialized job. Trailers, for example, have to be chosen to be capable of being manoeuvred into the unloading area at the venue. They have to be of a type that allows the easy unloading of equipment. Much of this will be in metal cases on wheels and so a ramp is needed to get them off the trailer. Specialized vehicles may be needed for electrical equipment to ensure that it reaches the venue undamaged.

If the event is to be staged abroad, then the driver has to be conversant with the intricacies of the appropriate Customs documentation and must know how to deal with the Customs authorities in different countries.

In short, as some very large clients have found in the past, trying to save money on transport can result in extra costs in the long run. One client decided that he could save money by hiring the transport himself. The conference was taking place abroad and, when the trucks arrived to be loaded up with all the equipment for the show, they turned out to be refrigerated vehicles that usually carried soft fruit. There were no fixings inside which could be used to secure all the equipment. Added to that, the drivers were not familiar with the documentation that they were given. That was bad enough, but, when it came to bringing everything home, the fruit market had picked up and so a proportion of the trucks did not arrive for the return journey. In the end, this attempt to save money resulted in a great deal of aggravation and some extra expenditure.

Crew costs
The question of crew costs is also one that gives rise to grumbles from clients. The fact is that good sound and lighting engineers, riggers, showcallers and all the other specialists involved in running a show are expensive to hire. Even so, they are usually worth their fee because they will do everything they can to make the show a success.

The question of their on-site costs is less easy to explain. What it amounts to is that, even if the client pays all hotel and meal costs, the crew will expect a daily expense allowance, referred to as *per diems*. The amount will depend on where the show is to be staged. *Per diems* in Geneva will be more than in Harrogate for the simple reason that prices are higher in Geneva. The official reason for *per diems* is that a member of the crew working away from home will need to get laundry done, make phone calls home and buy drinks in bars because he cannot put his feet up in front of the television as he would at home.

The only advice that can be offered in this instance is to haggle with the production company and agree a price. It should be remembered that the crew may be less willing to pull out all the stops for the client if the level of *per diems* is too low. The degree of unrest that can be created by the parsimonious client can be so bad as to mean that the level of *per diems* has to be increased on-site. Unless other costs are cut back to compensate, this will mean a budget overrun.

Site surveys
Site surveys are another part of the planning process and no client should object to paying for them. They are a good insurance against things going wrong during the conference. When things do go wrong, costs almost inevitably rise. This aspect of planning a conference is far from being the brief holiday that some clients believe it to be. It is the only opportunity the client will have to check the facts that have been presented in brochures. These are notoriously unreliable in some places and the client must check the facts.

Venue hire
One other factor that an inexperienced client can easily overlook is the length of time for which the venue is to be hired. Adequate time must be allowed for rigging and rehearsing the show before the audience comes in. Even the simplest of shows will need at least half a day to set up properly and the rest of the day and the evening to rehearse. Sufficient time must also be allowed to pull the set out at the end. This does not need to be as much as is allowed for the get-in. One show in the National Exhibition Centre in Birmingham took nearly seven weeks to rig. It was ripped out in a matter of a few days. Even so, cutting down on this time will affect the quality of the finished show.

The same applies to the cabaret. If this is to be a polished affair, then adequate time must be allowed at least for the sound engineer to balance the sound system for the artists and the room, and for the lighting technician to find out where light is needed and when.

Office equipment
It is necessary to include the cost of providing office equipment that will be needed on-site. If the event is to be held overseas, it may make sense to hire items like photocopiers and typewriters locally (provided the typewriters have English keyboard layouts!). Directors and senior staff who are attending a conference will probably need to

continue their day-to-day work, especially if they are away from the office for any length of time, and the equipment for this has to be provided.

Some venues also charge for the installation of telephone lines, and the cost of telephone calls is obviously an extra item. So there needs to be a miscellaneous section of the budget to cover these things.

Insurance

The equipment that is used in a conference is often extremely expensive to replace should it be lost, stolen or damaged. Losses of major items of equipment are fairly rare but, sadly, the risk of theft is not. Damage is also possible while the equipment is in transit to and from the venue. So it is worth finding out whether the company supplying the equipment has insurance cover for all these risks. If they do not, then it may be a matter of the client paying for the necessary cover.

The backstage area of a conference can be a hazardous place, with cables lying around, lights being hauled up into the roof and unexpected obstructions waiting in the darkness. If a freelance rigger or dancer were to fall over and hurt themselves, then they could be unable to work for some time. Once again, the client's liability in such a case must be considered and insured against.

Incidentally, it is fairly common practice for there to be a celebration for the crew after a successful conference. After such a celebration at one conference, a rigger fell and was disabled for some time. Because alcohol had been provided for the crew, the insurance company withdrew cover and a long legal battle resulted.

Delegates, too, can be injured, so any insurance policy should also cover them.

The final insurance factor to be considered is the abandonment of the event for reasons outside the organizer's control. A major air traffic controllers' strike, for example, may make it impossible to get the delegates to the venue. Whatever the client decides to do as a result will almost certainly cost money. It may be possible to insure against this type of eventuality.

Simultaneous interpretation

If the audience is to include delegates from other countries, it may be necessary to allow for simultaneous interpretation. The cost of this will depend on the facilities at the venue to some extent. If there are no interpretation facilities available on-site, the necessary equipment will have to be hired. In addition, of course, the interpreters will have to be hired.

The number that will be needed will depend on the number of languages to be used. Two interpreters will be needed for each language into which the text is to be translated. This is because the mental concentration needed requires that an interpreter works for thirty minutes and then relaxes for thirty minutes. The cost of hiring them will depend on a variety of factors, and the best way to get a guide price is to talk to one of the agencies providing interpreters.

Stage Two: The working budget

Production companies' budgets

A rough estimate of the overall cost of the event having been made, it is necessary to begin refining the budget in the light of firm quotations. This will involve entering into detailed negotiations with all the suppliers.

Quotations will have to be obtained from the venue, the hotel, the production company, the travel agent and any other companies who will be supplying goods or services. (Negotiations with the venue and hotel form such a major part of this process that they are dealt with separately in Chapter 6.)

If an outside production company is to be used, then their production budget will form a major part of the overall budget. They should present a breakdown of their costs at a very early stage. The way in which this is done will vary from one company to another. Some will quote on the basis of time put in by their staff and, if the staff need to put in more time, then the cost will go up. Other companies quote on the basis that they can produce the show at a certain price and, unless there is a fundamental change to the show, this is the price that will be charged. Production companies gain their profit in two ways: they will charge a production fee in addition to 'marking up' the cost of bought-in equipment and services.

The production budget should therefore be analysed against the known factors. If a ten-minute film is shown as costing only £5000 then the production company should be asked to explain how that cost has been determined. Sitting back in the belief that you have got a bargain will usually result in a budget overrun. Similarly, if speaker support material is shown as allowing for only ten slides in a fifteen-minute speech, an explanation is called for since most speakers will need at least one slide every thirty seconds.

When it comes to the set, sound and lighting equipment, although it may not look like it, the client is actually only hiring the majority of the equipment and materials. Stage flats (the pieces used to build the walls of the set), rostra, carpet, lecterns, screens – all will usually be on hire, as will all the hardware used in the show.

An outside production company will probably want to be paid in stages. The reason for this is that its cash flow is probably not all that it should be, usually because clients take so long to pay their bills. In addition, most of them are relatively small. As soon as they begin work on a show, they will have to begin paying their suppliers. Conferences usually take several months from conception to completion and so, unless the client provides some cash, the companies can find themselves unable to fund the development work.

The way in which the stage payments are worked out is very much a matter for discussion between the client and the production company. Neither company should be expected to fund the other, so the size of the payments should be calculated on the basis of the amount of work that the production company is having to pay for at each stage of the production process. Monthly stage payments are probably appropriate.

A properly calculated and laid out production budget should be very comprehensive and will take some time to peruse, digest and argue about. What the client should be aiming for is a price which includes all the cost elements in order that no one can come after the event with unexpected bills.

So far as the other suppliers are concerned, the organizer has to be sure that they understand precisely what is wanted and quote on that.

Air travel
There is little advantage in approaching airlines direct. Some will not deal with the organizer without involving a travel agent. Even if they will, the organizer is unlikely to be able to get a better price than a travel agent, and he will be making a considerable amount of work for himself which the travel agent is better equipped to do. After all, the travel agent will be paid a commission by the airline, and it is that fee that pays for his efforts.

Obtaining competitive quotes for air travel can be difficult. Some airlines claim that they will always quote the same price to different travel agents bidding for the same job. That should not prevent the travel agent obtaining quotes from more than one airline. If the organizer's company has an officially appointed travel agent, then he or she may have to work through them. The danger with this is that they do not all recognize the differences between company travel, conference travel and inclusive package holidays, so the organizer has to be sure that the travel agent knows what is required.

The ground agent
Ground agents do vary in their abilities and their prices. If more than one reliable ground agent can be found at the destination, then competitive prices should be obtained.

Stage Three: Controlling the budget

No matter how carefully the organizer constructs the budget, there will often be extra costs. The trick is to keep track of them and to have sufficient funds available to cope with them. This is part of stage three of the budgeting process.

If the planning has been done properly and no one calls for extra wine or orders cigars and drinks for all the delegates when there was no budget allowance for them, the catering and accomodation costs should not rise.

On the production side, the client should set up a system, either in-house or with the production company, to keep track of any changes to the budget which should only be brought about by the client making changes to the show. Obviously, if an extra film is added after the production budget has been agreed, the money for it has to be found from somewhere. Under such circumstances, it is the conference organizer's responsibility to warn whomever is demanding the change that there will be an extra cost involved.

This will mean that he or she has to persuade the company supplying the goods or services affected by the change to communicate roughly how much any change will cost as soon as possible. The client can then decide if the change is important enough to warrant the increase. This same system can be used to keep the client informed if the budget has been reduced. It does happen sometimes and it is worth knowing about it because that money may be needed elsewhere.

Tipping
An area that can be one of the most difficult to handle for a big company is the question of 'extra fees' to get things done. Stories abound in the industry of foreign Customs men demanding payments for 'paperwork'. Sometimes these are matched by open demands for cash inducements. Needless to say, receipts for these items are very rare.

Sometimes it will also be necessary to pay out cash tips to people in the hotels or the conference venue in order to get work done quickly. This appears to be very much the case in the USA, where some venues are very heavily unionized. This will often mean that the union has to be paid off in order that the necessary work can be done. It is very difficult to account for these items on the standard expenses form. It is an unfortunate fact that this sort of expenditure is sometimes necessary, especially if things have to be done in a hurry. It is worth sorting out beforehand how it is to be handled.

Reducing costs
Inevitably, there will be pressures brought to bear to reduce costs. There are indeed, some areas where this is possible.

Obviously, when an outside company buys in goods or services, they will add on a percentage before passing the cost on to the client. It may be possible for the client to arrange for some of the items to be paid direct. This will immediately reduce costs. Although this can be a workable option, it must be made clear to all concerned that the instructions to the supplier will still come from the production company.

Revenue
The organizer must not forget that it can be possible to earn revenue which can be offset against the cost of the event. Some conferences are set up as profit earners, and so delegates are charged a fee which must allow for all of the budget costs to be covered with the required amount of profit being shown at the end. As mentioned in Chapter 1, this is more often a feature of association meetings; but it is possible for corporate meetings organizers to learn something from the association meetings side of the business. In the motor industry, for example, it is now more acceptable for manufacturers to ask their dealers for a contribution to the costs of staging the conference. The trick here is to avoid saying that the fee is for any identifiable part of the event. By this means, the problem is avoided of dealers who

live close to the venue wanting to reduce their contribution because they will not be staying overnight.

Companies in other areas may also feel that they can charge their audience for attending a conference in this way. If they can, this can make a significant contribution to the budget. Obviously, if the conference is being held abroad, the level of contribution requested can be substantially higher than for a UK-based event. This is one of the factors that can make an overseas event more cost-effective.

There may be other companies who are interested in talking to your audience, and they may be prepared to pay for the privilege. For example, a finance house that wants to promote its services to the delegates can be asked to sponsor a cocktail party or a meal. Similarly, if there is to be an exhibition as part of the conference, outside organizations that want to promote services or goods to the delegates can be charged a fee in return for space within the exhibition.

These are all legitimate ways of reducing the costs for the client; but, in the end, the most important advice for the client is to make sure that every item in the budget is fully understood. No respectable production company, hotel or conference centre should object to having to explain how their costings have been calculated.

Use of a computer
All of the above may sound complicated and will take time to work out. However there is one way to reduce the amount of time taken to calculate the budget and, at the same time, reduce the scope for mistakes.

Many client companies today have some form of computing capability. If a standard spreadsheet program such as Visicalc is used, then the time taken to calculate the budget can be reduced. For example, the budget for a major product launch can take as much as half a day or more to calculate. By using a computer, this can be reduced to around thirty minutes or so.

At the same time, a formalized method of calculating a budget can ensure that items are not forgotten. For example, it is not unknown for an organizer to forget to double the hotel room costs because delegates are to be provided with two nights' accommodation. It is obviously important to remove the possibility of such mistakes.

Records
Even if a computer is not used, then a standard conference budget calculation form should be devised to make sure that no costs are

Sample food and accommodation budget calculation form

Date budget calculated...

Name of event...

Date of event...

Venue...

Budget calculated by...

Numbers to be catered for:
A. Number of delegates   ......
B. Number of partners   ......
C. Number of company personnel ......
D. Number of suppliers' personnel ......
                                 ‾‾‾‾‾‾
E. Total number of people
    (A + B + C + D)   ......

Bedrooms needed:
F. Total number of singles   ......
G. Total number of twins   ......
H. Total number of suites   ......

I. Number of nights per delegate ......

J. Cost of single per night   £.....
K. Cost of twin per night   £.....
L. Cost of suite per night   £.....

Total accommodation costs:
M. Single rooms (J × F × I)   £.....
N. Twin rooms (K × G × I)   £.....
O. Suites   (L × H × I)   £.....
                                 ‾‾‾‾‾‾
P. Total (M + N + O)   £.....

Catering cost per person:
Q. Breakfast   £.....
R. Coffee   £.....
S. Lunch   £.....
T. Dinner   £.....
                                 ‾‾‾‾‾‾
U. Total catering cost per person
    (Q + R + S + T all × I)   £.....

V. Total catering cost
    (U × E)   £.....

W. Total accommodation and catering
    (P + V)   £.....

overlooked. This form should allow the organizer to put in writing the assumptions that were made in calculating the budget. Six months after the budget has been calculated it is very easy to forget how certain figures were arrived at. By writing it all down this problem can be avoided. The sample calculation form shown here for the food and accommodation budget can be extended to cover the production budget etc.

Even more important is to put everything in writing to suppliers. No matter how well they are known, if figures are not put down on paper, suppliers have far too much scope for misunderstanding what the client was prepared to pay. They should never be given that opportunity.

A footnote

In summary, then, the budget should be calculated by defining the number of delegates; defining the delegate costs that the client is going to pay; calculating the amount that the client is willing to pay for the production of the conference and other variables like cabarets; and then, most important of all, making sure that everyone understands exactly what is being paid for and how much it will cost.

The points that have been covered here on budgeting can be taken to apply to even the biggest of conferences. However, every manager who is told to organize a conference must approach it in a structured fashion. While the sums of money involved in a one-day sales conference for a small audience will be less, if the manager constantly exceeds the budget on that sort of event, the finance department are likely to begin casting doubts on his or her ability. So the approach has to be the same for every conference, no matter how big or small it is.

• CHECKLIST •

- Establish the estimated budget

- Define the numbers of people attending:
    - *a* how many delegates?
    - *b* how many delegates' partners?
    - *c* how many staff and hosts?
    - *d* how many crew?

- Is overnight accommodation to be provided? If it is:
  - a single or double rooms?
  - b how many nights per person?

- Estimate cost of:
  - a single rooms
  - b double rooms
  - c suites

- Calculate total accommodation costs

- What food and beverage will be provided?
  - a breakfast?
  - b morning coffee?
  - c pre-lunch drinks?
  - d lunch?
  - e wine with lunch?
  - f afternoon coffee?
  - g cocktail party?
  - h dinner?
  - i wine with dinner?
  - g after-dinner bar?

- Estimate cost of those items to be provided

- Identify items on which VAT is not reclaimable

- Calculate cost of food and beverage for each delegate including VAT where appropriate

- Multiply delegate food and beverage cost by number of delegates

- Decide what travel is to be provided:
  - a coaches?
  - b train (either chartered or scheduled)?
  - c aircraft (either chartered or scheduled)?

- Estimate travel cost per delegate

- Multiply individual travel cost by the number of delegates

- Identify items of print needed:
  - a initial letter notifying delegates of conference
  - b official invitation
  - c delegate pack
  - d room packs
  - e delegate badges

  f daily schedules
  g menu cards for each meal
  h place cards
  i transcripts of speeches
  j product information packs

- Estimate cost of print

- Establish reasonable cost per delegate for conference production

- Multiply cost per delegate by the number of delegates

- Establish whether entertainment is needed

- If it is, establish reasonable cost per delegate

- Multiply cost per delegate by the number of delegates

- Establish likely daily cost of meeting room hire

- Establish the number of days for which the meeting room will be needed

- Multiply daily cost by number of days

- Estimate cost of transport for equipment

- Establish likely daily expenses allowance for each member of crew

- Multiply daily allowance by the number of crew and by the number of days on-site

- Estimate cost of site surveys

- If simultaneous interpretation is needed, estimate cost

- Add figures together and then calculate 10 per cent for contingencies

- Add contingency to total

- If delegates are to be asked to contribute to the costs, calculate revenue

- Deduct revenue from total to provide estimated working budget

- When production company and venue is known obtain firm quotation from all suppliers to provide actual working budget

- Establish a means of controlling the budget

3

The venue

One of the most difficult problems that any conference organizer faces, no matter how experienced he or she may be, is that of finding a suitable venue. This is not made any easier by the number of hotels and conference centres which all claim to be the answer to an organizer's prayers. In reality the chances of any of them being exactly right for a specific conference are very remote. Indeed, some of them may not even be suited to staging a corporate conference of any sort. Inexperienced organizers can also find difficulty in obtaining information about venues; and even when information is forthcoming it is often inaccurate or incomplete.

There are many different types of structure that are used for conferences. Hotels and conference centres are the most common, but stately homes, exhibition centres, marquees, film studios and many other buildings have been pressed into service in the past and will undoubtedly serve the needs of organizers again in the future. What the organizer has to do is to find a way of narrowing the choice in order to select the venue that most closely meets the need.

This is done in four stages. The first is to decide the geographical location; the second is to establish the criteria that a venue has to meet; the third is to carry out paper research in order to compile a short-list of possible venues; and finally, visits to the venues on the short-list will have to be arranged.

Choosing the location

In theory the organizer has available all of the conference facilities in the world from which to choose. In fact, the choice will be limited for a variety of reasons.

The budget

Using an overseas venue will usually be more expensive than using one in the home country because of the extra cost of transport. However, there are exceptions.

Some overseas venues will provide conference facilities at no charge. That will obviously help to offset the extra cost of travel. The timing of the conference can also help to reduce the cost of an overseas venue, because if the conference is to take place at a time that is out of season – for somewhere like Monte Carlo, for example – then the hotel rates that can be negotiated may be better than could be obtained in the home country.

In addition, if the organizer is going to ask delegates for a contribution to the cost of running the event, it may be possible to ask more for an overseas conference than for one at home.

Policy

Some companies have a policy of not taking conferences overseas. If the company makes a great publicity point of being British-based and making British products, using an overseas venue may seem to be out of line with the overall thrust of the publicity and so the choice will be limited to UK venues.

Attraction

Delegates can be more willing to give up time to attend a conference in an exotic location, and so using an overseas venue can make the event more effective because more of the target audience will attend. In some cases the conference will form part of an incentive campaign and these almost always use overseas locations as an enticement to better performance. On the other hand, some delegates may be reluctant to devote extra time to attending an overseas event and so will prefer a home-based conference.

Weather

If the event is to be held during the winter months, the organizer may want to use a venue where the weather is more reliable than at home. Conferences have been disrupted by heavy falls of snow in Britain in January. Similarly, if the conference is to be during the summer, southern Europe can be uncomfortably hot.

Proximity to Head Office

Conferences often involve directors and senior managers who are reluctant to be away from their offices for any length of time. This may mean that the venue has to be close to Head Office.

Factory visits

If a factory visit is to be an integral part of the conference, then the venue obviously has to be close to the factory, whether this is in Birmingham or Munich.

Risks of overseas venues

There are some aspects of using an overseas venue that involve an increased risk. Any event that relies on air travel is more likely to be upset than a UK-based event. There are a wide range of events that can delay or cause the cancellation of flights, ranging from strikes to bad weather. In addition, overseas venues often carry other risks: power supplies in some regions are notoriously unreliable; customs authorities can delay equipment; and most overseas locations will be working on a different time to the company's offices at home, making it difficult to get hold of people on the telephone.

Few of these potential problems are insuperable, but the organizer has to recognize their existence when choosing between a UK and an overseas venue.

Travelling in the UK

If the factors are pointing towards a UK destination, then the organizer has to consider the question of travel to and from the venue.

If the audience is coming from all over Britain, then it may be appropriate to search for a venue in the midlands. Alternatively, the organizer may decide to settle for a venue that is easily reached by air from the more remote parts of the country.

If the audience is coming in from abroad, then it will probably be best to use a venue near to an airport with scheduled services to those countries from which the delegates will be travelling.

Travelling abroad

When an overseas location is preferred, the organizer has to consider the length of time that the delegates will be at the conference in order to narrow the choice.

Long-haul destinations like North America and the Far East are best for conferences that will last for at least five days. It takes at least a day to recover from the effects of time changes and jet lag. Incidentally, it should be remembered that jet lag has a greater effect when travelling from west to east.

If the conference is to include no more than two nights in the venue, then the flying time should be limited to no more than three hours. When time is added on for the check-in and transfers from the destination airport to the hotels, a journey such as this will involve around five hours travelling.

One-night conferences are best limited to locations that are no more than an hour or so from the UK. Destinations like Amsterdam, The Hague and Paris are obvious possibilities for this type of conference.

Establishing the criteria

Having narrowed down the choice of destinations to either the UK or overseas, it is now necessary to set out the criteria that the venue will have to meet. These fall into two areas — the venue itself and the hotels.

Venue criteria

Most conferences involve gathering the audience together before the event starts. From there, they will enter an auditorium of some sort for the conference itself. In addition, an area for catering and space for an exhibition will often be needed.

When the organizer begins the process of selecting the venue, he or she needs to consider all of these criteria to establish what is needed in each of them. Some conferences will require special facilities. For example, a car manufacturer launching a new product may want to provide the opportunity to drive it. Other companies may want to include a factory visit in the programme. All these elements have to be marshalled into a list of criteria to be met.

These criteria will fall into two categories. There will be some features without which the event cannot take place. The existence of others will enhance the conference but they are not vital. So what is likely to be required of a conference venue?

Gathering space

The audience for most conferences will arrive over a period of time. This may vary from an hour or more if they have had to travel any distance, to a few minutes. Either way, it will usually be necessary to hold them before opening the doors to the auditorium. Very often they will need to be given coffee at this point.

So a gathering space or foyer is needed and this must be capable of taking the full audience. Unfortunately, some venues do not have this facility and some form of compromise may have to be accepted. This may involve taking a section of a public area and turning that into a reception. There is a danger, under these circumstances, of the public becoming mixed up with the audience. That must be avoided. Apart from the confusion caused by an individual who only came to buy tickets for a pop concert finding him or herself sitting in the auditorium, listening to the chairman's state of the nation address, there are security implications. Many conferences today involve confidential information and so it must be as difficult as possible for outsiders to get into the auditorium.

One of the requirements, then, is going to be the existence of a suitable gathering area.

The conference room
Once the audience has arrived, they will be led into the room where the conference is to take place. Obviously, this has to have sufficient seats for the whole audience. While that may seem obvious, some clients may be more flexible in this matter than others.

Seating capacity
For example, if a client is inviting 500 people to the conference, and everything about a particular venue is exactly right except for the fact that the conference room has only 250 seats, he may decide to run the conference twice. On the other hand, there may be very strong reasons for gathering the whole audience together at one time.

There is, however, one caveat to the inclusion of large audiences. There is almost inevitably an element of 'herding' involved and some will leave not having had the opportunity to talk to any of the senior staff of the sponsoring company. Some will not mind that, but others may feel slighted unless they have been personally greeted by the sales director.

Large venues
At the other end of the scale, conference rooms that are too big for the audience have to be used with care. An auditorium that can seat 2000 will feel empty and 'cold' if there are only 350 seats in use. This depends to some extent on how many seats are visible. Some auditoria have seating on two levels, and so only half of them will be visible to any member of the audience. Even so, it is a matter that has to be considered.

The shape of the room

This is equally important. Some purpose-built conference centres have semicircular auditoria. Nightclubs that are used for conferences often have shallow, wide rooms. Both of these shapes have the same drawback.

Most conferences use slide, film or video projection. It is a characteristic of projection screens that the further you are off the centre-line of the screen, the more degraded is the image. That is why cinemas tend to be long and narrow. If a wide auditorium has to be used then some of the seats will have to be left vacant, or two or more screens used. That will mean two or more sets of projectors, with a consequent increase in costs.

Whatever type of room is to be used, there will be a stage area. This may already exist or the client may have to build it. Either way, there are various requirements that have to be considered.

Back-projection or front projection?

Many conferences place the projectors behind the screen. Under some circumstances there are good reasons for doing this. A large auditorium may involve a long throw for the projector beams if they are to be at the back of the audience. This creates problems in the brightness and stability of the image on the screen. The reason for that is that the further the projectors are from the screen, the more the effect of any movement of the projector is emphasized.

These problems can be overcome by using back-projection, but then sufficient space has to be allowed for the projectors at the back of the stage. The amount of space will depend on the number of people in the audience, but the minimum realistic space is the equivalent of twice the width of the projected picture. What that means is that if the picture is to be eight feet wide on the screen, there needs to be sixteen feet of unobstructed space behind the screen for the projectors.

The width of the screen also determines the distances that the front and back rows of the audience should be from it: the front row should be no less than twice the picture width away, the back row no more than six times the picture width away. The picture width is the width of a thirty-five millimetre slide when it is projected.

The above relationships apply in the same way for front-projection in general terms. The calculation of these distances is important because projectors should not be placed in the middle of the audience.

In reality, of course, some projectionists will be able to cope with less space behind a screen, and others will handle a greater projector throw from in front. Even so, these rules should be regarded as a good guide.

The combination of seating space and the area needed for projection will provide a guide to the overall minimum size of room needed.

Access

Accessibility is one aspect of the venue that is often overlooked, yet it can have a disastrous effect on the build-up time or involve extra costs.

There is at least one hotel where the function room is on the fourth floor. The lift going to that floor is the size of a normal passenger lift, and so large pieces of set have to be carried up through the hotel or even handed up the fire escape outside. This will slow down the get-in.

At least two conference centres on the Mediterranean coast have doors only at the back of the auditorium. As a result, a ramp has to be built over the seats in order to get large items of equipment in and out. This will push up the cost of the event since the venue is likely to charge for building a ramp.

Ideally, the venue should have large doors outside where trucks can be parked for unloading. The parking area should be flat because conference equipment is often carried in metal flight cases which are on wheels.

If the room is on a higher level than the loading bay, then a large lift will be needed to get all of the equipment up to the conference room.

So the organizer has to consider what equipment will have to be placed in the conference room in order to decide what degree of accessibility is needed.

Catering

In most instances the catering facility must be capable of holding the whole audience. If there is to be a speech after lunch or dinner, then the delegates need to be all in one room and most of them should be able to see the top table. L-shaped rooms may not be acceptable. A speaker who cannot be seen is much more difficult to understand.

Banqueting capacity

Some venues will make optimistic claims about the number of people who can be served in a room.

Banquets tend to be held in rooms with round tables because people can talk to more of their fellow diners with this arrangement. However, these are less efficient than oblong tables since less space is needed for 350 people at long tables than the same number at rounds. Either way, the tables will usually seat ten people; the average venue will assign one waiter or waitress to ten people, so it is relatively easy to calculate the number of tables needed.

If there is any doubt about the capacity of the room, the venue should be able to produce a plan that shows how everybody can be fitted in.

Cabaret space

If there is to be a cabaret, then space must be allowed for this to take place. The amount of stage space needed will obviously depend on the content of the cabaret. For example, if a dance group is to be a major feature they will need space in which to perform. Sound and light will also be needed but, of course, this can be brought in if necessary.

Proximity of banqueting and conference rooms

The importance of the proximity of the catering room to the conference room depends on the programme. If the conference involves a morning session, lunch and then an afternoon session, the lunch room needs to be close to the conference room. Gala dinners can, of course, be held in a different building if necessary, since the delegates are unlikely to need to return to the conference room in the early hours of the morning.

Surroundings

A different building may be needed for the catering. Style is important to the catering because it can have an effect on the image of the meal and of the company that is paying for it. So it has to be considered when selecting a venue.

Exhibition space

Many conferences are run in conjunction with an exhibition. It has to be admitted that the designers of some conference centres have obviously forgotten about this until fairly late in the building programme. That is why some exhibition areas look like carpeted car parks: after all, that is what they are.

Size of the exhibition room
The size of the room is important and the organizer must calculate the area that he or she needs. As with conference rooms, too much space can be as much of a drawback as too little.

Access
Accessibility is important for the same reasons as for the conference room. It must be possible to get all the equipment and displays into the room without resorting to hauling heavy objects up flights of stairs. It is true that this can be done; but it takes time and, again, costs more money.

Allowing for catering and an exhibition
There will often be a conflict between catering and exhibition spaces because many venues have only one room that can be used for both functions. Indeed, there is at least one conference centre in Britain where it is not possible to hold an exhibition alongside a conference at the same time as serving lunch to the delegates. There are ways around this particular problem, but they may involve delegates in an hotel room sitting at round tables during the conference in order that the hotel staff can lay them for lunch quickly. This is not ideal; but if the hotel staff can lay up the tables during the time the delegates are taking pre-lunch drinks, then it may be acceptable.

Accommodation
When a conference is to involve overnight accommodation for the delegates, this needs as much attention as the other aspects of the venue.

Deciding the hotel standard
The standard of accommodation needed must be decided and the maximum acceptable distance from the hotel to the conference centre can then be established. This needs to be a matter of travelling time rather than distance, for the simple reason that it can take much longer to cover two miles in city-centre traffic than in a rural area.

In fact, this is likely to be one of the areas in which compromises will have to be made. This may be a matter of accepting that there is no way of reducing the travelling time if a particular conference centre is to be used unless a lower category of hotel is accepted. Once again, it is a matter of establishing what must be provided and what would be an advantage.

The image of the hotel is important because it should reflect the style of the conference. For example, if the event is being organized to launch a new product that will be promoted with reference to traditional qualities, then a traditional style of hotel may be favoured. A conference for a computer company, on the other hand, may fit more comfortably into a modern setting.

At the same time it is necessary to consider the characteristics of the audience. A group of senior directors will probably be used to high-quality hotels, whereas a group of salespeople may feel uncomfortable in such surroundings. More to the point, they may object to the bar prices that such hotels charge.

If the delegates are likely to indulge in high-spirited antics, then an hotel that is liberally sprinkled with antiques is probably best avoided.

Number of bedrooms

The number of bedrooms that will be needed is obviously of prime importance. However, this is another area in which there are likely to be choices that can only be made by the organizer. If all the delegates are to be accommodated in four-star hotels and there are insufficient rooms in any one of the properties in the town being considered as a destination, then it may be acceptable to use more than one hotel.

Using more than one hotel

If this is done, care should be taken to ensure that all the hotels being used are of comparable standard and style. Delegates visit each others' rooms and comment to each other on the excellence or otherwise of the accommodation. If there is a noticeable difference in either standard or style, then the organizer will have to deal with complaints from delegates who feel that they have not been treated properly.

Of course, this is a problem that can also arise within one hotel, particularly the older properties. The sizes and standards of their rooms vary, whereas a modern hotel will be more likely to have all its rooms to exactly the same standard. While this avoids some of the complaints, it does carry a penalty: bedrooms in a Holiday Inn in Slough, for example, will be nearly identical to those in a Holiday

Inn anywhere else in the world, and many people may feel that an opportunity has been missed if the only way in which it is possible to tell what country the hotel is in is by looking out of the window.

If more than one hotel is to be used it is generally inadvisable to use more than two or three. Using more than that number will require more staff on information desks, more liaison with hotels, and a greater risk of differences in standards and style.

Breakfast rooms

Very often, the main meals will be taken away from a delegate's hotel with the exception of breakfast. This meal is often taken for granted by organizers, and yet, if it is badly handled, it can create chaos just as easily as any of the other meals.

If there are 100 people in an hotel who all have to be at the conference at nine o'clock, they will probably all arrive for breakfast at eight. This is likely to stretch the hotel's resources to breaking point and some delegates will either be late at the conference or arrive having had no breakfast.

The breakfast space should be large enough for the whole group and, if necessary, it will have to be provided in a function room rather than in the restaurant.

Leisure facilities

The organizer must also decide whether or not leisure facilities will be needed. Hotels and conference venues are beginning to provide leisure clubs, golf courses, tennis courts and swimming pools. It may be that the organizer will want to provide his or her delegates with time to relax and take some exercise.

Assembing a short-list of venues

Ideally, everything that has been discussed so far should be assessed on paper in order to assemble a short-list of possible venues. Information must be obtained from the venues in order to do this. This information must include the availability of the venues for the dates that the organizer needs.

Sources of information

In fact, gathering of information can pose something of a problem. The first part of that problem will be to find venues that may be suitable. In the UK, help can be found in the pages of the Conference Blue Book which lists many of the hotel and conference-centre facilities throughout the country. That will be a good starting point for gathering information. The Blue Book shows the numbers of bedrooms, the seating capacities of function rooms and auditoria and, in some cases, floor plans of conference rooms.

If overseas venues are being considered, then it is a different story. There is no guide to conference facilities outside the UK. However, there are a number of guides to hotels. None of them lists all the hotels in any one country and the level of information that they provide varies. Most give a general impression of each hotel listed and some provide basic information about conference facilities. Good company travel agents should have one or more of these guides, prices for which can be more than £100. They can be a good starting point for enquiries, but for conference centres it is a matter of finding people who can supply the necessary information.

The national airlines of the countries under consideration are a good source of information. Many of them have departments which concentrate on the conference market. They will usually know the locations, telephone numbers and addresses of the various convention bureaux in their countries. These convention bureaux vary in their efficiency. Some are very good while many are of little use; but it is worth trying them, because they may be able to help.

Once the possible venues have been identified, they must be asked to send information on their conference facilities and bedrooms. The organizer may find it difficult to make direct comparisons on the basis of these brochures because many of them do not provide all the relevant information. If any facts have been missed from the brochures, the venue has to be contacted in order to get answers to specific questions.

The organizer should thus be able to establish how closely each venue under consideration meets the criteria, discard some of them and arrive at a point where a short-list of suitable venues can be visited.

Venue inspections

It is vital to go to see the short-listed venues. Unfortunately, some companies have a very short-sighted view of such inspection trips, especially if they involve overseas travel. In fact, the inspection trip is the only way in which an organizer can be fully satisfied that the information provided on paper is accurate. The refusal to allow a proper inspection trip to be carried out is putting at risk a programme costing thousands of pounds for what is, in comparison, a paltry sum, even if it does involve overseas travel.

Getting a true impression of the hotel
Some companies also have a policy which forbids their employees to accept free travel and accommodation when they are looking for a conference venue. In some respects this is helpful because an organizer is more likely to be able to gain a true impression of an hotel by booking in like any other guest. If he contacts the sales manager and asks for a reservation so that he can come and talk about a conference, he is likely to receive VIP treatment. While this is very pleasant it is best avoided; the organizer will then find out if the reception staff tend to look on guests as being there for the hotel's convenience rather than the other way round.

Touring the hotel
At some stage it will be necessary to tour the hotel in order to assess its suitability. Usually this will be a carefully arranged affair with a sales person showing the best bedrooms. It is true that an organizer can demand to be shown the worst room in the hotel, but he will not have any way of knowing that he has actually been shown it until one of his most important guests complains about his room. It is one of the laws of conference organization that a particularly important delegate will have one of the worst rooms in the hotel.

One trick that may work is to stop by doors at random and ask to see the room behind. The snag with this is that hotels often refurbish their rooms floor by floor, so that all of the rooms on any particular floor may have been gutted and refitted within the last year while all the rooms on the floor below are not due for the treatment until after the conference. So it is worth having a look at all the floors. If any of the corridors seem to be tatty with the marks of trolleys on the walls and worn carpet, an organizer should ask to see rooms on that floor. One tip here is to watch for fitted carpets in corridors that have loose carpet runners on them. The chances are that the carpet is worn but has not been replaced, and this is a possible pointer to an inadequate refurbishing programme.

In the tour of the hotel the organizer should try to keep properly orientated so that he or she can see if all the rooms being shown are on one side of the building. If that seems to be the case, ask to see rooms on another side. Sometimes the reason they are not shown is because they look out on to the backs of neighbouring buildings or on to a well in the hotel. Such rooms are often described as 'quiet'.

Checking the kitchens
A guide to how well the hotel is run can sometimes be seen from the state of the kitchens, which should be included in the tour. Unsavoury kitchens are fairly easy to recognize, but even those that appear to be clean can have tell-tale signs such as a coating of grease on the floors. The kitchen staff can also be a useful guide. If their uniforms look clean and the staff appear to be happy, the chances are that the hotel is well-run.

The influence of the manager
Of course, as with any business, the attitude of the hotel staff is heavily influenced from above. The general manager is an important factor in any conference, and if he or she is in any way offhand or unhelpful, it is unlikely that the staff will provide the sort of assistance that is needed.

The client liaison person
For the conference organizer, the key member of staff will be the person who is the main point of contact with the hotel. These people have a variety of job titles, but there should be someone whose sole function is to make sure that the organizer gets what he or she wants.

Banqueting manager v chef v waiters
When it comes to catering, the hotel world is divided into three groups. The banqueting sales manager will want to provide whatever the client demands and will complain that he does not get the support that he needs from the chef. The chef, on the other hand, probably believes that the sales people don't understand either his problems or food, and will often curse about the unimaginative menus that have been sold or the impracticality of the menus. While a degree of his ire will be directed at the sales people, he is also convinced that, as soon as a dish leaves his kitchen, it will be ruined by the waiters. The final link in the chain is the banqueting head waiter, and he knows that his staff are the ones who are in the direct line of fire when the delegates are unhappy with the food they are served.

Part of the answer to this state of affairs is to demand a meeting with all three individuals to discuss menus. In that way, the organizer can be reasonably sure that practical meals are being suggested that can be cooked and served in the right way. One banquet involved a dessert that included spun sugar. The banquet was for nearly a thousand people and the chaos that was caused by the waiters being unable to serve the dessert in a decorous fashion came close to ruining what was otherwise a very good event.

Catering for staff and crew

It is also worth considering what catering facilities are available apart from those for the delegates. All the people working on the event will have to be able to eat in the days before the delegates arrive, and if the only restaurants are several miles from the venue then special arrangements will have to be made or extra time allowed for meal breaks. Alternatively, if the event is to be staged in an upmarket hotel, the management may demand that jackets and ties be worn in the restaurants. Some conference crews seem not to own such garments.

Breakfast is particularly important at the crew's hotel since it often needs to be served at an early hour. This is particularly worth checking if the crew has to work on a Sunday. Hotels tend to assume that everyone gets up later on Sunday and breakfast often starts an hour or so later than on other days.

The conference room

The organizer should consider how easy the conference room is to find. Once he or she is inside the room, it is worth standing and listening for a few minutes in order to check how quiet it is, and then listen for echoes.

Features like mirrored walls have to be viewed with extreme suspicion. The interior designer may have thought they looked good but they can cause havoc for a conference organizer. One hotel redecorated what had been a very good conference room and covered the ceiling with mirrors. They were very proud of it and could not understand why the first organizer to go into the room after the redecoration was complete threw up his hands in horror. It had never occurred to them that mirrors reflect light and those on the ceiling allow the audience to see behind the set!

The blackout

It may seem very obvious to say that it must be possible to achieve a full blackout. In fact, there are some venues where a blackout cannot be provided. Others will only provide it at extra cost. In fact, of course, it will never be possible to get total blackness. There will always be some leakage of light through doors and from emergency exit lights, which must always be left on. However, the effects of those leakages will be accentuated if the room is light in colour or if it has been liberally decorated with mirrors. It must be possible to reduce the light level in the room to allow for good projection and for the stage lights to be noticeable.

The golden rule is that if a blackout cannot be demonstrated, another venue should be found. Some sales people have been known to promise a blackout and then try to achieve it by sticking plastic waste-bin liners to the windows.

Noise levels

After extraneous light, one of the worst interferences a conference organizer has to cope with is noise. Most hotel function rooms are also used for meals. That means that the kitchens have to be alongside them and kitchens are a great source of noise. Some chefs seem to exert their authority by the power of their voice alone, and a surprising number of hotels seem to hold their annual plate throwing contests during conferences.

Many hotel function rooms can be divided into several smaller units. The sales manager will make extravagant claims about the sound-insulating properties of the partitions, but these very often do not live up to the claims made. It seems that the sound of a teaspoon on a saucer will defeat even the most efficient soundproof door. An easy way to check the soundproofing qualities is for someone to go to the other side of the closed partition and shout. If they can be heard, the soundproofing is not good enough.

Both of these problems – kitchen noise and sound spill from the next room – can be overcome to some extent by forward planning. The kitchens should have double doors and the moving of crockery in the next room should be banned during the conference. If the soundproofing between rooms is not good enough, then the organizer has to seek an assurance that there will not be another conference running at the same time.

On the other hand, the phantom hammerer who afflicts many conferences cannot be removed. The best that can be done is to get a written guarantee that renovation work will be suspended while the conference is running.

Of course, some venues have noises that are unique to them. One

Spanish conference centre has a roof that is built on runners so that it can expand and contract. The sound of this happening provides an interesting addition to the audio side of any conference. There is no solution to this problem except to find another venue if the noise is intrusive.

There are other noise problems too. One hotel conference room in Rome was next to a dancing school and all the budding tap and disco dancers could be clearly heard going through their paces beyond the dividing wall.

Air-conditioning is a source of noise. However, this will usually only become apparent when it is switched off, because the human ear will accept a steady background hum as normal until it is no longer present. In practice an audience gives out so much heat that the air conditioning is likely to be operating throughout the conference, but it should be checked out.

Noise is also a two-way affair. There is at least one hotel which has guest rooms above the function room. As a result, when sound checks have to be carried out in the early hours of the morning, the guests complain and with good reason. In this case the hotel should make every effort to keep those rooms free.

Acoustics
A room with poor acoustics will involve extra cost in terms of sound equipment. A good sound engineer will be able to overcome all but the fiercest echo, but he will need better amplifiers, speakers and electrical boxes of tricks to do it.

Room temperature
Temperature is very important. If the audience is confined in a warm, stuffy room, they are more likely to fall asleep than listen to speeches, so an efficient air-conditioning system is necessary. By the same token, an audience that is cold will be concentrating more on their discomfort than on the content of the show, so the room has to be kept at a reasonable temperature. Ideally, this should be around 70 °F.

Security
Security is also important these days since many conferences involve confidential information. The conference room must be capable of being sealed off. If the room provides a short-cut for the staff from one part of the building to another, then they must be told that the

room is out of bounds from the day the client moves in until he has left.

Power
The power supply has to be considered because some conferences today require large amounts of electricity. This will often need to be a three-phase supply and in a place that is easily accessible from the backstage area. The main power supply cable will be very thick and is not the sort of thing that should be running down the middle of the seats.

Hotel room size
The size of the room needs to be approached with particular care when an hotel conference room is being considered. Plans for these rooms will often show a minimum ceiling height of fifteen feet but conveniently forget to mention the chandeliers that hang down to within ten feet of the floor. Sometimes it is possible to work around obstructions like this, and sometimes it is possible to have them removed − at a price.

The height of the room in these venues is important because it will have a flat floor. If the audience members at the back of the room are to be able to see over the heads of the people in front, the screen has to be raised off the floor so that its lower edge is visible from the back of the room.

Other simultaneous activities
Finally, it is worth checking to see what other functions are being held in the venue at the same time as the conference. It would be embarrassing, to say the least, if a prime competitor was holding an event in the same venue at the same time.

It is also worth checking to see what other organizers will be moving in or out at the same time as the conference. If the venue has an exhibition space with exhibitors either building or removing their stands during the build-up to the conference, then there will be fierce competition for any lifts that have to be used and for parking space in the loading bay.

Checking unfinished rooms
Organizers should also beware of assessing rooms that are not finished. There is an hotel in Britain where a very good conference room was built. An organizer went to see it before it was finished,

was very impressed and booked it. He was the first to use it and had been assured that the front of the projection booth was to be all glass. When he began to prepare for his event he found that the booth was indeed all glass at the front, but it was heavily tinted. The interior designer had thought that the audience should not be able to see the projectors behind it. It never occurred to him that the projection beams could not penetrate it either.

Another organizer in the USA booked a venue on the basis of drawings and a site visit carried out before the building was complete. When he moved his conference in he found that all the rooms were about ten feet smaller each way than was shown on the plans.

Decorations
The state of the decorations in the conference room and adjacent areas has to be looked at very closely. Very often a venue will be chosen months or years ahead of the event and, unless there is a constant programme of renovation, the venue is likely to deteriorate further before the conference moves in.

Exhibition areas
If an exhibition area is needed it should be seen during the check-out trip. The amount of space needed, the state of the decorations, the location of the exhibition room in relation to the conference room, and access, are all as important here as in the conference room.

Dimensions
Some exhibition areas can be reduced by means of moving partitions; but they need careful inspection since they are often damaged, showing the scars of having been moved back and forth many times.

Power supply
The amount of electricity needed for exhibition lighting and specialized equipment cannot usually be drawn off a thirteen amp plug on the wall. The exhibition contractor will often need three-phase power and this must be in a position which makes it accessible.

Proximity to the conference room
The exhibition room needs to be close to the conference room because even an enthusiastic audience will begin to lose interest if they have to undertake a hike along endless corridors and up and down staircases in order to reach the exhibition. If this is the case for

the designated exhibition area, then it is worth finding out if another area can be pressed into service.

Spouses' programme
With many conferences today involving the delegates' spouses, consideration has to be given to what they will do if they do not want to attend the conference sessions. This may require advice from people at the venue, but the success of the event can be affected to a very considerable degree by a well-planned and executed spouses' programme.

The location of the hotel is important because, if it is remote from shops with little in the way of on-site facilities, the delegates are likely to feel trapped as if on a desert island.

Facilities for the handicapped
This is one factor that must be considered in relation to all the facilities at the venue. If any of the delegates are handicapped, they must be able to gain access to all the areas without feeling that they are having to be treated as special cases. This means that there should be ramps and space in the auditorium for wheelchairs.

Seeing what is happening
The main point that any organizer should remember in a check-out visit is that he or she should keep eyes and ears well and truly open. If something is not seen, then its existence must be doubted. This is, perhaps, a sad reflection on the business, but it is true. He or she should also watch and listen to how regular guests are treated. This may demonstrate that there is a vast difference between his or her VIP treatment and the welcome extended to an ordinary guest.

Alternative venues

The final matter to consider in all of this discussion about venues is that there are many facilities that can be used for conferences apart from the usual hotels and conference-centres.

In-house facilities
Many companies holding conferences have suitable facilities themselves. This may be a showroom or even a warehouse. It may seem a little prosaic in comparison with some of the outside venues

available, but there may be real benefits in using such a facility since a factory visit can be included as part of the event.

Universities
These have to be used with care because few of them have facilities that are suitable for corporate meetings. The conference rooms are not usually set up for the sort of equipment used in business meetings and the accomodation tends to be somewhat spartan. Added to that, they can usually only be used during vacations. There are exceptions and they may be able to provide exactly the facilities needed.

Stately homes
Country houses and stately homes can provide the space for conferences and lend a unique air to them. However, they often do not have the space for more than a handful of delegates, and they can be very expensive. Even so, they have been used very successfully in the past.

Temporary structures
Where covered space is scarce, as in stately homes, a temporary structure – what used to be called a marquee – can often be used. However, these have to be chosen with care because they are often made of white material which means that they cannot be blacked out. There are some which are specifically designed for conference use and they can be very successful. The point to remember with them is that everything usually has to be brought in – power, telephones, toilets, water, catering and all the rest. In addition, if the conference is to be held at any time other than in the summer, heating can be something of a problem.

Theatres and cinemas
Theatres would seem, at first glance, to be ideal. Some are, but often they do not have sufficient catering or exhibition facilities and it may be necessary to work around a show that is being performed every night. The same applies to cinemas but they are often worth investigating.

Film studios
Film studios are sometimes thought of as being suitable venues but, in practice, the owners tend not to want to commit themselves to a

conference too far in advance in case they have to turn down a major feature film. The reason for this is that they are more than just the sound stages. A film will be much more profitable for them because a film company will often use the power house, on-site carpenters, the scene dock, the preview theatre and cutting rooms, none of which will be of interest to the average conference organizer.

Sporting venues
Some sporting venues are now looking to conferences to increase the return on their expensive land. Racecourses, football and cricket grounds can all be used for conferences and can be very good venues.

Venues converted from other uses
There are an increasing number of venues that are converted from a previous use. Old breweries, the cellars of inns, old department stores can often be very useful; but it is necessary with these to make sure that they are really suitable. A venue on the top floor of an office block with only a passenger lift can be extremely difficult to use. In addition, the character of these buildings will often dictate the style of the meeting at the same time as lending it a unique air.

Exhibition halls
The owners of exhibition halls are also now using conferences to fill their halls when there are no exhibitions on. Those that are accustomed to these events have become very professional with the support services that they provide; but it must be remembered that these are 'black box' environments. Everything for the conference usually has to be brought in.

Ships
The shipping companies are also promoting their cruise ships as suitable conference venues. These are, in fact, very good if the event is to recognise effort. Under the right circumstances they can also be used for product launches. For example, the Austin Metro was launched on board a cruise ship and the event was very successful. However, they are expensive to use and they do have particular problems. It is risky, for example, to drill holes in the deck in order to fix a set in position. The on-board currency will often be dollars and, if the ship does not 'go foreign', there are considerable complications with duty on things like drinks. Against that, they do provide

the ultimate captive audience. While the ship is at sea, there is nowhere else for the audience to go.

Nightclubs
Nightclubs are also often seen as suitable venues, and they can be. However, the catering may leave something to be desired and the set-up time may be limited if the club is unwilling to close on the night before the meeting. Even so, they can be effective venues and should not be discounted out of hand.

The importance of selecting the venue carefully cannot be over-emphasized. The character of the conference room and the quality of the hotel will affect the audience's perception of the event. The organizer must always be aiming to send the audience home having enjoyed the conference as well as having learnt from it or been influenced by it in the way the organizer wants. The right venue can help to achieve all of this.

• CHECKLIST •

- Decide on the most suitable geographical location

- Establish the venue criteria:
    a how much space for gathering the audience?
    b how many seats will be needed in the auditorium?
    c how much space will be needed for a stage and projectors?
    d are there any special needs for access?
    e if catering is to be provided, how much space is needed?
    f is space needed for a cabaret?
    g if an exhibition is to be mounted, how much space is needed?
    h if hotel accommodation is to be provided, how many rooms will be needed?

- Research suitable venues

- Establish availability of suitable venues

- Carry out a site inspection

4

Do-it-yourself production?

Every conference makes a statement of some sort about the sponsoring company. If it is well-executed, the reputation and image of the company will be raised in the eyes of the audience. On the other hand, any conference that staggers from one crisis to another with a succession of incompetent and inaudible speakers backed up by badly produced slides will damage the reputation of the company. So the decisions that affect the staging of the event are extremely important.

There are many ways in which the production of a conference can be handled, but they all come down to two basic methods.

The manager who has been given the responsibility of organizing the event can choose to make all the arrangements, or he or she can decide to use the services of an outside company that specializes in conference production. Whichever course is chosen it should be the result of a conscious decision. As with so many aspects of conference organization, neither course should be taken by default. The organizer must weigh the pros and cons of the alternatives and then decide on one or the other.

This is just as true with a small conference as with a big product launch. If it is to reflect well on the sponsoring company, even a small sales conference must be produced well.

There are two major elements to a conference: the equipment or hardware and the content or software.

Selecting the equipment

First impressions
If the organizer chooses to arrange the event, he or she must first consider the impression that the audience gets as they walk into the

68

conference room. That impression will usually be gained from the setting against which the speakers will be seen. This is true whether the event is being held in the works canteen or in the more salubrious surroundings of an hotel function room.

All too often the audience enters the room to find a projector balanced precariously on a chair, which is itself standing on a table, with cables running across the floor. The projector will be pointed at a tripod screen alongside which the hapless speaker will stand to deliver his script. The combined effect is to suggest the very worst kind of home movie show. Most people will have been to conferences, too, where the speakers were inaudible from half way down the room because no public address system was used, and the lighting often provides a choice between a darkened room in which the slides can be seen but the speaker cannot read his notes and bright lighting that will defeat any slide projector. A show like this will damage the image of even the most dynamic company.

If the correct impression is to be given, then all of these basics have to be right. The organizer has to recognize that fact and obtain the right equipment.

The set
There are various inexpensive ways of creating a very basic set. Some of the exhibition systems that clip together can be used or, alternatively, a purpose-built set can be hired.

The advantages of a set are twofold. On the one hand a set provides a professional focus of attention and blots out any distracting backgrounds to the speakers. On the other, a set with the right sort of screen can be used to hide the projectors.

The types of set that can be hired complete will usually be offered in a variety of colours and with the option of having the client's name or company logo applied to it.

The other element of the set that needs attention is the lectern. Most speakers will need one, partly to put their notes on and partly to hang on to. It seems to give them a degree of physical support that many are in need of when facing an audience. Once again, it is worth obtaining one that looks good. It is likely that, if the conference is being held in an hotel, they will have a lectern. Very often these are of wood and show signs of heavy use.

If a set has been hired, the company providing it can often supply a lectern to match. Some of these have a range of controls that would rival the instruments of an aircraft in their complexity. Such sophistication is not necessary and can be counter-productive. The average company speaker should only have to concentrate on delivering a good speech, and so the controls are a distraction.

One other point that is worth considering is that it is relatively easy to personalise it to the company responsible for the conference. This is usually done by having the company name or logo cut out of polystyrene, which is then stuck on to the set. This is both cheap and effective.

Projectors

There are two methods of projecting an image on to a screen. The most widely known, largely because it is the only method possible with a tripod screen, is to place the projector in front of the screen. This may mean that the projector will have to be positioned in the middle of the audience. That is not ideal because the noise can be distracting. Some audiences may find it more interesting to watch the projectors stepping through their slides than to listen to the speaker. Added to that, if anyone moves across in front of the projectors a shadow will be cast on the screen, and there is always the more serious risk that someone will trip over the cables to the projector.

The alternative is to place the projectors behind the screen. This is known as back-projection and means that the projectors are out of sight of the audience. Generally this is the better option, especially if there are so many slides that more than one magazine is needed. If the projectors are out of sight, the magazines can be changed without the audience knowing.

It is worth using at least two projectors because that will mean that the slides will dissolve from one to another without the blank screen that is a characteristic of the single projector. The most popular slide projector is the Kodak Carousel or its stablemate, the Ektagraphic. Two of these can be linked together very easily with a variety of equipment, none of which is expensive to hire.

This assumes that only slide projectors will be used. In fact, film and video projectors can usually be used in either a front- or rear-projection format. However, the supplier must be told which is to be used in order to avoid having a back-to-front image on the screen. This is not a problem with slide projectors since the slides can be inserted either way round. Film and video tape is not reversible in the same way.

Film projectors

Many conferences use film in addition to slides. If this is the case then a film projector has to be hired. The guide for hiring these is to obtain the best possible. Saving a few pounds will seem to be a very foolish tactic when the projector chews up the organizer's film.

There are two types of film that may be used, 16 millimetre and 35 millimetre. Of these, 35 mm is less likely to be used except in the case of television commercials which may only be available on 35 mm. In fact, it is worth having these transferred to 16 mm in order to avoid having too much equipment behind the screen.

Sixteen-millimetre projectors are available in three forms. The most common is for projecting a film with an optical soundtrack. With this, the sound is reproduced by means of a signal that is laid alongside the picture as a strip of varying width.

Magnetic soundtracks are less often used, but they have a strip of magnetic recording tape applied to the side of the film.

When a film has to be shown before it has been completely finished, the picture and the soundtrack will be on two separate rolls. This is a double-head film and needs the third type of projector.

These three types are not interchangeable, and so the organizer must be clear as to the type of film that will be used on-site.

Video projectors

Television technology has not yet reached the point where a video image can be projected with the same degree of quality as film. Even so, it may be necessary to use video tape in a conference, in which circumstances a video projector must be hired. They work together with a playback machine and so both will be needed. Picture quality varies enormously from one type of video projector to another, and the organizer will be well-advised to see a demonstration of any machine that he or she is thinking of hiring.

Sound system

When film or video is being used, the organizer must make sure that the sound from the projector is fed through a good sound system. Film projectors do have the ability to reproduce sound through a small speaker, but this is not of good enough quality for a conference. The same applies to video projectors which have a sound system.

Apart from that, any audience of more than thirty people is likely to need some form of sound system if they are to be able to hear every word the speakers utter. The golden rule for sound is: if in doubt, bring in a public address system. It is far better to have it and not need it than to have the audience straining to hear what is said. At the same time, if film or video is to be used within the conference, the sound system must be capable of feeding the soundtracks off them through the loudspeakers.

A simple sound system will involve at least one microphone on a stand, an amplifier, possibly with a sound mixer that allows several sources to be fed into the speakers which are the final part of the system. The speakers need to be hired with suitable stands so that they can be lifted above the heads of the audience to make sure that the sound carries to every part of the room. Once again, all of this can be hired at reasonable cost.

Stage lighting
When it comes to lighting, it is necessary for the audience to be able to see the speaker and for the latter to see his or her notes. However the light that allows this should not be allowed to fall on the screen because then the slides or film will not be visible. It may be that the room in which the conference is taking place has the sort of track lighting that enables the organizer to direct spotlights on to specific areas. If that is not the case, then a small amount of stage lighting needs to be hired.

This will involve at least two lights for the speaker and a few others to light the set as the audience enters the room. They will need to be mounted on stands, and there must be a control board along with the electrical equipment to fade the lights up and down.

Equipment packages
All of this equipment – projectors, sound and lights – can be hired from a number of sources, either individually or as packages which are designed for audiences of specific sizes.

Some hotels operate a system called the Guaranteed Venue Scheme which is intended to make sure that all the basic hardware needed for a successful conference is readily available.

Whether the equipment is hired from an outside company or the venue, a technician should be hired to set up and operate the equipment. In this, some of the hotels offering the Guaranteed Venue Scheme are not working to the standards that the designers envisaged. Any organizer using the scheme has to be satisfied that the hotel will have someone on hand who genuinely knows how to use

72

the equipment. A written guarantee is needed from the venue because it is not unknown for the technician to be unavailable outside working hours because the hotel will not pay overtime.

Unfortunately, there are some companies that object to paying even moderate hire charges for equipment that will help to give a good impression. This is a very short-sighted attitude because of the damage done by a badly presented conference. After all, a conference for fifty people, all earning around £10 000 a year, will cost at least £1000 in wages for their time alone once they have travelled to the event, spent an hour listening to the conference and returned to their offices afterwards. Against that background, a couple of hundred pounds spent on good presentation is relatively insignificant.

Content

Hiring the equipment is not, of course, the end of the story. Any conference that is organized in-house will take up a considerable amount of the organizer's time. Not only will he or she have to spend time coordinating the equipment; but it will also be necessary to badger people into producing scripts, finding someone to produce the speaker support material, overseeing its production and the production of any films, video tapes or audio-visual modules that have to be produced for the conference. At first glance this may seem a daunting list of tasks. The reality can be different if they are approached in a logical fashion.

The whole conference will begin with the scripts. These will form the content and, to a large extent, reflect or dictate the style of the meeting. Scripting is dealt with in detail in a later chapter and so, for the moment, we can leave that aside. Once the scripts begin to take shape, the organizer has to consider the visual elements of the show.

These will usually be in the form of slides with the possible addition of film and video tape. Generally speaking, overhead projector cells are not suitable to the type of conference we are considering: while they may be fine for small meetings and seminars, they are not usually of good enough quality for a significant sales conference.

Slides – their choice, design and production
The commonest form of visual aid used in a conference is usually called speaker support. This is a misnomer because any speaker who

needs support from his slides should think twice about standing up in the first place. Slides that accompany a live speech must be used because they add to the understanding of the messages contained within the speech or because they can reinforce the strength of what the speaker is saying.

So the key to these slides is the script. It is a fact that some speakers prefer to decide what slides they want to use and then write the script around them. Inevitably, this will be much more of an evolutionary process than other methods because the slides will begin as little more than subject headings. For example, a speaker may want to talk about the size of next year's market and ask for a slide that says that. As the script develops, it may transpire that the forecast market should be shown on screen as a bar chart, illustrating the month-on-month figures. The speaker may then want to add in the company's forecast share of that market and express the market share in volume terms. So the original single slide becomes a series of three or more.

The alternative method of designing the slides is to take the script and read it through several times in order to pick out the key points that need illustrating on the screen.

It is likely that both methods will produce the same result, which is why neither method is clearly right or wrong. Indeed, if there is not much time in which to produce the slides, it may be that they have to be designed and the artwork begun while the script is still being written; not an ideal state of affairs, but one that does occasionally happen in a business world where developments can occur very rapidly.

Slide types – words, graphics and pictures
In order to demonstrate the way in which the various slides can be used, let us take a section of a fictional speech to be made by the manufacturing director of a company. The figures in brackets show where a slide may be needed.

Let me now turn to the question of manufacturing capacity (1) for the next five years. Output has been restricted recently by the type of machinery that exists in our main assembly building. We are addressing this problem in several ways.

Next January, a new, computer-controlled warehousing (2) system will come on stream. The main benefits of this will be tighter control on the

74

stocking (2a) levels of components, along with the ability to make sure that all work stations have a consistent (2b) supply of components.

This will be followed by the installation of (3) robotic materials handling which will reduce the damage to components. That will be matched to redesigned workstations (4) which are aimed at producing a better working environment. The result of these two phases of the investment plan will be to ensure a higher quality of finished product.

Together, these new developments will also bring about an increase in productivity from 100 units per man-week to (5) 150 units per man-week. Obviously, this will not happen overnight. The increase will build up steadily from the current levels of productivity in (6) January to the new levels which will be reached in June.

Slide (1) would be a straight word slide reading MANUFACTURING CAPACITY. Slide (2) would be a heading reading COMPUTER CONTROLLED WAREHOUSING. Slide (2a) would carry the same heading as slide (2) and add BETTER STOCK CONTROL under the main heading; and slide (2b) would be the same as slide (2a) with the addition of CONSISTENT COMPONENTS SUPPLY.

On the face of it these three slides contravene one of the golden rules of word slides: that no slide should contain more than five words. The reason for this is that more words inevitably mean that each individual word has to be smaller and the resulting slide becomes very confusing and difficult to read. However, in this case the number of words is just acceptable because each of the three points is very closely linked and the audience is not being hit with more than five *new* words at a time.

Slide (3) would be either a word slide reading ROBOTIC MATERIALS HANDLING or a picture of the type of robot to be installed. Slide (4) would be a drawing or photograph of the new type of workstation. Slide (5) would be a simple bar chart showing the current and projected levels of productivity. Finally, slide (6) would be a bar chart showing the build-up, month by month, to the new levels of productivity.

It can be seen that this list, if extended through a complete script, will mean a very considerable number of slides. In fact there are probably too many for the length of script shown, but it does illustrate the main types of slide that can be used. In reality, slides (3), (4) and (5) could probably be dropped in favour of one which would read IMPROVED QUALITY AND PRODUCTIVITY. If that were to be the case, then an extra line would need to be added to the script in order to make the new slide appropriate to the text. For example, the new text might read, 'That will help to improve quality and productivity, but we are also going to install new robotic materials handling...'

Adding extra lines, or changing existing text, is an important part of developing a script and the associated slides for a presentation. No one should regard the words in a script as unchangeable because there will often be times when the sense of the text will be improved by minor amendments.

The storyboard

The list of slides to be produced will be best laid out as a storyboard. This is a series of hand-drawn or written pictures, each one representing the content of a slide. These will be used only as a guide to producing the artwork and so there is no need for artistic talent in drawing a storyboard.

Slide formats

Having decided on the content of the slides, they need to be produced. One of the important factors to remember in doing this is that all the slides must be made to the same format.

There are two types of slide used for conferences – the familiar 35 mm slide which has an oblong format, and the newer 46 mm or Superslide format. This is square, and so it does not matter which way up it is produced. However, 35 mm slides must be produced in either all landscape or all portrait format: mixing the two formats will mean that the screen has to be too deep for landscape and too wide for portrait.

One of the groups that commonly mixes formats is the advertising industry. Faced with the need to show a single-page advertisement, they will often photograph it within a portrait format slide. This will then be mixed with double page spread ads that are photographed landscape. The resulting mess does no one any favours. A better solution would be to photograph the single-page ad within a landscape format and against a black background. Quite apart from the improvement to the projected images, it maintains roughly the same sense of scale between the two types of ad.

Filling the screen

The business of filling the screen is important to the production of slides in other ways. If, for example, a word slide is produced as type on a coloured background, it will be very obvious if the projected image does not fill the screen. An inadequately filled screen does not look professional and is relatively easy to avoid. The obvious way to avoid the problem is to ensure that the projected image spills over the edges of the screen slightly.

However, if the organizer is not able to control the placing of the projectors, an alternative is to use coloured type on a black background. The same can be done with slides that use graphs, pie charts or bar charts. The reason for this disguising of the area of the screen filled by the slide is that sometimes a speaker will be performing at a conference organized by someone else. Under those circumstances, he or she will have little control over the screen size and the ability of the projector to fill it. Indeed, the organizers of some conferences with guest speakers allow for both landscape and portrait slides. If colour graphics on a black background are used, then the result will still look professional instead of being a coloured oblong which clearly does not fill the screen. A guest speaker using this ruse will appear more professional than others at the same conference, with a consequent benefit to his reputation.

Quality of origination

Just as important as the use of colour on word slides is the need to produce the original material as artwork rather then hand-lettering. It is difficult to produce good freehand lettering; and when it is enlarged on the screen, any slightly ragged edges that are not noticeable on the original will become glaringly obvious.

Computer graphics

Over recent years another alternative has been developed. There are now a variety of systems that use computer graphics to produce slides. On the face of it these are a real boon because many of them can be used with existing computers or installed in the organizer's company offices.

In reality these systems are not usually that good. A computer capable of producing the kind of graphics seen on television is a very powerful and expensive beast. The limitations of the technology mean that the small machines sold for in-house slide production have inherent drawbacks. In particular, diagonal lines and circles will not be completely smooth. Indeed, with some systems there will be a noticeable 'stepping' effect on any lines that are not either horizontal or vertical. This may be unimportant for some conferences; but the organizer must get hold of some examples of slides produced on any system and project them on to a screen before agreeing to buy it.

Relevance to the words
The words on screen must be relevant to the words that are being spoken. While that may sound painfully obvious, it is a fact which is often forgotten. People frequently project a list of bullet points which the speaker works through. The problem is that the audience will race on ahead of the speaker and they cannot read one thing while absorbing a different message that is being spoken. Similarly, some speakers will have a slide on screen which says, for example, PRODUCTIVITY when they are talking about 'production efficiency'. There is thus the potential for confusion in the minds of the audience.

Filler slides
In most scripts there comes a time when the speaker moves off one subject which is illustrated by a slide but has not reached the subject of the next slide. Once again this can cause confusion, and the solution is to use a 'filler' slide bearing the company's logo or the title of the conference. Once the tactic of using slides has been established, it is better not to leave the screen blank.

It is also worth while to have available a quantity of these 'filler' slides that can be used to cover points that are added during rehearsal. Speakers have a habit of changing their scripts in rehearsal and, even if the organizer is only using one projector, the need to remove a slide from the tray causes a considerable amount of work at a time when there are better things to do. If more than one projector is in use, then the problem will be greatly compounded. When a slide does have to be removed, it is much easier to drop in a 'filler' to take up the space. Having said that, the organizer must impress upon the speakers that no slides can be removed or added once they have all been placed in the projector trays. It is this sort of work which, when done in a hurry, can result in slides appearing in the wrong order, back-to-front or upside-down. No organizer can accept anything that jeopardizes the conference in that way.

Use of graphics
Graphics slides should always be used in preference to columns of figures. They are much easier to understand quickly. In the example above, the rising rate of productivity would be better illustrated by

a simple bar chart than by a column of figures that gives the same information.

Pie charts are useful to show, for example, the proportion of a company's output represented by each of its product lines. Once again, this is much more powerful than a list of figures.

As with word slides, colour is very useful in graphics slides and the same rules apply about the advisability of using colour on a black background. One aspect of using colour that has to be approached with care is its visibility and the effects of different colour combinations.

Yellow, for example, is a very weak colour and can be difficult to read on screen. When colours are combined on screen, it should be remembered that some will dominate others. Under some circumstances a red area will overpower a blue one. In addition, the organizer has to consider the possibility that some of the audience may be colour-blind, so red and green should be used with care.

In order to gain some insight into the ways in which colour works on screen, it is worth getting hold of some demonstration slides from a slide production house. By projecting these on screen the organizer will be able to see how the professionals use colour.

Captions for graphics

Most graphics slides will need a caption of some sort as an explanation. These should be kept to the minimum necessary to explain the slide and should be big enough to be readable. As a rough guide, if the type cannot be read on the original slide without the aid of a magnifying glass, then it is too small.

Pictures

Pictorial slides will often be necessary and these must always be landscape format if the slides are 35 mm. If possible, they should be copied from two-and-a-quarter inch square transparencies or larger so as to achieve the best possible quality on the screen. The copying of printed pictures should be avoided as far as possible because the dots that make them up will be visible on the screen. If a picture that has appeared in a brochure is to be shown, then the original transparency should be used to make a duplicate.

Handover

There should always be a slide to cover the handover from one speaker to another so that the first person's last slide does not stay on screen until the next person begins speaking. This may be the company logo, the title of the conference or the next speaker's name.

If a film is to be used, then a black slide should be inserted at the appropriate point in order to avoid having to turn the slide projector off and on. The time when a projector bulb will fail is when it is switched on.

Producing the slides

When the content of all the slides has been determined, they need to be produced. This is best done by a specialist with equipment designed for the job.

Companies exist in many cities which can take a typed list showing the content of each slide and then produce the slides for use in the show. This list must be carefully checked for accuracy. Discovering a typographical error after the slides have been made will increase the cost of slide production. It is worth contacting the slide producers at an early stage in order to establish how long they will need to do the job. Time can then be allowed for producing the slides early enough for the organizer to arrange them in sequence, place them in the projector trays and project them on to a screen in order to check them well before the conference. This will allow for corrections to be made if necessary.

It is very important to the quality of the conference for the slides to be checked in this way. Shows have been run successfully with the projectionist dropping a speaker's slides into the projector trays as he is talking, but this does no one's health any good and is likely to affect the smooth running of the whole show.

Film and video

Film and video are frequently used within a conference and people have been arguing for years about which medium is best. The one undeniable fact, however, is that while video is easier to use on-site, the picture quality is not as good as with 16 mm film. Unfortunately, the argument is much more complex than the simple matter of deciding which is easier to use.

The factors to be taken into account include cost, the time available to shoot the film or video, the locations to be used, whether or not the organizer has access to in-house production facilities, and many others. The best solution is for the organizer to talk to some producers of both film and video, and try to decide which is best for the particular application in mind.

Film and video production
Once the decision is taken, the processes of producing a film or video
are very similar. They start with the briefing which will form the
basis for a script. This will usually need to be done by a specialist
writer because the script has to be produced with pictures in mind.
The production company will usually suggest a writer who they have
worked with before. The writer will need a very comprehensive brief
and will produce a draft for the client to see. Once that has been
approved, the shooting can begin.

The crew
A film or video crew will usually contain a surprising number of
people. There is a temptation for the client to wonder if they are all
strictly necessary. Even a simple interior location shoot will need a
director, a camera operator with an assistant, a sound engineer,
possibly two lighting people and a gofor or grip. The best way of
understanding why all these people are necessary is for the organizer
to try to shoot some film. Only then will he or she realize that
someone, (the director) has to consider the whole film, particularly
since the shots will usually be taken out of sequence before being
edited together. Someone else has to concentrate on each shot (the
camera operator), without having to worry about having loaded film
magazines handy and marking each shot (the assistant does that as
well as making sure the camera is focused). It is quicker to judge the
effect of the lighting if the camera operator can stand by the camera
while the lighting people move the lights around. The grip humps
equipment around and literally goes for food, coffee, sticky tape and
helps keep unwanted people out of shot.

The business of actually shooting a film or video is unutterably
boring. It can take an hour or more to set up a shot that lasts only
a few minutes. This is one of the reasons why film and video are so
expensive.

Using company people
Very often a company will want to have its own people on film,
explaining something connected with their work. This can be very
successful but, unless they are amateur actors or are used to making
speeches, it is better not to give them a script. Faced with a camera,
several people that they do not know and sweating under the lights,
the average company person will become wooden on film. To avoid
this it is better to tell a quality-control manager, for instance, that

he or she needs to explain a piece of equipment and its benefits. The speaker will then need a few rehearsals before the director tries to get the shot completed. As a rough guide, half a day with such a person should be allowed for shooting five minutes or so of film. Some people will be able to do the job much more quickly, but most will need all of that time.

Editing

Once all of the shots have been completed, the film or video tape will need to be edited together. The production company will usually go away and do this before showing the rough edit to the client. Slight modifications can then be made before the final edit is done, the pictures married to a soundtrack and the finished film or tape is available for use.

This is a very simplistic description of the process of shooting and editing which will take possibly weeks to complete and cost many thousands of pounds but, for a novice organizer, it is sufficient.

Transfers from video to film

It is also worth remembering, when deciding whether to use film or video, that video can be transferred to film by using a laser scanning process. It is more difficult than transferring film to video, and the result is not as good, but it can be done.

Audio-visual modules

Finally, in the do-it-yourself conference, it may be necessary to use audio-visual modules. These are programmes that use slides which change in a predetermined sequence with a soundtrack. There may be as many as fifteen or more projectors, all pointing at the screen and all controlled by a minicomputer. The tape that carries the sound usually has at least four tracks. One — or perhaps two — will provide the sound. The third will be left blank and there will be a time code on the fourth track. The computer is instructed to change slides at precise times measured against this track. The fourth track is often left blank.

As with film, the production of a module is usually best done by an outside specialist company. The process is remarkably similar to that for film and video, but it is unusual for a film production company to be capable of producing audio-visual modules.

The main difference between a film and a module is obviously that the images in the module do not move. They can change at an astonishingly rapid rate, but they will always be a sequence of still photographs. It is possible to achieve animation, but it is done with a series of slides which have to be shot in a careful sequence.

Once the script for the module has been agreed, the slides will be produced and a soundtrack recorded. Some companies will then place the slides on a lightbox and the client will have the opportunity to check through them before they are put into projector trays and the computer programmed to run the projector in the desired way. Once again, this is a very simplistic explanation of what can be a complex operation. Since the work will almost certainly be done by an outside company, however, it is sufficient.

On-site

Once all the hardware for the conference has been booked and the software (scripts, slides, film, videos, a-v modules and soundtracks) has been produced, the remaining tasks for the organizer will be on-site. The equipment has to be available in order to rehearse the show at least twice − once without speakers for the benefit of the technician(s), and once for the speakers. If possible, the speakers should be persuaded to rehearse more than once.

Handling slide changes
It is best for the slide changing to be handled by someone behind the scenes. A speaker has more than enough to worry about without having to remember to press a button at the right moment. The projectionist should be given a script with the slide change points marked so that the speaker can concentrate on the script without being concerned with what is happening on the screen. The speaker must then be told not to *ad lib* too much. If words are spoken that are not in the script when the slides are changing, then the speaker will invariably be saying something that has no relevance to the slide on the screen. The speaker also runs the risk of confusing the projectionist, and that can mean that several slides will be out of sequence.

The actual rehearsal and the show itself will be dealt with later.

Outside production companies

One of the main benefits of using a specialist conference production company is that much of the preceding work is done by them. They will arrange all the hardware and the technicians to operate it. They will make sure that it all gets to the venue in good time and oversee its installation. They will arrange for the production of all the software and, if necessary, the scripts, and get it running ready for the rehearsal.

With a simple show, the advantages of using a production company are less clear than they are for a complex production. The decision on whether or not to use an outside company for a small show depends, as much as anything, on how important the show is. If it would be disastrous for it to go wrong, then it is probably better to be safe and use a specialist. However, this presupposes that the production company will do a better job than the manager given the task of organizing a conference. Not all of the companies claiming to be conference organizers can do a better job, so it is important to make the right choice of company.

Before considering production companies, it is worth mentioning advertising agencies. Some of them will claim to be able to handle conferences for their clients. Very few can. Many will simply subcontract the work to a specialist and then make a mark up on the price. The result is that the client pays more.

Choosing a production company
There are many specialist production companies around the country. They vary from the excellent to the incompetent. Distinguishing one from another is not always easy and depends very much on being able to start from a list of reliable suppliers. Compiling such a list can be difficult if the organizer has never had any contact with the conference world before. If he or she has absolutely no knowledge of production companies, then it can be helpful to call people who use them regularly. These will be car manufacturers, computer manufacturers, insurance companies and pharmaceutical companies. Most of them will be happy to tell an organizer who they have used and what they thought of them. Those comments can be used to compile a list of 'possibles'.

The Audio Visual Directory published each year by *Audio-Visual* magazine lists programme production companies, but the list is not complete and includes many companies that do not produce conferences. Existing clients are a better guide.

Visiting production companies
A list of interesting companies having been compiled, it is then necessary to go and see some of them. The first visit will usually follow a predictable programme. A sales pitch will be given first,

before a tour of the premises. The duration of this will obviously depend on the facilities that the company has, and the importance that they attach to the various facilities will depend on whether or not they have them in-house.

Very few companies have scriptwriters permanently on their staff. Good writers tend to be few and far between and few production companies have sufficient work to provide full-time employment for writers. Added to that, writers often specialize, so the lack of a scriptwriter on the staff is not necessarily a drawback. Some companies use their producers to write scripts. The wisdom of this approach depends very much on the number of scripts that he or she will be expected to produce. Scriptwriting can be a very time-consuming process, which may mean that the producer is unable to devote sufficient time to coordinating other aspects of the show.

Some of the smaller companies have only one producer and often he will be the proprietor. Again, this is not necessarily a disadvantage since freelance producers can be hired. The bigger companies often claim that this is inadvisable because the company does not have ultimate control over the quality of the freelance producer's work. There is an element of truth in that, although the conference world is very small and a freelancer who is not good does not last long.

The bigger companies will have an art department along with a specialized camera for slide production, their own projectors, tape recorders and even a recording studio. None of this is absolutely essential, and some huge shows have been produced by companies who have nothing more than a couple of offices and a telephone.

What is important is the quality of work they produce. This will be seen when they show some of their work. In viewing this, the organizer has to consider the objectives each piece was intended to achieve and whether or not it succeeded. The organizer should not be dazzled by the number of projectors in use. The technicalities of what was done are not as important as the effect on the audience.

Probably one of the best ways of judging a production company is to talk to some of their clients. The fact that a company has worked for a client only once is not important because of the way in which jobs are placed. Generally, this will involve a client asking three companies to pitch for a job.

Competitive pitches
The best time to handle a competitive pitch is when the organizer does not have a conference in view. When a conference is looming

the pressures often result in hasty decisions. It has to be admitted, however, that the average manager who will be appointing a production company will only be able to do so in response to a demand for a conference. Under these circumstances, he has to choose at most three companies to pitch. More than this is time-consuming and carries no benefit. Each company must be told what the conference involves and be given the opportunity to ask questions.

Putting together a pitch is an expensive process, so the organizer should actively discourage the production of models of the set and video tapes produced especially for the occasion. The cost of these elements will inevitably be fed back into production budgets as part of the overhead of running the company.

When the companies present their concepts for the show, the organizer should consider which company has created an idea which will help to achieve the objectives. In addition, he or she should bear in mind that there is a great deal to learn from a professional production company: once the choice has been made, then the production company must be taken completely into the organizer's confidence. All of these companies regularly deal with material that is of a commercially sensitive nature. If they make a habit of divulging it to outside parties, they will not last long in the business.

Production company costs

Conference production companies gain revenue in two main ways. Everything that they buy in for a client will usually carry a mark-up, the amount of which will vary from one company to another. The second method is for the production company to charge a production fee. These are not alternatives. Usually a company will charge a fee and charge a mark-up as well.

The ways in which overheads are recovered varies, too. Some companies recharge everything from travelling costs to staff time and photocopying. Others charge these items selectively. The extent to which this is acceptable by the client is a matter for the organizer to decide.

• CHECKLIST •

- **Establish sources for:**
  - a the set
  - b a lectern
  - c slide, film and video projectors as appropriate
  - d a suitable sound system
  - e appropriate lighting

- **Establish the content:**
  - a source the scripts
  - b determine slide content
  - c create a storyboard
  - d produce all necessary slides
  - e if film or video is needed, establish content
  - f source script(s) for film or video
  - g produce film or video treatment
  - h produce film or video
  - i if slide/tape programmes are to be used, establish content
  - j source script(s)
  - k produce storyboard(s)
  - l record script and produce slides
  - m programme projectors against soundtrack

- **Using an outside production company:**
  - a draw up a shortlist of suitable companies
  - b visit those on the short-list
  - c either brief one or select three to pitch for the job
  - d write a brief for the three and give it to them
  - e assess response and choose the best

5

Planning the conference sessions

Whether a conference is to be produced in-house or by an outside production company, a brief is a necessary part of the production process. For the in-house show, it helps the organizer to get his or her thoughts in order. For the outside production company, it is vital that they be told what is required and why. It is then their job to tell the organizer how they propose to go about the job.

The brief

The brief must contain certain information that may, on the face of it, seem obvious. The dates of the event, the numbers in the audience and the location are all obvious facts. However, for some, the need to set out the objectives of the meeting may be less apparent.

Objectives

Unless everyone involved knows what is to be achieved through the conference, it will lack direction and may appear woolly to the audience. It is important that the objectives should not be confused with the content. The two are not interchangeable. The objectives explain why a conference is being organized and what is to be achieved. The content is the message to be communicated.

A conference being staged to launch a new product may also be required to motivate the audience to take advantage of the opportunities being presented. Thus, one of the objectives will be to motivate. The content will probably include the specification of the new product, the advantages that it has over its competitors, and the sales volumes expected of it.

Alternatively, it may be that the company has been going through a rough patch in the market, and under these circumstances one objective may be to build the confidence of the audience in the ability of the client to weather the storm and succeed in the future. The content would involve showing how the company plans to overcome its difficulties.

Conference content
The content of the conference should also be spelled out in the brief along with the reasons for including the information to be communicated. For example, it may be that the client wants to explain marketing plans for the next twelve months in order that the audience can link their own promotional activities to those of the client. The second part of this requirement could affect the style of the conference and so it has to be shown in the brief in order that it is properly considered in producing the event.

What is the audience used to?
Less obvious than the need to set out the objectives and content may be the need to explain who will be in the audience and the type of conferences that the client has organized before. If the audience sees conferences staged by other clients, then it is worth trying to find out what sort of event these are.

The reason for declaring both of these factors is that each audience has an expectation level. For example, car dealers attending the launch of a new car will probably expect a fairly lavish style of event because that is common practice within the industry. Another audience may have been used to fairly low-key conferences in the past and so, not only is it not necessary to use adventurous staging tricks, they may actually get in the way of the message of the conference.

Speakers
This is also the time to address the question of who is to speak in the conference. Ideally, this should be done by first deciding how the content should be divided into manageable sections. If specific parts of the conference need to be dealt with by live presenters rather than with film, video or audio-visual modules, then the organizer should be able to decide who would be best suited to speaking to the various subjects. Part of this task involves achieving a good balance between live speakers and pre-recorded material. If an outside production company is going to handle the event, then they should be given the freedom to recommend the best mix of the available media.

Budget
The available budget should also be shown in the brief. Some clients object to doing this on the grounds that the production company will happily spend every farthing that is declared available. Maybe that is true; but the alternative is the equivalent of telling someone that you want him to sell you a car and then refusing to tell him how much you are prepared to pay. Under the circumstances, it would be hardly surprising if he offered a Jaguar when you only had enough to pay for a Metro.

A compromise would be to declare to the production company only 90 per cent of the budget so that there is a contingency which the organizer can choose to spend at a later date if it is necessary.

Although that will ensure that funds are available to pay for unforeseen expenditure, the practice of not telling a production company how much money is available is fairly pointless. Within reason, a good production company will be able to devise a show within whatever budget is declared. The fact that they know that more money is available does not mean that they will only produce the same show as they would have done on a smaller budget but charge more for it. Responsible production companies will devise a show that uses the budget as efficiently as possible.

What does the budget cover?
It is, however, necessary to lay out in detail what is to be included in the budget. Typically, this would be the design and building of a set; the design and production of software; the hiring, installation and operation of hardware connected with the show; transport to and from the venue. If the client is going to pay for crew travel and accommodation separately, then this should be pointed out.

What is excluded from the budget?
Whether the show is being produced in-house or by an outside organization, it is necessary to make sure that everyone knows what is being paid for out of the production budget and what is to be funded from elsewhere. If a production company is being used, it will be unusual for a client to expect them to book hotel rooms, design and produce printed items or arrange catering and travel for the delegates. Part of the reason is that most production companies do not want any part of these activities. They prefer to stick to what they know. Some do have departments or associated companies that handle these aspects of the event, but they are in a minority.

Date for the response

Finally, if the brief is a competitive one then it should tell the production companies when they are to present their concepts. Ideally, they should have around four weeks to assemble their responses.

Delivering the brief

The best way to give a brief is in a meeting between the production company and the organizer. If the brief is part of a competitive pitch, each company should be seen individually and they should have the opportunity to ask as many questions as they feel are necessary. They may ask which other companies have been invited to pitch. There is no reason for the organizer to refuse to tell them. After all, the conference world is very small and everyone will know quite soon who is involved.

Receiving the proposals

For a competitive brief, the production companies should be given the opportunity to present their proposals individually. From the organizer's point of view it probably does not matter very much whether this is done at their premises or at the production companies' offices, since the organizer should have already been to see the facilities of each production company.

Once the organizer has decided which company is to produce the show, all concerned should be informed whether they have succeeded or failed.

Briefing without objectives and content

Some conferences involve very long lead times. This is most often the case with a new product launch. Under these circumstances the client will probably not be able to give detailed information about the product. Indeed, for security reasons he may well not want to tell outsiders anything about the product when they are not yet closely involved with the client.

One solution to this problem is to ask the production companies to explain why they should be chosen to handle the event. That will be an interesting exercise for all concerned. Some production companies find this type of response the most difficult to put together for the same reasons that advertising agencies are usually not very good at advertising themselves.

The production schedule

After the brief has been written, the next part of the planning is the writing of the production schedule. If an outside production company is used, they will produce the schedule. It is equally important for an organizer who is going to handle the show himself or herself to establish a production schedule. This sets out the dates when various key events will happen. The sequence is likely to involve the following:

Briefing
The brief that was prepared for the pitch will need to be extended for the detailed planning stage. By this time, if an outside production company is being used, they should have appointed a producer. His or her task is to liaise with the client and produce a show that meets the client's needs in full. The producer who has been assigned to the job has to be given all the information that is relevant. If the producer is kept in the dark on any aspect of the content of the show, he or she cannot be expected to do a good job.

If possible, the producer and the writer must be briefed by the company departments that are most closely involved in the various elements of the show. In deciding what to tell the producer, the general rule is: if in doubt, give the information and let the producer decide whether or not it is relevant.

So if the show is to explain an advertising campaign, the advertising manager and the agency must be involved in briefing the production company. In this instance, the producer must be told what the campaign is trying to achieve and why the particular creative platform has been chosen. While this may not form a part of the conference, understanding the thought processes that led up to it will help the producer and the writer to represent the campaign in the right way.

Site survey
The organizer must have visited the venue before making the final selection. Even so, another visit is necessary now that the outline of the show is known to confirm that all of the planned activities are

possible within the conference. This survey must take place before the set design is finalized so that the designer is fully aware of the limitations and potential of the venue.

Set design approval
A suggested design for the set will probably have been shown in the original proposal. The design that will be shown now will be much more detailed as a result of the briefing and a site survey.

Budget
Once the set design has been approved, it should be possible to produce a breakdown of the budget. This should show in detail how the money will be spent, setting out the costs of the set, the numbers of slides to be produced and all the rest. (see also Chapter 2.)

First draft scripts
This is the date when the writer will finish the first draft of the scripts for the client's approval. If there is anything wrong with the scripts, this is the time to say so. If it is a complex show, or if the client is particularly demanding, there may need to be a further date for second draft scripts. Either way, there must come a point early on when the client agrees to the scripts in order that work can progress.

Storyboards
Once the scripts have been approved, storyboards for the speaker support and for any audio-visual modules can be designed. These will take the form of a series of hand-drawn pictures representing the images that will appear on the screen. If anything is wrong with them, this is the time to get it put right. After this stage, corrections will start to cost money unless they are the fault of the production company.

Photographic shoot
Any studio or location photography that has to be done must be scheduled into the programme. If it is too late, it will delay the production of slides. The dates for any shoots that are necessary will often be dictated by the availability of the material to be photographed. New products are often not available until fairly late in the production schedule. If this is going to be the case, the production company must be made aware of the problem so that they can plan for it.

Soundtrack recording

If soundtracks are needed, then the business of supervising the recording is best left to the producer, except for the initial recording of the narration: the client should be present for that in order to make sure that pronunciation and emphasis are correct. The rest of the session will involve the choosing of music and the mixing of music, sound effects and narration. This is a long, tedious process and it is unlikely that the client will be able to make any significant contribution. If the organizer is handling the production, it is likely that there will still be a specialist production company producing any audio-visual modules. The same guidelines apply.

Whoever is responsible for recording the soundtracks must be aware of the laws relating to copyright. Basically, every piece of music that is likely to be used on a soundtrack will be in copyright, and permission must be obtained to use it. Usually this can be done through the Mechanical Copyright Protection Society (MCPS). This will involve the payment of a fee; for a very popular piece of music the fee can be steep.

Some composers will not allow their music to be used at all. That is their prerogative. If this is the case, nothing can be done. But it is vital that permission be obtained because, if it is not and the MCPS finds out about it, a court action is likely to follow with stiff fines being the usual result.

Lightbox review

This will involve laying out all the slides on a lightbox to check them for accuracy. Some production companies omit this stage of the production process. However, it is an opportunity for the client to check all the slides for content. Any changes that are required as a result of information changing or the client supplying the wrong items for photography — or simply because he does not like something that he sees — will involve extra costs but should be called for at this point. Later on, changes will cause more disruption and may involve increased charges because of work having to be rushed.

Walk-through

Once all the slides have been mounted and loaded into projector trays, the production company will show them on screen for the client's approval. At the same time, any audio-visual modules, video tapes or films should be seen in a rough form. This is 'walking-through' the show. Minor modifications will still be possible, although anything that requires major changes – like rerecording part of the soundtrack – will involve extra costs. In the same way, changes to speaker support slides that the client calls for will involve extra costs. If, on the other hand, he wants a slide change to happen earlier in a script, for example, that will not usually be a problem and should not involve any cost.

The get-in
Time must be allowed for the set and the equipment to be set up. Even for a small, simple show, at least half a day needs to be allowed for this. The bigger the show, the more time will be needed.

Rehearsals
The importance of a rehearsal cannot be overemphasized. Any company that has any respect for its audience must make sure that the whole show works properly. This is the prime purpose of the rehearsal. It is held for the benefit of two groups of people. The speakers need to get used to the feel of the environment and the sequence of events in the show. The crew need to prove to themselves that they can achieve what they set out to do, and they also need to know how the presenters are going to work on stage.

Normally there will be technical rehearsals, which are principally for the crew to work through all the sound, projection and lighting cues. While the organizer may wish to be involved in this stage, he or she must make every effort to keep others out. A technical rehearsal can look very messy and will only serve to worry the average organizer's company directors: they should only be present for the speaker rehearsals when all of the elements of the show are brought together.

One of the elements of a show that can create chaos is smoke. If this is to be used, the organizer must make sure that it is permitted and that the venue knows when it is to be set off. Many conference rooms have smoke detectors and, if no warning is given before the smoke guns begin their work, the organizer may be in the embarrassing position of having caused the evacuation of the building while the fire brigade arrives in force outside. This needs to be remembered, too, with other equipment like fork-lift trucks and cars which produce smoke.

The performance
Everyone concerned with the show should be in the auditorium at least half an hour before the start time. The crew will be there before

that, but thirty minutes is enough to make sure that the speakers are present and ready.

The get-out
Once the show is over, all of the set and equipment must be removed from the venue. This will not take as long as the get-in, but time has to be allowed after the audience has left the auditorium.

Stage payments
The dates for stage payments may also be included in the production schedule, but this depends on the individual production company.

The above production schedule is the type of sequence that would be involved in a fairly large show handled by an outside production company. However, it is worth producing a similar schedule for in-house shows so that everyone understands what is to happen, and when. Obviously, smaller shows will not involve all the stages shown above. There may be no soundtrack recording, for example, so it can be scaled down to suit the event being organized. The important fact is that every show, no matter how small, should be approached in this structured fashion.

Scriptwriting

Even when the production is being handled outside, some of the elements may be handled by the client. The most likely of these is the scripts for company speakers.

Script length
The commonest mistake that is made when writing scripts is to decide that director A will have ten minutes and director B will have twelve because he or she is more important. What should happen is that the content of the speakers' scripts should be determined and then an allowance made to give them time to cover all of that material. This may show that director A only needs seven minutes. If that is the case, then any attempt to increase the length of time that he or she is standing up will mean that there are several minutes of padding. That will not help the speaker and it may mean that another speaker who genuinely needs more time will be cut short in order to keep the length of the conference to manageable proportions.

Following on from this, no conference should run for more than one hour without a break for the audience. After an hour, people tend to get restive and need to stretch. Individual scripts should be kept, so far as possible, to no more than ten minutes. The attention span of the average audience will mean that their minds will begin to wander if anyone talks for more than ten minutes.

Ordering the script content

The process of writing a script should begin with a list of headings covering the points to be made. These should then be organized in a logical sequence so that each idea leads sensibly into the next. Once these headings have been written down, they can be fleshed out so as to form a speakable script.

Writing the words

It is important to remember that a script is being written to be spoken, not to be read, so the style will differ considerably from a written report. The acid test is to read the words aloud and see if they sound contrived, pompous or laboured. The style of the speaker has also to be considered when the script is being written. Styles vary from the Churchillian to conversational. To take an extreme example, if a speaker sounds like a Welsh Methodist preacher, then the style of words that will have to be written down for him will need to be very different from those for a person who has a more formal style. The rule is that the script must be written to suit the speaker. The speaker should not have to adopt a new style to suit the script.

A script is like a newspaper article in many ways. The first line has to grab attention. Instead of starting a script by saying, for example, 'I want to talk to you today about our advertising and sales promotion plans for the next year', it would much more effective to say, 'Ladies and gentlemen, you have already heard that next year we are going to achieve a 20 per cent increase in sales volume. That's quite a task, but the plans for advertising and sales promotional activity that I am about to explain will help us to achieve the increase.' The first sentence grabs the attention of the audience while the second points to the subjects that the speaker is going to cover.

Comedy in scripts

Some people like to use comedy in scripts. It can be a very useful tool, but it needs to be used carefully. Not everyone is capable of delivering a funny line, and overt jokes can be extremely embarrassing for all concerned if they fall to the floor with an almost audible thump.

Motivational tricks

If the script is to be of a motivational nature, then the devices used by politicians can be useful. The politicians call one of these strategies 'the clap line'. A conference speaker will be unlikely to get the same level of applause as a politician, but the technique is useful. As an example, one politician concluded a section of an election address by saying, 'You may remember they tried the same tactic in the 1979 election. It didn't work then and it won't work now.' The line signalled that the speaker had finished speaking about one subject and was moving on to another.

A significant point can be emphasized if it is the third in a series of related points; so, if the sales director wants to say, 'Ladies and gentlemen, next year we shall achieve a 40 per cent share of the market. Given total commitment, we shall achieve that', it would sound more dramatic if he were to say, 'Ladies and gentlemen, next year we shall achieve a 40 per cent market share. I know it won't be easy, but we have the right product, we have the right price and, with total commitment, we shall achieve our goal.'

Final words in a script

The last passage also demonstrates the technique of bringing a script to an end. It summarizes the major point of the script and, by the structure of the words, clearly signals to the audience that the speaker has finished.

Using a scriptwriter

It should not be assumed that scripts for company people have to be written in-house. A good scriptwriter will be able to bring benefits to the conference: a fresh approach to the subject, picking out salient facts that the company people cannot see because they are too close to the subject; and suggestions for a better method of communicating the message.

Speakers

Company speakers

Whoever writes the words, sooner or later someone is going to have to speak them. Nine times out of ten this will be a company person, who will have to recognize that he or she is on stage to give a performance. This is dealt with in more detail in a later chapter, but there are one or two points to consider in choosing the speakers.

First, is there any choice? It may be that the organizer will be told who is to speak, and then all that can be done is to try to ensure that they do a good job. On the other hand, if the organizer does have a choice the job may become more difficult. There is no way of knowing if a person will be a good speaker merely by talking to them. Some individuals who can entertain a bar full of people will freeze on stage in front of an audience. Others who seem to be rather retiring off stage can be riveting when the lights are on them. The only real guide is that technical types tend not to be good speakers. Apart from that, the organizer will only find out who is good when they are put on stage.

Outside speakers

There are other people who will be used in conferences from time to time. These are actors and guest speakers. As with any other element of a conference, these people should only be used when they have a genuine function to perform.

Linkmen

One common use of outsiders is to link the conference. An outsider may be the right choice because there is no one in the company who could do the job as well. A television presenter could be used, and the type of programme that he or she is associated with on television will have a bearing on the suitability of the individual for the conference. The presenters of *Tomorrow's World* have, for example, been able to supplement their television earnings by linking shows about new products, advanced technology and the future for the very simple reason that millions of people automatically connect them with subjects of that nature.

Interviewers

Occasionally it may be desirable to use a television interviewer to ask questions of speakers instead of or in addition to a speaker's presentation. Once again, this is a good reason for using an outsider. The word 'interviewer' is important here because clients have used newsreaders for this task in the past. In fact, the disciplines of newsreading and interviewing are very different, and newsreaders are not always good interviewers unless they have a background in journalism.

Actors

Television presenters are unlikely to be suitable in sequences that have to be acted out, and actors should be used. Once again, the two disciplines – acting and interviewing – are quite different. Actors do not usually make good interviewers and vice versa.

Where to find outside speakers

If the show is being produced by a production company, they will suggest suitable actors or presenters. If the job is being done in-house, then the organizer has to track people down: there are various books that list these people and their agents. If they cannot be found by that means, television companies will often give agents' addresses.

Guest speakers

There are other people who are neither television people nor actors, but who can add to a conference. These are either specialists in a particular field or are well known for some other reason. The recognition event is one instance where such people are commonly used. Themes like 'success' or 'winning' will possibly suggest an athlete or perhaps a visibly successful businessman. In these cases, it will be necessary to go to the businessman's company to make contact. Athletes who make a practice of speaking at such events often have an agent now.

In choosing a speaker of this type, the organizer has to be aware that many successful businessmen are not successful presenters. The best way to find out about any individual is to try to establish whether or not they have spoken at conferences before and then talk to someone who was there.

So far as athletes are concerned, it is worth watching to see how they perform when they are being interviewed on television. A shy, retiring runner is unlikely to be a good presenter, whereas one who is obviously articulate and able to explain his tactics in a race will probably be a success on stage.

Some people in the sports field who are regular contributors to conferences will arrive complete with a prepared presentation that includes slides and film. If such a presentation is available, it can be a benefit so long as it fits the theme of the organizer's conference.

If there is doubt about the ability of an individual, whether a businessman or an athlete, it may be safer to use them in an interview rather than expecting them to make a presentation.

100

Briefing outside speakers

Whoever is chosen must be properly briefed on the event and their part in it. This is equally important, whether the individual is using a stock presentation or preparing material especially for the event.

It is also important to meet outside speakers before their contracts are signed in order to try to establish their attitude. Actors or presenters who are going to be difficult on-site are to be avoided: the organizer will have enough to do without having to cope with a prima donna as well. In fact, there is no reason to use such people. There are more than enough cooperative performers in television who will be easy to work with for it to be totally unnecessary to use those who are 'difficult'. As a guide, any guest speaker or presenter who is more concerned with the way that they will appear than with the content and objectives of the conference is best avoided.

The sad part about this question of attitudes is that an actor who has never worked in a conference before may not realize that demands that might be made as a matter of course in a film studio will be seen as totally unrealistic in a conference. The answer may be to explain the way in which a conference works: the company speakers are the 'stars', and everyone else is hired for a job and very often seen in just that light.

Question and answer sessions

One aspect of conferences that has not been considered yet is the question and answer session. This can be a valuable opportunity for the audience to clarify points that have been made or to make observations or criticisms on the company's business operations.

If a question and answer session is to be included, there needs to be a chairman who will be seen to be firm but fair. A chairman who appears to adopt bullying tactics and to bridle at the merest hint of criticism will soon stifle a question and answer session. He should have no more than four other people on stage with him; panels that are bigger than this become unwieldy and some of the panel will never be asked a question.

Microphones

The chairman must have a microphone to himself. For the others on the panel the minimum must be one microphone between two.

The audience, too, must have microphones and must be made to use them. Questioners at the front of the auditorium often speak without a microphone because the panel can hear them. That leaves everybody behind them playing the game of guessing what question gave rise to such an incomprehensible answer. Even if all the questioners use a microphone, the chairman should still repeat the gist of the question.

There are two ways of providing microphones for the audience. Two or three can be placed around the room on floor stands. This will have the advantage that questioners have to stand up to speak and so everyone will be able to see who is asking the question. It does mean, however, that there will probably be a delay while an individual walks to the microphone after he has been called by the chairman. There are ways around this, usually involving the chairman calling one speaker and naming the next at the same time. In this way the next speaker can be making his way to the microphone during the preceding question. If this tactic is used there should be a vacant chair near the microphone for the next questioner.

The alternative is to provide microphones that are handed down the rows of seats until the questioner has one in his hand. If this is to be done, then there must be ushers who are fully briefed on their job and who know how to control the microphones. Obviously radio microphones can be used, these avoid cable trailing across people's knees as it is passed down a row of seats, but they are more expensive.

Plants
A few questions should be 'planted' so that the awful hiatus that always seems to occur when questions are invited may be avoided.

A footnote

Whether a conference is being produced in-house or by an outside company, the organizer's role is to coordinate all of the many elements that make up a successful show. Even if an outside producer is being used, the organizer will still have a great deal to do. It will be necessary to obtain all the information that the producer needs, make sure that items or locations to be photographed are available on the appropriate days, chase people to produce scripts, agree to scripts and storyboards – and much else besides.

If the organizer is doing the job himself, or herself, there will be a great deal more than this to do: overseeing the design and production of a set, deciding on the amount of sound and lighting equipment that is needed, and hiring it, as well as making sure that the venue is right, menus are chosen, staff briefed and all the thousand jobs that have to be done in a conference.

Contingency planning

Part of the job will involve that old management technique of contingency planning – in other words, 'What do we do if this happens?' Pressure at conferences is such that, when something does go wrong, there is a tendency for some people to rush around making split-second decisions which may not be right. If the problem has been anticipated and a course of action agreed to overcome it, the conference will be much more successful.

Nevertheless even with the best planned shows there are likely to be unforeseen problems. This is where the skills of the organizer really show, making the right decisions under pressure. If he or she can instil calmness in others at the same time, then so much the better.

The secret of good conference production is to approach it in a careful, planned way. If the plan is laid down at the beginning and then adhered to, there is less chance of things going wrong. At the same time, in the planning stage, high-risk elements can be identified and contingencies laid down for use if the plan begins to go wrong. It is the carefully planned conference that will be successful. No matter how creative it is, no conference can be judged a success unless it runs like clockwork from beginning to end.

• CHECKLIST •

- Write a full brief to include:
  a objectives
  b content
  c location of the conference
  d dates of the conference
  e nature of the audience
  f what the audience has seen before
  g any speakers who must be included
  h budget and what it includes
  i the date for the response

- **Create a production schedule to include:**
  - *a* briefing date
  - *b* site survey
  - *c* set design approval
  - *d* budget agreement
  - *e* script approval
  - *f* storyboard approval
  - *g* photographic shoot
  - *h* soundtrack recording
  - *i* lightbox review
  - *j* walk-through
  - *k* get-in at the venue
  - *l* rehearsals
  - *m* shows
  - *n* get-out

- **Scriptwriting**
  - *a* arrange 'bullet points' in a logical order
  - *b* write words to be spoken
  - *c* check for length

- **Determine speakers**
  - *a* company personnel?
  - *b* professional link people?
  - *c* actors?
  - *d* guest specialist speakers?

6

Eating, drinking and sleeping

While the conference sessions have to be carefully planned, they form only a part of the total event. The other elements − leisure time, food, beverages and bedrooms − all have to be planned with just as much care as the conference. The aim must be to allow sufficient time for each activity and to avoid making the delegates feel that they are being rushed from one part of the programme to the next.

Planning the programme

Each part of the programme has to be laid out with the time needed for each activity alongside. The timetable can then be determined.

As an example, the programme for a group of delegates flying to the south of France for a conference at Cannes could look like this:

Day One
08.50	Final check-in time at UK airport
09.50 (GMT)	Flight departure
13.00 (Local time)	Arrival Nice airport
17.00	First conference session
18.00	Cocktail reception
18.45	Buffet dinner

Day Two
08.00	Breakfast
09.30	Second conference session
10.00	Spouses' tour departs
10.30	Exhibition
13.00	Lunch
14.30	First workshop sessions
15.30	Coffee
16.00	Second workshop sessions

17.00	Workshop sessions finish
19.30	Cocktail reception
20.15	Gala dinner
22.45	Cabaret

Day Three

08.00	Breakfast
	Morning free
13.00	Lunch
14.00	Depart for Nice airport
16.00	Return flight departs
17.00 (GMT)	Arrival at UK airport

Taking this programme from the beginning, the final check-in allows one hour before take-off. This is required by the airline and it is unlikely that they will agree to reducing it. Indeed, some airlines demand a final check-in one and a half hours before take-off. It may be possible to negotiate this down to a more reasonable hour.

The take-off time will be determined by the availability of time at the departure airport and the availability of landing times at the destination. While the organizer has to be flexible to some extent, it should be possible to negotiate a take-off time within an hour or so of the ideal.

Many destinations will be on a different time to the UK, both in summer and winter. If this is the case then the delegates' notes should warn them of the time difference. In the above example the destination is one hour ahead of the UK.

Four hours have been allowed between landing and the first conference session. This allows for the delegates to pass through immigration before the forty-five minute drive to Cannes. With an efficient ground operation, they should arrive at their hotels at around 2.15 p.m. Since this conference involved lunch on the air-craft, the rest of the afternoon is available for delegates to unpack and have a brief look at the town before arriving at the conference venue for the first conference session.

In this instance, the delegates will go directly from the conference to the cocktail party. Since they are expected to have their partners with them, those wives and husbands that do not go to the conference have to be told what time they should arrive for the cocktail party.

A buffet dinner is shown and this is because many of the delegates will have had a very long day, having had to drive to their departure airport before joining the flight. Under those circumstances, many people prefer a relaxed first evening.

The start time for breakfast allows sufficient time for everyone to eat before the start of the second conference session.

Starting the Spouses' Tour half an hour after the second conference session allows the staff at the hotel to concentrate on one task at a time. All the delegates attending the conference will have left by the time the tour starts.

It is likely that coffee will be served when the exhibition opens. If the exhibition is not large enough to occupy the delegates for the full two and a half hours shown, then the whole day-two programme should start later.

One and a half hours has been allowed for lunch and this should be more than adequate.

The two workshop sessions have been planned to last one hour each, with a coffee break in the middle.

The break of two and a half hours between the end of the workshop sessions and the cocktail party will allow delegates time to relax and get changed. This is particularly important if delegates are expected to wear dinner jackets for the gala dinner.

The dinner itself will probably take up to two hours to complete. A further thirty minutes has been built in to allow for speeches and a short break before the cabaret starts.

With a one-hour cabaret, the programme will end at 11.45 p.m. The organizer may choose to provide a band for dancing then, or simply let the delegates amuse themselves in the bar.

Once again, sufficient time has been allowed for breakfast on day three, although serving of breakfast should continue later than on day two. Delegates may have celebrated the night before and not want to appear too early in the morning.

The morning of day three allows time 'at leisure', as the travel trade calls it. This is time for the delegates to wander around the town and do any shopping that they want.

A casual lunch would complete the arrangements at the hotels before the delegates are returned to the airport for their return flight.

It can be seen that this programme allows for all the work sessions to be completed, adequate time for eating and time for delegates to enjoy the destination. Delegates tend to take a dim view of any organizer who takes them to an exotic location without time to explore it. Obviously, a one-day business conference in London would be much shorter; but it still needs to be planned in the same way in order to make sure that there is enough time for all the activities.

Although this programme is for a business conference, a recognition event needs to be planned in the same way, with the various entertainment activities built in.

Food and Drink

It is necessary to understand that, as in so many areas of business, you get what you pay for. Many organizers have congratulated themselves on screwing the hotel down on the cost of the gala dinner only to find that the hotel actually reduced the cost by cutting down on the standard of the food and service. That is not to say that deals cannot be negotiated. Of course they can, and any responsible organizer must try to get the best possible price for what is wanted. However, there is a limit to how much an hotel can trim off its price.

Coffee breaks
The venue, whether it is an hotel or a conference-centre, will quote a price for this and possibly include biscuits. Surprisingly, the price will usually be per head rather than per cup. This is because it is more difficult to keep track of the number of cups of coffee that are served and because the venues know from experience how many cups the average delegate will consume.

Probably the best way to cut the cost of the coffee breaks is to dispense with the biscuits. The chances are that no one will notice if they are not there and a few pence per head will be trimmed off the cost if they are not provided. While that may seem a small benefit, if it is grossed up for the numbers attending, it can be a significant sum of money.

Cocktails
Pre-lunch drinks will be priced in the same way. The venue will usually quote a cost per head for a thirty-minute session. This will vary depending on the type of drink to be provided. Obviously, the most expensive is a full bar. When the drinks are free, most peoples' tastes go up by several notches and many will discover a liking for double brandies when they would not buy those for themselves in a pub.

A straight choice of red or white wine will be cheaper, although

108

organizers should not accept a cheap but undrinkable house wine merely on the basis that very few people will drink it because it is so foul. Nor should he or she be bamboozled into paying for an excellent wine, being ashamed to admit to not knowing the difference between a Chablis Grand Cru and Beaujolais Villages. In fact it is probably not worth paying for a really good wine because most people will not appreciate the extra quality in a conference environment.

It is a curious fact that one of the cheapest forms of pre-lunch drink is Champagne or sparkling wine. The reason is because most people will drink no more than half a bottle before they begin to feel bloated by the bubbles.

The way in which the drinks are served will also affect the amount that is drunk. Service from trays will usually mean that the delegates will drink more because it is very easy to grab a drink from a passing tray. It takes longer to go to a bar and wait for a barman to serve a drink.

Whichever method of service is chosen, the organizer should make sure that the drinks are as far as possible from the doors to avoid people gathering at the entrance.

One of the factors that has to be considered when deciding whether or not to have pre-lunch drinks is the form of the conference programme after lunch. If there is to be another conference session and the delegates have drunk freely at the bar and then taken wine with the meal, they are less likely to be alert when the first speaker stands up after lunch. Obviously this is not usually a consideration with a cocktail party before dinner. However, the rules shown above still hold good for an evening cocktail party.

Special cocktails
One possibility that can be considered is the creation of a special cocktail for the event. This could reflect the company's corporate colours by the judicious use of different ingredients, or it could simply be a matter of creating a different drink. The chief barman in any venue will be likely to be flattered to be asked to create a special drink. However, the organizer must try any concoction before inflicting it on his delegates.

Food
When considering food, it helps to understand how the hotel arrives at the price for a given menu. Many venues work on the basis that

the raw food will cost around one-third of the menu price. Departmental overheads for things like heat, light, refurbishment, redecoration and so on will take another third. The final third will cover labour, including the waiters and profit.

From this it can be seen that, if an organizer chooses a particular menu and then negotiates down to a very low price, the only area in which the venue can cut its costs is in labour.

There is one basic and inescapable fact about the menu: no matter how hard the organizer tries it will never be possible to please everybody. Even with a traditional standby like roast beef and Yorkshire pudding there will be those who do not like beef, and there may be strong-minded Lancastrians who refuse to eat the 'foreign' addition. An additional factor to consider is that beef is expensive and so, for that reason, if for no other, the organizer would be well-advised to choose another dish.

There is also likely to be a proportion of people who are on special diets. These fall into three groups: those who are forbidden to eat certain foods because of a medical condition like diabetes, and people on a salt- or fat-free diet; religious groups such as Jews and Muslims; and people who choose not to eat certain foods. The last group will usually be vegetarians, although they come with various tastes: some will eat fish but not eggs, others will eat eggs but not fish. Vegans, of course, will only eat vegetables; fortunately they are rare.

Most venues will be able to cope with all dietary requirements but they do need to be told well in advance.

The chef

For the majority of people the normal range of menus offered will be sufficient. When choosing these, the organizer should realize that the cooperation of the chef is essential to make the meal a real success. Chefs have to train for many years and work very peculiar hours. Very often they regard themselves as being highly creative, and some undoubtedly are. A chef is likely to feel that his or her talents are wasted if asked only to produce a slice of melon, followed by roast chicken and crème caramel. Chefs like to be able to exercise their talents and this can often be to the advantage of the organizer because food that is cheap in its raw state can be transformed by a talented chef into a dish that will look extremely expensive when it is served.

Choice of dishes

It is best not to offer delegates a choice of dishes — with the exception of those needing special food — because this will make the service slower and it will be more difficult to estimate how many portions of each of the dishes to prepare. Because of this, some delegates will find that they do not have the choice shown on the menu and they will feel cheated.

Cuisine à trois

When choosing menus, it is worth insisting on a meeting with the banqueting head waiter, the banqueting sales manager and the chef. Part of the reason for this stems from the attitudes of these people.

For example, the banqueting sales manager will be convinced that he does not get the support he deserves from either the chef or the banqueting head waiter. The chef will be certain that the sales staff do not understand the first thing about banqueting food and he will know that, as soon as a dish is handed over to the waiters, it will be ruined. The banqueting head waiter, for his part, will tell anyone who will listen that the other two do not know what goes on in the banqueting room. It is his staff who get it in the neck from the diners when something goes wrong.

The best way to overcome these animosities is to demand a meeting with all three. It may be difficult to arrange this because the sales manager may well be reluctant to ask the chef to attend such a meeting. Chefs are very often autocratic and the shortage of good chefs means that everyone lives in fear of crossing them. Even so, pressure should be put on the venue to arrange a meeting at which all those involved can discuss the event and find the best programme for the organizer.

Between them, they may be able to suggest a theme for a meal. This may relate to the company, the product or the venue. Many hotels regularly arrange themed evenings and have the necessary equipment and contacts to arrange this, so a conference during which an incentive campaign with a prize of a holiday in the Caribbean could finish with a dinner with a Caribbean theme. The range of themes is limited only by the imagination of the people involved in the planning.

At the same time, by involving all three in the discussions the organizer should get a better result. The chef will know what dishes can be provided at a price the organizer is prepared to pay and may be able to suggest variations and additions that will enhance the meal. The banqueting head waiter may be able to suggest ways of introducing drama to a dinner. For example, if Baked Alaska is served, it will be much more dramatic if all the waiters enter at once with some sparklers in the Baked Alaskas. If a buffet is being provided, then the chef may want to produce a centre-piece that represents the company's main product or their logo.

So each of the three should be given the opportunity to understand what the organizer wants and to suggest ways of improving the programme.

Buffets
If the meal has to be served and eaten within a certain space of time, then a buffet may be quicker than a meal with silver service. Either style will be quicker if the first course is one that can be placed on the table before the delegates sit down. If a buffet is provided, there is a characteristic of British audiences that has to be taken into account: they make queues.

One Spanish banqueting manager was very distressed to find that his buffet was taking much longer to operate than he had expected. It was simply that he had laid it out as he would for a Spanish group who would quite happily gather all round the buffet, helping themselves to what they wanted. The British made an orderly queue. So the buffet has to be laid out in such a way as to make it plain that delegates can go to whatever point on the table they want; either that, or be designed so that people can pass down the buffet quickly.

What about the quality?
Judging the quality of the food that is likely to be served is difficult. Venues have a habit of inviting organizers to lunch in order to sample the standard of food that can be provided. This is a pointless exercise because a lunch for two or three people is a very different logistical matter than for a dinner for 200. The organizer must also recognize that it takes longer to serve a gala dinner than would be allowed for a meal in a restaurant. The best way to judge the standard of food and service is to ask to see a similar meal being served to a group of similar size.

Wine
Wine is habitually served with dinner and very often with lunch too. The venue will suggest a suitable allowance per head and quote on that basis. This may be as much as half a bottle or more of red and

a similar amount of white. This is a matter for the organizer to decide on; if he or she is too parsimonious in his allowance, there will be complaints. Many after-dinner speakers have gained a heartfelt laugh by proposing a toast to absent friends, 'On this occasion linked with the name of the wine waiter'.

Company directors will often give orders for more wine to be brought without any thought for the cost implications of what they are doing. This sort of late demand can also cause untold problems since there may not be enough chilled white wine available.

After-dinner drinks

Drinks after dinner are a difficult area to deal with. If the delegates are to stay at their tables for a cabaret, then they will almost certainly want drinks. This can be a very expensive matter since some individuals can consume a surprising amount of liquor in an hour. It may be that the organizer decides that all drinks after the meal will have to be paid for by the delegates. If this is the case then it must be made abundantly clear to all concerned. At the very least, the menu should carry the line 'cash bar' after the last part of the meal for which the client is paying.

If the client is going to provide drinks, then it may be best to supply one liqueur per person and then place jugs of beer, soft drinks, whisky and gin on the tables with an appropriate number of mixers.

One other point to remember is that, if there is a cabaret, then the drinks service should be suspended while it is on. This must be made clear to the delegates since they can be very annoyed if all the waiters disappear after dinner, or if those who stay to watch the cabaret fail to respond to demands for more drinks.

Breakfast

Breakfast will almost certainly be served in the delegates' hotels. Many people still like a traditional English breakfast, although this will be called an American breakfast by some continental hotels. The interpretation of an English breakfast varies from country to country. Bacon will usually be cooked to a crisp and English sausages will be unobtainable. Those that will be provided may have a flavour that is distinctly odd to a British palate.

Even boiled eggs can be a problem. At least one Spanish hotel seems to prepare these by loading raw eggs into a metal dish full of lukewarm water. One delegate at this hotel opened seven eggs that were still raw before settling for toast and jam. (Marmalade is a peculiarly British product and is unlikely to be available abroad.)

Whatever form the breakfast takes, it must be capable of being served quickly. This will usually mean that it needs to be a buffet style of operation. If the room in which it is served can accommodate all the delegates in the hotel, then it should be possible for all of them to have breakfast at the same time before leaving for the conference. If they have to be at the venue at 9 a.m. they will probably all arrive for breakfast at 8 a.m.

Fiddles

Of course, fixing the cost of the various meals and drinks sessions is only one part of the cost element of food and drink. Any barman will be likely to know a range of ways of supplementing his earned income with various fiddles. These range from the equivalent of an office worker using the photocopier for his own needs, to overt theft. It is highly unlikely that any venue will condone such activities, but they cannot always even find a well-constructed fiddle that is being operated on their premises. The fiddles are usually operated for the benefit of a barman.

In its simplest form, the fiddle is simply a matter of the staff helping themselves to drinks. One organizer went behind the set during a dinner and found a waiter with a bottle to his lips. The waiter looked at the organizer and said, 'Waiter's perks sir' and went back into the room.

Others fall into two main categories. When the bottles are set out for a bar it is possible for the organizer to check that there are as many as were promised; and at the end of the evening to check the number of empties. However, only extreme vigilance would reveal if a barman was substituting the odd empty bottle for a full one and pocketing the full one.

The other fiddle tends to be operated with a cash bar. The hotel will expect a sum of money equivalent to the number of empty bottles returned after the bar has closed. If the barman buys a bottle of Scotch in an off-licence and sells the contents of it over. the bar, he can pocket the money paid for those drinks by the delegates. The books are kept straight but the barman will have picked up extra cash.

When an organizer is trying to figure out whether the bar prices are fair, it helps to know that the average hotel will squeeze 32 measures out of a bottle of spirits, 12 to 16 measures out of a bottle of sherry, up to 30 out of a bottle of liqueur and around six glasses out of a 75 centilitre bottle of wine.

One final point on drinks. If it appears that everyone has drunk everything that was offered and has taken the full allowance of wine, then there is something wrong. Unfortunately, by the time the organizer notices this, it will be too late: it will not be possible to prove that the venue's figures are wrong.

Tipping

Tips are another source of problems. The hotel and catering businesses use these to an extent that is unknown in most other areas of commercial activity. For example, in the past the Concierge may have had to pay for his job. Although this is not the case now, he will be paid a pittance because he and his employers know that he will have a considerable income from tips. The banqueting staff also expect tips. These may be accepted and kept by an individual, or they may be placed in a common pool or tronc. This will then be divided between each member of the staff, the amount they receive depending on their seniority.

However it is operated, the practice of tipping is an anachronism. Nevertheless it exists and the conference organizer has to accept it and play along. If a tip is not given there is nothing the staff can do on that occasion; but they may have their revenge if the organizer ever returns to the venue in the future.

In-flight catering

The final part of the catering that may have to be considered is that provided on aircraft being used for overseas venues.

If an organizer is chartering a complete aircraft, then the range of meals available is limited only by the catering facilities at the departure airport. Many people today are familiar with the pressed meat and limp salads that seem to be staple airline fare. Organizers need not accept that since full first-class standard catering can be provided − at a price. Arranging this will be one of the services that the travel agent will be able to provide.

With scheduled flights the choice is more limited. Airlines are reluctant to give special treatment to one group of passengers even if it has been paid for, since it creates problems with other passengers wanting to know why they cannot have the same food. Added to that, anything that changes the normal routine for the cabin staff increases the chances of things going wrong. So, with scheduled flights, it is probably best to accept the normal catering.

Feeding the workers
It should not be forgotten that the people organizing and running the event need to eat too. Conference crews often have to work long and difficult hours, and this will mean that they have to eat at strange times. The organizer must make sure that the venue can provide a good standard of food at those times. Similarly, coffee and soft drinks should be readily available throughout working hours.

This is particularly important for breakfast. Crews often have to start work very early in the day and the organizer must make sure that they can get breakfast before beginning their day's labours. Arranging this is a small price to pay to make sure that the event comes together properly.

Accommodation

This is one area in which the organizer does have some leeway for hard negotiations. The bulk of the cost of providing bedrooms has to be paid whether or not they are being occupied. As a result, negotiating a better price on bedrooms will not have the potentially disastrous effect of similar action on meals.

The time of year that the conference takes place will affect the room rate. If a conference is to be held in London in September, it is likely that the organizer will have to pay a higher price than four weeks earlier or later: it is all a question of market demand.

If the hotel will have no problem filling its rooms with full-price business, why should it provide discounts to a conference organizer? Apart from the revenue involved, if the hotel is full with conference delegates, the hotel's regular business guests who come back time after time will have to be turned away during the conference. There is aways a risk that they will decide to take their custom to the alternative hotel they go to as a result. So it pays for the organizer to be flexible on dates if possible.

Bedroom rates
Most hotels operate several different tariffs. There will be a RAK rate which is the most that they charge for any given room. Then there may be a range of business rates which depend on the volume of

business provided by any individual company. This is the same as a bulk discount. Travel agents bringing tours in will get yet another rate, as will airlines for their staff when they appoint an hotel to provide crew accommodation.

The hotel may begin the ritual bargaining by offering a discount off the RAK rate. The amount of this discount will depend on some of the factors already mentioned. Even so, the organizer, in trying to get a lower price, should point out the volume of business, particularly if this is to be provided in the low season or at weekends in a city centre.

The hotel should also be reminded about the amount of food and beverage business being brought in. The amount of discount that is offered in the end depends on the organizer's negotiating skills as well as the time of year, the amount of catering involved and the health and mood of the sales manager.

Obviously, the overall cost of the rooms can be reduced if it is acceptable to put two people in twin bedded rooms. However, this is an option that will not be open to many organizers.

What does the organizer pay for?
Once all the deals have been struck, it is necessary to decide what the organizer is prepared to pay for.

Many hotel rooms today have direct dial telephones, mini bars, and some have in-house movies for which the guest has to pay.

With international telephone calls being so easy to make, direct-dial telephones are risky if it is not made very clear that each individual delegate is responsible for extras charged to his or her room. The same goes for mini bars, in-house movies, valet and room service and all the other costs that a delegate can charge to the room.

The golden rule with these charges is to make sure that delegates know what they have to pay out of their own pockets. Some staff will be allowed to charge costs to their rooms. If this is so, they should ask to see all the bills that they sign before signing or paying the room bill. The conference crew should be encouraged to avoid signing anything to their rooms. In that way, there can be no disagreement about what they are being charged for.

How many delegates?
One of the key factors in both catering and accommodation is the ability of the organizer to tell the hotel or venue how many people will be arriving for meals and how many bedrooms will be needed.

Since the organizer will be doing this negotiation some time before the event, it may be necessary to revise the original figures as the event gets closer. Hotels and venues are well aware of this and will often provide a date by which the numbers have to be confirmed. Any reductions in numbers after that date are unlikely to be matched by a reduction in the bill.

The reason for this is that an hotel cannot usually fill rooms that it suddenly finds are going to be vacant if it does not know this until the day that the guests are supposed to be arriving.

Food is just as susceptible to cancellation charges, but for different reasons. If the organizer has booked a meal for 200 and, twelve hours before it is to take place, informs the hotel that there will be only 180, there is likely to be a cancellation fee equivalent to the full cost of the food for the missing delegates. This is because the food will already have been bought and the waiters hired.

Whether or not the food is eaten, it has to be paid for. Similarly, the waiters will have to be paid. While most hotels will allow a 5 per cent variation in numbers, it would be as well to tell them the actual numbers at least three days in advance. There should not, then, be a cancellation charge.

Some hotels will build a variation into their contracts and this needs to be carefully noted.

Numbers of delegates are important for another reason. An hotel or conference-centre that is offered a conference that will occupy a substantial proportion of their space in a quiet time of the year will often be prepared to move other bookings around to accommodate the business. By the same token, if the conference is relatively small and the hotel is busy at the time chosen, then it is likely that nothing the organizer can say or do will persuade them to take it. To some extent this will depend on regular business. Some hotels, for example, are popular venues for bar mitzvahs. These are good business because, if an hotel gets a good reputation for handling them well, it will be likely to get many of them. Regular business like that will be protected by the hotel.

Paying the money
Finally, hotels and conference venues will want a deposit at the time of booking. Some may demand the balance before the delegates even arrive. This will vary from one venue to another and it is up to the organizer to decide what is acceptable.

Medical services

The organizer must know where a doctor can be obtained quickly. More than one delegate has caused a stir by collapsing at a dinner or even during a conference, the result of being 'tired and emotional'.

It is possible to hire a doctor to be on duty throughout an event, although he or she will have to be paid. It is to be hoped that the doctor will not be needed, but it is worth having one there in case. At one conference a delegate suffered a brain haemorrhage; because a skilled doctor was immediately on hand, the delegate made a full recovery and was probably better off than he would have been had the same thing happened at home, simply because the doctor was attending to him within a few minutes.

• CHECKLIST •

- Plan the total programme allowing sufficient time for all activities

- Discuss menu content with venue

- Determine what drinks are to be provided

- Negotiate prices for food, drink and bedrooms

- Check availability of medical services

7

The printed word

The overriding factor concerning printed matter is that the ability of the average delegate to misunderstand instructions cannot be underestimated, no matter how intelligent they are in other ways.

One organizer sent registration forms out to delegates and one of the questions asked for the delegates' passport numbers. Several delegates forgot to fill in that particular box. When one of them was contacted by telephone to find out what his passport number was, he said that he did not have one. He had not needed one the last time he went abroad and saw no need to have one now. It transpired that the last time he had been abroad was to go with the army to France in 1944! He was a successful businessman and could have been expected to know that a passport is needed for international travel.

Faced with that sort of possibility, the organizer has to consider the printed material very carefully. What needs to be produced and why? In this chapter the print needed for a fairly complex conference will be considered. Obviously some of it will not be needed by many conference organizers, but it is a question of picking out what is wanted and using that.

First requirements

Announcing the date
On the print side, the first thing that an organizer must do is to tell the delegates that a conference is to take place. Business life today is very hectic and people need a considerable amount of notice of these meetings, particularly if they are to be held over a period of several days.

Because of this, the initial notification may have to go out months before the programme for the conference has been finalized, and so it may not be possible to print a full invitation. In addition, by sending out a letter, followed by an invitation, the organizer has two chances to recruit delegates.

The objective of the letter is merely to persuade the delegates to note the date in their diaries. Even so, the letter must include any information that will generate interest among the potential delegates. It should not be merely a matter of saying, 'There will be a conference on 1 April at Wembley'. The recipient has to be told why it would be beneficial to attend.

The formal invitation

The second stage of the notification process is the sending out of formal invitations. These do not need to be expensively produced in order to be impressive. Obviously it will look better if the invitation is printed on card (what the printing trade calls 'board') rather than paper. Using coloured board will be cheaper than multi-coloured printing and can be just as effective. If the conference has a theme, whether that is a title or a visual style, the invitation should reflect it so that it begins to establish that style.

Providing for replies

In its simplest form the invitation will remind the delegates of when and where the conference is to take place. However, if catering, travel and hotels are to be provided, the organizer needs to know how many people are going to attend. For this reason the invitation needs to have a reply section. The complexity of this will vary from one conference to another, but it can be made to perform several functions.

First, it can be used to tell the organizer how many people are likely to attend the conference. This is obviously important for planning catering and accommodation.

Second, it can be designed so as to give delegates an opportunity to make known any special dietary requirements.

Third, it can be designed to help to save time at the hotel check-in. Hotels usually require guests to register with pertinent details like their name, address and nationality. If there is to be a substantial number of delegates, this process will take some time and is to be avoided if possible. This may be done by designing the reply section of the invitation in conjunction with the hotel so that it can be used as a registration form. Obviously this will mean that the organizer will have more information than really needed; but provided the form is well designed that is not a problem.

The final potential function is when a charge is to be made on delegates. In this case, the reply card can also perform the purpose of a self-billing invoice.

If all of these functions are to be performed by the one form, then the organizer needs to have the cooperation of the hotel and the company's accounts department in designing it. The problem then is to make sure that all the interested parties get a copy of the form. The best way of doing this is to have it printed as a set of self-duplicating forms. This can easily be done by printing three copies of the form on NCR (No Carbon Required) paper. All of the copies are then glued at the head so that a delegate writing on the top copy makes all of the other copies needed. This will avoid the need for someone to make endless photocopies of the forms as they come in.

If the form is to perform all these functions, then it must be very carefully designed. If it is too complex the organizer will have to spend time answering telephone queries on how it is to be filled in. Further time will then have to be spent returning forms to people who have not filled them in correctly.

Reply-paid envelopes

Some organizers provide a reply-paid envelope with the invitation. The decision on whether or not this is to be done is the organizer's. It will not necessarily mean that more replies will be forthcoming. However, if a reply-paid envelope is to be produced, the organizer will need to talk to the Post Office in order to get the necessary licence. It may be that his company already has one, in which case it will be a matter of designing the envelope to conform to the regulations. Even if a reply-paid envelope is not provided, it can be useful to send out an addressed envelope. What a pre-addressed envelope will provide in a large company is reassurance that the replies arrive in the right office and are easily identified.

The delegate pack

The next item that the delegates should receive is an information pack. This needs to go out only a matter of a couple of weeks before departure. If it goes out further in advance than that, delegates will lose the bits and pieces. Obviously, if the conference is a simple internal briefing or a straightforward business conference, a single sheet reminding the delegates of the date, time and location of the conference will probably be sufficient, although it may be necessary to include simple instructions on how to find the venue, the location of car parks and so on.

Overseas events need an altogether different approach. It should be remembered that people have a remarkable ability to lose individual sheets of paper, even if they are included in a folder. That means that it is advisable to design a pack that can be sent out as a complete booklet which includes all the information that they need. Ideally, this booklet should be about four by eight inches (10 cm × 20 cm) so that it can easily be slipped into a pocket or handbag.

Colour-coding

If there are to be several groups going to the venue on different dates, each booklet needs to be identified by date. This may be a matter of colour-coding the covers. This can be done much more cheaply by using different coloured cards rather than coloured printing. Similarly, if different departure airports are to be used and different hotels, these should be clearly shown on the cover.

The delegates should be able to see, from the front cover, the dates of the conference, the departure airport and the hotel.

Laying out the information

Inside, the booklet should be laid out in a logical fashion. It may be that this will be in chronological order, in which case the first section should deal with what the delegate has to do before departure.

Before departure

This will cover items like making sure that a passport is valid, checking whether or not a visa is required and, if it is, where one can be obtained. On this subject, if it will take some weeks to obtain a visa, as it can for the USA, then the delegates must be warned. If an international driving licence is needed, then the delegates must be told where they can get one. If there is a need to register for any special trips or seminars, the delegates have to be told how to do that. Finally, notes should be given on dress, particularly if any of the dinners will be formal. In this respect, it is better to say that dinner jackets will be needed rather than simply say 'Gala Dinner – Black Tie'. One invitation that said that the gala dinner was 'Black Tie' resulted in people arriving in lounge suits with a black tie. Some people will not be upset by that, but others will have the evening ruined by not being appropriately dressed.

Venue information

This is also a good point at which to give some information about the venue. If the climate will be very different from the UK's, delegates should be warned so that they can have the right type of clothing with them. Similarly, if it is advisable for delegates to be warned of potential problems at the venue, as can be the case in North Africa, they should be told what the problems are. In this case it may be a matter of telling them that they should not venture into certain areas unaccompanied.

Baggage labels

The old joke about 'breakfast in London, lunch in Cannes, baggage in Bahrain' can be avoided by the inclusion of baggage labels. They should be colour-coded to the hotels if more than one is to be used. This will make it much easier to sort the baggage when it arrives at the destination. It will help the make-up of the book if they are self-adhesive rather than the tie-on type or the fancy plastic clip-on labels that some incentive companies use.

In designing baggage labels the organizer must consider whether or not to 'advertise' the conference at departure airports. Some companies are sensitive to publicity about their organizing 'jollies' abroad, and so they leave the company name off baggage labels, identifying them only with the conference logo.

Directions to the airport

Next will come information on how to find the departure airport, both by car and by public transport. For car drivers information about car parking should be included. A map showing the immediate area around the airport with appropriate motorways marked will help, as will a plan of the airport area showing the car parks.

Check-in and take-off times

Delegates must be told very clearly the time of their flight and the last time for check-in. Many will want to know the flight number, and most will be interested to know the arrival time. In addition, if catering is to be provided on the flight, then delegates will appreciate knowing about this in advance.

If the organizer has made special check-in arrangements, these must be clearly explained along with the maximum baggage allowance. It is now fairly common for organizers to arrange for the check-in to take place at an hotel adjacent to the airport. This avoids much of the queueing that is an inescapable feature of air travel; if this is to be done, it must be spelled out. Delegates will not take kindly to wandering around an airport check-in area looking for the right desk if they should have been at a nearby hotel enjoying a cup of coffee. As with all instructions, the details of what the delegates must do when they arrive at the airport have to be spelled out unambiguously. Wording such as 'You can then pass through to the departure lounge where you can pick up your duty-free goods' will lead some delegates to expect that the organizer is going to give them free cigarettes and whisky.

Emergency telephone numbers

One extra item of information can be extremely useful. This is the provision of an emergency telephone number at the check-in that delegates can call if they are delayed. If the check—in is at the airport, the telephone number will have to be arranged with the airline; but the organizer has to be sure that, if anyone does call the number, their message will be relayed to the person in authority at the check-in desk.

Check—in slips

Because tickets for travel to conferences are often not sent out to the delegates, one page of the booklet should be perforated with space for the delegate's name and address. These details may be added by the organizer in the form of a label or the delegate may write his own details in. Whichever method is used, it will speed the flight check-in. Obviously, if delegates are taking their spouses with them, two check-in slips will be needed. Check-in staff can then compare these to the list of known delegates to make sure that they are all present and that there are no extras arriving. It is not unknown for delegates to arrive on the wrong day and at the wrong airport.

Equally important is the need to tell delegates that they will not receive a ticket. This will avoid an avalanche of telephone calls pointing out that the air ticket has been forgotten.

In-flight information

Information relating to the flight, meals to be served, time differences between the UK and the destination should be shown on a different page.

Arrival at the destination airport
The next page should then show what will happen on arrival at the destination airport. If the organizer has made arrangements for the luggage to be passed through customs *en bloc*, then delegates should be told this so that they do not wait in the baggage reclaim area while they should be boarding their coaches. If separate coaches are to be provided for different hotels, the delegates need to be told how to identify them.

Arrival at the hotel
Similarly, they need to be told what will happen on arrival at their hotel and the programme for the rest of the day. It is useful, at this point, to add in the details of the programme for the whole conference, with times and locations of various activities.

The return journey
Finally, similarly detailed information for the return journey should be set out in the rest of the booklet. This should begin by telling delegates when to leave baggage outside their rooms for collection by the hotel staff. There should be new baggage labels for the return trip, which may need to be colour-coded for different airports if the delegates will be returning to, say, Gatwick and Manchester. Arrival times must also be shown so that delegates can make their arrangements for their return journey from the airport.

All of this may seem very complex. In fact, it is simply a matter of making sure that everyone knows exactly what is going to happen and what they are expected to do. If it is clearly set out, the delegates will be greatly reassured in knowing precisely what is going to happen, and when.

Delegate room packs

Some delegates will either not read the original booklet, lose it or forget what they read, even if they did not misunderstand it in the first place.

To overcome this, as they arrive at their hotels they should be given an envelope containing the key to their room, a key card, a timetable for that day's events, and any other items they may need such as name badges.

The envelope itself should have the delegate's name and room number on the front. The schedule for the first day's activities should be very simple, providing information on the time, type and location of the various activities. Once again, the design of this should reflect the 'style' of the conference.

Delegate badges

Badges are available in a bewildering range of styles and sizes. The main purpose of them is to enable people to identify each other easily, and so they need to be big enough for the delegate's name and company to be clearly printed or typed.

The simplest form of badge is a piece of card that will slot into the top pocket of a jacket. The problem with this will become apparent if delegates remove their jackets. Apart from that, ladies' dresses tend not to have breast pockets so it may be necessary to use another type.

There are many badges that can be pinned or clipped to clothing. These may be a simple plastic sleeve with a pin or clip at the back. A piece of card with the necessary information is then slipped into the sleeve. The cards can be printed with the organizer's company name or logo or the logo of the conference in addition to the delegate information.

Metal clip-on badges are also available. These will usually be printed with a logo on the front and a self-adhesive label with the delegate's name will be stuck on to the badge. These look much better than the other type but they can be expensive.

The final type of badge is the self-adhesive paper or fabric style. Again, these can be printed and the delegate details typed on to them. They are cheap but have to be used with care since they can damage some materials like fur and leather.

Whichever type of badge is produced, the organizer must consider whether or not it is desirable to be able to identify different groups. Staff, for example, can be picked out by giving them different coloured badges. It can be useful to give VIPs yet another colour if the staff at the venue know that a person wearing a red badge has to receive special treatment.

Daily schedules

So the delegates will now be in their rooms, knowing what they are expected to do for the rest of the first day. The organizer now has to make sure that they know what to do on all the succeeding days. This is best done by delivering a schedule for the following day's activities to the rooms while the delegates are out at dinner. If the sheets are delivered earlier than that, there is a risk that people will become confused.

Other requirements

Menus
For the rest of the programme the printed items needed will vary. Menus will almost certainly be required, and these should be understandable by the average British delegate. This may mean that a translation of some *haute cuisine* French phrase has to be provided. Of course, if there is a simple English language equivalent this should be used in preference to the French. Many people will not know what flageolets are, but they will recognise kidney beans and will probably prefer to be told in a comprehensible fashion what they are going to be given.

Menus, like most of the print to be used, can be personalized to the client by the use of corporate colours and the company logo. In addition, the menu should tell the delegates what will happen during the dinner. If there is to be Grace, after-dinner speeches and the drawing of a raffle prize, these should all be shown.

Table plans
If a table plan is to be produced it needs to be well-presented. This should include an alphabetical listing of delegates showing their table numbers. In addition, people often like to know who they will be sitting with, and so a similar list by table should be provided. However the human mind has an enormous capacity for forgetting simple facts, so it will be useful to have someone on hand in the dining room with a copy of the alphabetical list.

Place cards
Table plans will usually bring place cards in their wake. These should again have the company or event logo on them, and it is useful to have the name on both sides of the card so that people know who is sitting opposite them.

Reserved signs
On a larger scale, most organizers will need signs with which they can reserve certain seats in the conference room. These are often forgot-

ten until the last minute. Many venues can supply them, but it is better if the organizer can remember to have some good ones produced and take them to the venue. Even so, they should not be *too* good: they are often left behind in the post-event mêlée.

Direction signs and flags

Similarly, large direction and No Smoking signs may be needed. These must be identified by the organizer during the site survey. The best way to handle this is to follow the delegate's path and see where signs will be needed. It may be that a welcome sign is needed outside the building, along with company flags and the flags of any nations which are represented among the delegates. The welcome sign and the house flags will need to be supplied by the organizer. Most venues with flag poles will be able to supply, at the very least, a National Flag. Other flags may have to be obtained from a specialist supplier.

One-day events will usually have a check-in desk. This may need to be divided up, either alphabetically, by sales region, department or some other means in order to speed the check-in process. Signs for this must be at a high level so that they are visible over the heads of the crowd.

Questionnaires

At the end of the event some organizers like to know what effect they have had on their delegates and so issue questionnaires to be completed during the closing stages of the conference. This is a mistake since it is impossible to guage the true effect when everyone is flushed with euphoria. It is much better to send these out two or three weeks after the delegates have returned to their offices. The results may not be as glowing, but they will be more accurate.

Transcripts of speeches

In some cases, too, organizers like to provide their delegates with transcripts of the speeches made at the conference. The only thing to watch here is that speeches change. The transcripts will probably have been printed before the rehearsals take place and so may not be entirely up-to-date. This may not matter; but again, it may be better to send these out after delegates have returned to their offices.

Product information packs

Delegates attending new product launches often want something on paper to take back with them. This can be a sensitive area since many organizers will not want their competitors to have the information so soon. It is, after all, practically certain that as soon as anything is committed to paper, someone will pass it to an organizer's competitor. Even so, it should be possible to provide a sheet that gives the barest minimum of information. At least people returning from a conference will have something to show to their colleagues.

Beyond the items shown already, there may be other pieces of print that the organizer will want to provide: souvenir brochures, book matches, headrest covers for aircraft, brochures to go out during an incentive campaign of which the conference forms a part to whip up enthusiasm – these and much else besides can be used. It is simply a question of the organizer recognizing opportunities to maximize the impact of the conference through the accompanying print.

Printing aspects

When the organizer knows what is needed it may be advisable to get quotes from two or three printers. Their prices do vary and savings can be made without any reduction in quality.

Sources of cheap print

Print can sometimes be obtained at a reduced price. For example, if an organizer wants to send out a brochure that extols the virtues of the destination, many towns have copies of their own brochures which can be supplied flat, with only the pictures printed so that the organizer can overprint the text. This gives the benefit of full colour printing at single-colour cost.

This is particularly useful for a trip that is a prize in an incentive campaign. This type of event also gives the opportunity for other gimmicks to be used. A postcard purporting to be from the hotel manager can be a useful 'teaser', while organizers in the past have sent out coconuts for Caribbean destinations and miniatures of brandy for a conference to be held in France. The potential range of items to send is limited only by the imagination of the organizer and the budget.

Printing processes

In overseeing the production of the printed items it will help the organizer to understand something of the printing processes. Of course, some will have the benefit of a print department who can be relied on to produce whatever is needed. Those who do not have such a department at their disposal will have to call in a printer and discuss the project with him. This must be done at an early stage, since printing a brochure can take a considerable amount of time.

There are several different methods of printing, but they all come down to three fundamental techniques. *Letterpress* is the least likely to be used today. It involves using individual metal letters to make up the text; ink is then applied to the letters and they are pressed on to the paper. *Lithographic* (litho) printing, in its various forms, uses a large metal plate which carries all the images and text to appear in the brochure. The method employed for transferring this to paper is of little importance to the organizer, except for one fact.

If letterpress is used the printer will provide a proof of the text and pictures. This will be printed on paper and it is perfectly possible to change the words at this stage because they are made up of individual metal letters. Indeed, that is the purpose of the proof. With the litho technique, on the other hand, a piece of artwork will be prepared and presented to the organizer. This is the stage at which any necessary changes must be made. Once the printing plates have been made any change will result in a whole new plate being needed and that can be expensive. It is not possible to cut and patch a litho printing plate.

The third method of printing is usually only used for surfaces that cannot be printed by either of the first two methods. It is called *silk-screen* printing and, in essence, is similar to using a stencil. As with litho, any corrections must be made at the artwork stage.

All of the printing methods will start at the same point. The organizer will brief the print buyer or the printer on all the print requirements. Designs can then be produced which demonstrate that all the elements have a common theme. This will involve the use of a common typeface, the common use of graphic devices and the common use of the conference title.

If the organizer is using an outside conference production company for the show, they may welcome the opportunity to either design the print or, at least, be involved in the design process so as to make sure that their concept is properly reflected in the print.

Once the organizer has agreed the designs, the next step is to provide all the copy and illustrations for the printer, and this will be turned either into letterpress proofs or artwork. They can be checked for accuracy and necessary changes made. Then revised artwork or proofs are called for or approval given for printing to begin.

131

In due course the printed material will be delivered, and all the organizer then has to do is to get it to the venue.

It may appear that the elements listed above involve a degree of hand-holding of the delegates by the organizer. That is absolutely right. Delegates to corporate conferences have a stunning capacity for getting things wrong. They arrive at airports without their passports. They go to the wrong airports. They arrive at the conference centre on the wrong day or at the wrong time. The possibilities are endless. Everything possible must be done to avoid all these mistakes without making the instructions sound condescending. When the event is under way, clear, concise instructions will reduce the organizer's problems.

As with every part of the business of organizing a conference, the most vital component in producing the print is detailed planning with sufficient time being allowed for the suppliers to do their work. The organizer must also remember that the printed material will reflect both on the conference and the company. For those reasons it has to be as good as he or she can make it.

• CHECKLIST •

- Send warning letter to delegates

- Send invitation

- Monitor replies

- Determine content of delegate pack

- Determine content of room packs

- Design delegate badges

- Determine content of daily schedules

- Determine content for menus

- Design place cards

- Determine content of questionnaires

- Determine requirement for transcripts of speeches

- Determine content of product information packs

- Obtain quotations for all print

- Arrange production for all print

- Source direction and reserved signs and flags

- Draw up table plans

8

Keeping the audience awake

For all too many people, the image of a conference is of a procession of speakers droning on about subjects of little interest or relevance in overheated rooms where it is impossible to fall asleep without being noticed. Part of the organizer's job is to get as far away from this image as possible.

The ways of doing this are many and varied, but they all demand a degree of understanding of the audience. For example, a group of senior bank officials will probably listen with rapt attention to a detailed evaluation of the inter-relationship of the pound with overseas currencies. Faced with this sort of presentation, the average sales executive's mind will begin to wander within the first few paragraphs. If that information is needed, then it has to be presented in an altogether different fashion which makes the content more interesting and explains its relevance to the audience.

So it is necessary to understand the attitudes and prejudices of the audience when planning a conference. It is also necessary to understand a little of the workings of the human body. These affect, probably more than anything else, the length and style of the conference.

Duration

No conference should run for more than one hour without a break of some sort. People expected to sit in one position begin to get restless after that long and need to stretch their legs at the very least. This is particularly the case if the conference is held in an hotel function room because the chairs commonly supplied by hotels have the appearance of having been designed by a sadistic dwarf with a deep and abiding dislike of conference audiences.

Chairs like these will demonstrate better than anything else the truth of the theory that the brain goes numb about ten minutes after the buttocks. However, even deep and comfortable chairs such as those provided by some conference-centres must not be used as an excuse to prolong conference sessions. People still need to be able to stretch, go to the toilet and generally rest their brains from the onslaught of information.

The hour that the conference sessions will run needs to be broken up into several different elements and each should last for no more than ten minutes. American research shows that the attention span of the average audience is no more than twelve and a half minutes. While it is true that a dynamic speaker who has an important message to deliver can hold the attention for longer, they are few and far between; and even then the circumstances in which they can push their luck are rare.

Sir Michael Edwardes, at one time Chairman of British Leyland, was able to hold an audience of 1500 in thrall for twenty minutes on more than one occasion. Part of the reason was his superb presentation, but he was helped by the fact that he was talking about a subject that directly affected the livelihoods of the audience and they could see that livelihood slipping away.

When it comes to speaking, it has to be admitted that although speaking at conferences is now a part of the working life of many senior managers, very few achieve any great degree of ability in this skill and so very few will be able to hold an audience for more than ten minutes.

This business of attention span is often misunderstood by people who point to the fact that a television programme will normally last for more than thirty minutes, as will a feature film. While that is true, anyone watching a television programme will usually comment on some aspect of it, get up to let the cat out or give their brain a few seconds respite in some way. This is what is meant by the attention span. After around ten minutes, the brain will relax for a few seconds. The closest parallel in everyday life is the reading of a book loaded with information. If it is read for more than ten minutes at a stretch, there will come a moment when the reader realizes that he did not absorb a paragraph and has to go back to re-read it.

If such a momentary relaxation occurs during a speech on sales figures or the excellence of a new product, the audience will run the risk of missing a vitally important piece of information.

Sequencing the subjects

The conference having been divided up into different elements, each of which must deal with a definable subject in a concise and interesting manner, they need to be arranged in a logical order. For example, if the conference is going to explain the need for increased sales, the advertising programme should be explained after the projected sales figure. The advertising will be an aid to achieving the desired increase and so it will be much more pertinent after the size of the sales task has been outlined.

Variation of pace and technique

It is necessary to build into the conference a variation in pace and technique. As with a play, a conference has to have light and shade – it should build to occasional peaks before slowing down to allow the audience to gather itself for the next build-up.

This is part of the process of retaining the attention of the audience. If the conference grinds along, slowly examining the minutae of a particular subject, it is likely that the audience will lose interest.

Similarly, if a conference begins at a cracking pace and does not relax until the lights go up at the end, the audience will get lost along the way. So there has to be a variation of pace. A section dealing with an exciting advertising campaign that is dealt with in a fast-moving way must be followed by at least a few moments of calm, and preferably by a more sober subject altogether.

Techniques must be varied too, in order to retain interest. If the conference is to use a mix of media – live speakers, film and audio-visual pieces, for example – then these should be arranged so as to help bring about a variation in pace. None of the elements should be bunched together so that there is a procession of speakers followed by a number of film and audio-visual inserts with no human intervention.

Even those conferences which rely entirely on live speakers can vary the technique. If possible, the speakers should be arranged so that those with similar delivery are separated. If the organizer can position an extrovert, lively speaker after one who is dry and less dynamic without destroying the logical flow of the whole conference, then this will help to make the event more interesting.

The scripts

Comedy

Very often there is a demand to use comedy in presentations. It is true that this can be very effective in communicating a point – as the Video Arts training films have so ably demonstrated – but it has to be used with care. Apart from anything else, very few companies have at their disposal anyone who genuinely has the comic talent of John Cleese.

Once again, the nature of the audience has to be considered. For many, they are attending a working session and tend to view comedy as an unnecessary intrusion. For this reason, overt jokes are probably best avoided unless the organizer can be sure that the audience will react to them. There are few sounds worse for either a speaker or an audience than a joke falling to the floor with a dull thud. Humour in the conference environment is often a matter of a humorous remark or comment rather than an overt joke. In that way, it will be less embarrassing for all concerned if the audience does not laugh.

It will not help, either, to plant someone in the audience who will laugh at the right moments in the hope that their mirth will carry the others along with it. The only effect is likely to be one person guffawing at what others think is singularly unfunny.

Having said all that, comedy can be very useful if it is used carefully. One senior director was making a presentation of a new car on one occasion and doing it very well. He was walking around the car as he talked and the audience was visibly impressed. He felt the mood of the audience and knew that he had them entirely under his control, so when he sat inside the car and wanted a drink of water, he said 'One interesting feature of this particular model is that it has a glass of water as standard in case the speaker needs a drink'. The audience was so in tune with what he was doing that they laughed and applauded, but such moments are rare. The fact is that it is not necessary to build jokes into a script and it can be very damaging.

Variations in scripting

The variation in technique can be carried over into the scripting. The two most important points in a script are that it should be written for an individual to speak, and it should communicate all the information that there is to convey. Beyond that, there is scope for variety.

A director who is to talk about research or development to a lay audience may find that the subject is communicated better by a conversational style of delivery. In order to achieve this, the speaker has to look on the audience as one individual, rather than to a room full of people. When it is written down such a speech will be littered with grammatical oddities because we do not all speak with due regard to the laws of English grammar. In speech, people begin sentences with 'and', 'but' and 'you know'.

English as spoken

It may even help to write the words as they are spoken, so that 'you know' becomes 'y'know'. English purists will probably be horrified at the suggestion, but it can be very effective for a speech. It must also be remembered that the sense of a phrase can be dramatically altered by the inflexion and timing used when it is spoken. The sense of the song title 'What Is This Thing Called Love?' changes if a pause is inserted in the wrong place, so that it becomes 'What Is This Thing Called − Love?'

Buzzwords and verbosity

One point to watch in scripts, however, is the use of buzzwords and phrases that are overlong. Many speakers are described as never using one word where three will do. Phrases like 'at this moment in time' must be avoided and replaced with a simple equivalent − in this case 'now'.

Many industries have their own language. Computers, insurance and even the conference industry use words that are incomprehensible to the uninitiated. So whoever is writing the script must be certain that the audience will understand the language. If there is any doubt, then spell it out. As an example, the car industry often refers to TIV. The fact that TIV is shorthand for Total Industry Volume and refers to the number of new cars registered in any one year will be understood by some of a car manufacturer's staff. Even so, it will be a mystery to many other employees and may not even be understood by some smaller dealers, so it should be explained when it first appears.

Multi-national audiences

The question of language is obviously a matter for careful consideration when multi-national audiences are present. The obvious point here is that simultaneous interpretation should be provided, and the

138

interpreters who do this will have to have an up-to-date copy of the script well before the event in order to be able to do their job properly.

Not so obvious is the need to recognize the differences in language existing between British and American audiences. Some words which are innocuous in Britain will have a totally different meaning in America. If large numbers of Americans are to be present, the scripts should be read through by an American national before they are delivered in order to avoid these problems.

Visual contributions

Slides

Many speakers rely on slides to help them to communicate their message. These can be a great help but, with no more effort, can actually work against the speaker. Many directors have called for slides that bear too many words. Obviously, it is possible to put on slide as many words as the speaker wants. This is called by some 'the Lord's Prayer on a pinhead syndrome'. It can be done but, if no one can read it, is it any use?

In fact the audience is likely to spend so much time deciphering a slide overburdened with words that they will not hear what is being said. The chances are that they will not absorb what was on the slide either. So slides have to be designed with great care.

Film and video

Film and video can be very powerful ways of communicating a message but, like slides, they can just as easily be detrimental. It is a curious fact that an audience is unlikely to notice technical excellence in the presentation of a projected image. However, if it is less than excellent, they will notice the technicalities. Out-of-focus pictures, poor sound quality, poor colour rendition and scratches on film or 'snow' on a video image, will all be remarked upon.

Any film that is to be used in a presentation must be to the highest possible quality. This usually means that at least two copies of the film will be needed: one for rehearsal and one for the show itself. During the show the rehearsal print can possibly be used as a back-up in case the show print gets damaged. For organizers less par-simonious, a third copy should be ordered. In fact, when considering how much the film will have cost to produce, saving a few pounds on an extra print tends to suggest a foolish degree of economy. If that much money has been spent on producing something, then it is worth spending a little more to make sure that the audience sees it in the best possible way.

For the same reason it is worth paying for a decent film projector. Cheap ones have a disconcerting appetite for raw film and also exhibit a remarkable ability to make even Lord Olivier unintelligible.

One final point is to make sure that the show print of the film is usable. This means showing it all the way through before the audience arrives, preferably far enough in advance to be able to take remedial action if it is wrong in some way. Even the best processing laboratories have been known to make a mistake and editors have been known to include the wrong shot in a film. Given enough notice, this type of error can be corrected.

With video, cheap video projectors are good only for demonstrating that a television picture is made up of three colours. Any image projected from these machines will have a colour fringe around it. It is true, however, that an incompetent operator can make even a good projector seem worse than this with the slightest turn of a knob. It is worth remembering, too, that a video projector will be needed for any audience of more than about fifteen people. Below that number, it is possible to get away with two or three large-screen televisions.

One technical point about video projectors and video recorders is that they need to be allowed to acclimatize themselves. If they have been brought in from a car that has just completed a couple of hundred miles in January, then they must be allowed to sit in the presentation room overnight before any attempt is made to use them. Even then, it is worth switching them on for half an hour or so before loading a video tape into the recorder.

Once again, it is worth having at least two copies of the video tape available, along with a sacrificial copy of a tape that is no use for anything except feeding into a machine that has just destroyed a show tape. If it destroys the sacrificial tape as well, then another machine must be obtained before using the standby tape.

Sound, light, and the element of surprise

Some organizers seem to work on the principle that if an audience has to work to hear what is being said, they will pay more attention.

This is rarely the case. If an audience cannot hear, they will mentally switch to another channel. So, whatever protestations may be heard from the speakers, a good sound system will be needed.

In considering sound levels, the organizer has to be aware that sound engineers seem, as a breed, to be deaf. Perhaps it comes from sitting in recording studios with the sound levels turned up high enough to be able to hear every defect in the soundtrack. Whatever the reason, many will turn the volume up to a level that is uncomfortable for the audience, particularly for product reveals. The only solution to this is to keep telling the stage manager to turn the sound down.

Production companies seem to be the worst perpetrators of the 'keep them awake by blasting them out of their seats' approach. They are great fans of the big finish, with bangs and flashes going off all over the auditorium. It is true that these techniques can heighten the drama of a conference; but, like everything else, they have to be used sparingly and with an appreciation of the effect they can have on the audience. This is particularly true if the audience had a heavy night before going into the conference!

The reason for including bangs and flashes is often to add an element of surprise in addition to the dramatic effect. The organizer should always be looking for other ways of doing this. Like a good book, a conference will be more interesting if it occasionally takes an unexpected turn.

When the Austin Metro was launched, this element of surprise was built into the actual reveal of the car. The high point of any new car launch is the moment when it is revealed for the first time. In the case of the Metro, the set had been designed to look as if there was nowhere that such a reveal could take place. As a result, when the car was revealed to the obligitory accompaniment of music, dry ice vapour and stage lights, it was a total surprise to the audience.

This is an example of the audience being led in one direction, confident that they know what is going to happen next, and then springing the surprise on them. A variation of this was explained by Alfred Hitchcock when he was talking about his techniques in making horror films. He said that the audience was classically led to believe for several minutes that something was going to happen. If it then happened, there was a moment of shock. On the other hand, if it did not happen, there was an even bigger shock.

Obviously, the speaker must be seen and yet a surprising number of organizers neglect the lighting that will be needed. The speaker must be lit without the light falling on the screen, so degrading the image that is projected.

Just as unwelcome as the blast of sound is the dazzling of an audience. The industry even has a name for these lights: blinders. Most people do not like to have lights shone directly at them. After all, this is the basis of the classic 'third degree' type of interrogation. Unless it is absolutely vital to a moment in the show, such techniques are best left to the pop music world.

Guest presenters

These are two very distinct types of people and they fulfil different roles within the conference. On the one hand, the guest speaker is used to talk about a specialist subject while, on the other, the professional presenter is used to guide the audience through the conference.

The reasons for using both must be very carefully thought out. For example, no audience will believe that a well-known personality is present because he or she believes implicitly in either the company or its products. We all see too many recognizable people in television commercials to believe that loyalty cannot be bought. The guest speaker must be used because he or she can speak on a subject that is outside the experience of the company's employees. If they cannot, then a company person should be used instead. The professional presenter can be used to help inept company people to give a good account of themselves or to relate the subject matter directly to the audience.

Guest speakers are very commonly used in what are called recognition events. These are conferences that form a part of an incentive campaign. If the conference is taking place in Rome, for example, then someone who is an acknowledged authority on Rome may be appropriate. Even here, care must be used to make sure that the person selected can speak in an entertaining fashion on the subject. Such a conference which takes as its theme 'Success' may need a demonstrably successful businessman or athlete. Once again, care has to be taken since not every businessman or athlete is a good conference speaker.

Professional presenters can be one of two things. They will either fulfil the role of a television-type presenter, such as those seen on current-affairs programmes, or they will represent on-stage the interests of the audience.

One of the functions that such people are often called upon to perform is to interview a company person. If this is to be done, then the company person must not be scripted, or his or her answers will sound stilted and wooden. At the most, the interviewee should know what questions are going to be asked and then have some means of being prompted to cover specific points in his reply. This will sound more spontaneous and believable.

Finding these outside contributors can be difficult. The best way to find good ones is to rely on word of mouth. If anyone in an organizer's company hears a good guest speaker or presenter, then they can usually be relied on to do a good job again. Alternatively, companies that regularly use such outside presenters will usually be willing to make recommendations on those that have been found to be good in the past.

When using such people, it is necessary to know how they react to direction. Some people in the public eye will quite deliberately do things that they have been told not to do. Why they do this will forever remain a mystery, unless it is pure cussedness. Whatever the reason, the result can be disastrous.

Briefing guest presenters
Any outside contributor to a conference must be as fully briefed as possible. By the time they arrive at the venue, they must have a good understanding of the company, its products or services and the areas that are taboo. One very straight-laced client, for example, hired a comedian to act as linkman in one of their conferences. He decided that the event was dying on its feet and so decided to liven it up with a part of his act which involved references to gynaecology. The client was far from amused but, once the comedian was on the stage, there was very little that could be done.

Such diversions can be catastrophic for the organizer, who will doubtless be blamed, but other mistakes can be just as damaging if more insidious.

Other important considerations

Ambient temperature
The temperature of the conference room must be right. If it is too warm the audience will become somnolent, too cold and they will

become irritable. If it is too smokey they will find the atmosphere irritating; and, with so many people being non-smokers today, it will probably be best to say that there should be no smoking in the conference room.

The right time of day
People are more likely to be naturally alert before lunch. If the event has to take place after lunch, or to have a lunch break built in, then it must not be a heavy, banquet-type meal with copious quantities of wine. This will make people want to go to sleep during the afternoon.

Allowing time for breaks
Conferences that run for more than an hour have to be timed carefully. Sufficient time has to be allowed for the audience to eat, take coffee or go to the toilet, depending on the purpose of the break. When it comes to food or coffee, then the catering manager of the venue will be able to advise on the length of time that should be allowed. For 'comfort breaks', the time allowed depends on the number of toilets available. Ideally, this sort of break should be between twenty and thirty minutes. That is just about enough time for people to be able to go back into the conference reasonably re-freshed, although the people running the conference may need more time to make changes to the set, films or slides.

All of these factors will help to make sure that the audience is in a receptive frame of mind throughout the conference. Achieving this state of affairs is just as important as choosing the right venue because an audience that is mentally alert will be more likely to hear and understand what is being said. Under those circumstances, it will be much easier to communicate whatever is necessary.

• CHECKLIST •

- Keep each session to less than one hour

- Keep individual elements to less than twelve minutes

- Determine a logical sequence of the elements of the presentation

- Brief any outside presenters

9

The company speaker

Virtually every corporate meeting that takes place will involve one or more of the company's directors or managers standing up to address the audience. Some will bore them to death. Others will be able to hold them rivetted even though they have a very mundane message to deliver. Whatever their effect on the audience, every conference speaker must be aware that several reputations will ride on the standard of their performance on-stage. Not the least of these is the speaker's own.

While it is true that some people will never be able to give a good account of themselves on the stage, most will be capable of at least a competent performance. This is something that usually has to be learned. In comparison with some management skills, it is not difficult and it begins with the recognition that conference speaking differs from public speaking in many ways.

The major difference lies in the fact that a conference speaker will usually be working from a written script, whereas in public speaking the speech is usually delivered 'off the cuff', sometimes with notes being used.

The immediate danger is that the speaker will sound as if he or she is reading. Good conference speakers deliver their scripts as if it was extemporized. Poor speakers are obviously reading from a prepared speech and, at their worst, lose all impact and sense of immediacy.

Part of the trick of achieving a good presentation is to have a good script to start with. Indeed, the script is one of the most important parts of conference presenting. Even a brilliant speaker will fail dismally if the material is poor.

Planning and producing the script

Length of script
Ideally, the script should be written for a speech lasting no more than ten minutes before the speaker gives way to either another type of

145

presentation – film or audio-visual module – or another speaker. The reason for the time limit is that most speakers will find it very difficult to hold the attention of the audience for more than ten minutes.

If an individual genuinely needs more than ten minutes to cover a subject, then the contribution should be broken up, with some parts of it being covered in a different fashion. For example, if the managing director is giving a run-down on the company's commercial performance which involves a report on the profitability of an overseas operation, then this part could be covered by a simple audio-visual module. The change of technique will help and the managing director can return to finish the presentation after the module.

While ten minutes may seem a very short time in which to communicate a complex subject, it is surprising to see how much can be covered. As a rule of thumb, seven pages of script, typed with double spacing on pages of A4 paper, will take ten minutes to deliver. That is only a rough and ready guide. Every script must be carefully timed, and to do this it is necessary to read the words aloud. Most of us read more quickly than we speak, and so simply reading the script will not give a proper guide to its true length.

Planning the script
The most important part of the planning stage is to decide what has to be said and then to arrange it in a logical order. An audience will find a logical sequence of ideas much easier to follow, and ordering the points to be covered in this way will also help to avoid unnecessary repetition.

Defining the content sounds a very simple thing to do; but any conference speaker is likely to be told that it might be worth while to mention a few additional facts. If they are pertinent to the subject being presented, then fine; if they are not, they must be ruthlessly excluded. They will destroy the flow of the presentation and disturb the concentration of the audience, who will be left wondering why that subject had been brought up at all.

There is often also a desire to include a rebuke to the audience if they have failed to perform in some way. This is highly unlikely to be successful because every member of the audience will assume that the rebuke is aimed at everyone else. In extreme cases, the speaker will simply alienate the audience and they will then be less receptive to the rest of the conference.

So the first stage of writing the script must be to write out a series of subject headings. To those can be added the points to be made under each heading, and then they can be shuffled around until they are in a logical sequence. Anything that does not fit into the sequence must be either excluded or moved to a different part of the conference where it will sit more happily. Unfortunately, corporate politics is likely to rear its head again here: a point that the sales director wants to cover may fit better into the research director's presentation, but the research director cannot be allowed to trespass on the sales director's territory. This is the sort of situation that will call for all the diplomacy that the organizer can muster. There is no easy answer; common-sense must prevail.

The first draft

Once a series of headings has been written down, the script moves on to the next stage – the preparation of the first draft. If a professional scriptwriter is being used the headings can form the basis of the briefing, after which the writer will go away and produce the first draft.

If the speaker is going to write his or her own script, it is probably easiest to dictate the words into a tape recorder, because the form of words is then more likely to sound like normal conversation. It should be agreed with the unfortunate secretary who is going to have to type all the script variations that the first dictation will be done without any instructions being given as to punctuation. The script can be typed with the secretary making a guess as to punctuation and paragraph breaks. In fairness, this should only be done if there is a word-processor available, because the first draft will undoubtedly have to be retyped when the punctuation has been corrected.

The advantage of missing out instructions on where to begin new paragraphs and so on is that their inclusion will destroy the flow of words, and there is a risk that the speaker will fall into dictating a script that sounds more like a formal report. This has to be avoided at all costs.

Writing for speaking

The actual writing is one of the aspects of producing a script that many people misunderstand. The main point to remember is that the words are being written to be spoken. They differ in this respect from a report which is written to be read. Reports are often written to impress, too, whereas the aim of a script must be to produce something that is easily understood.

Once the draft has been completed, it should be read aloud to a colleague to ensure that the ideas to be communicated have come across in the way that was wanted, without pomposity.

Delivering the script

When the time comes to deliver the script there will be a few technical aids available.

The lectern
This must be set at a height that is comfortable. If it is too low the audience will have a splendid view of the top of the speaker's head for much of the time. On the other hand, if it is too high the speaker will look like a dwarf.

Short speakers
Most conferences will involve several speakers of varying heights. If one or more of them is particularly short, then a low box can be provided that can be stored in the base of the lectern. This does mean that the shorter speaker will have to bend down to pull it out before starting to speak, unless it can be surreptitiously pulled out with a foot.

There are two ways of overcoming this problem. Arrange the programme so that the short speaker is the first after a break so that the box can be set during the break; the following speaker can then push it out of the way with a foot. Alternatively, the box can be made so as to provide a narrow platform which taller speakers stand behind. The only danger with this is that someone may fall off the back of the box.

Microphones
Ideally there should be two microphones in case one fails during the conference. They should be positioned one on each side of the lectern so that, as the speaker's head moves to look from one side of the audience to the other, words are not lost. The microphones must be floor-standing and insulated from the lectern. Most speakers need to hang on to the lectern, and any movements that they make will be picked up by the microphones and be heard as dull thumps over the sound system if the microphones are attached to the lectern.

Every speaker must have total confidence in the crew and assume

148

that when he or she begins to speak the microphones will be on. Under no circumstances should the microphone be tapped or blown into: it looks unprofessional and sounds awful at the same time as risking damage to expensive equipment. Returning Officers in elections may do it, but that does not mean that it is right. If nothing can be heard when the speaker begins, it is best to admit that there is a problem and wait for a signal to show that all has been corrected.

Lighting
There must be some form of stage lighting so that the speaker can see and be seen. The light must not spill on to the screen because this will make slides less easily visible. Ideally, these lights should be set at such an angle as to avoid them shining straight into the speaker's eyes. Speakers who squint at their audiences through narrowed eyes tend not to be popular.

Pointing aids
The final piece of equipment that is sometimes used is a pointer of some sort. This can vary from a billiard cue to a hand-held laser. These are to be avoided because, for one thing, they give the speaker something else to cope with. Apart from that, if the slides need the sort of detailed explanation that means the speaker needs a pointer, then they are too complex and must be redesigned so that they stand up on their own.

Methods of reading the script
There are three ways of delivering a script in a conference. First there is the 'postcard' method favoured by public speakers. This involves writing key points on a series of postcards which the speaker refers to. This has the advantage of making the speech more immediate since the speaker will appear to be speaking off the cuff. However, if slides are to be used, the person controlling the projectors will not know when to change the slide on the screen. Phrases like 'Can we have the next slide, please?' from the speaker smack of amateurism and must be avoided, and so this type of delivery should only be used by speakers who have no slides.

The second method is to have the whole script typed out with the speaker reading the script word for word. This overcomes the problem of slide changing, since the projectionist can have a copy of the script marked up with the change points. However, it does mean that the speaker must be familiar enough with the script to be able to look

149

up at the audience regularly. No audience will enjoy a speaker who spends the whole of the time addressing a point on the top of a lectern. The script itself must be a clean copy, double spaced and typed on one side of the page only. The pages should be loose rather then stapled together so that they can be moved aside as the speaker progresses through the script. Some speakers like their scripts to be typed all in capital letters, but this is purely a matter of personal preference.

It should be remembered, too, that some of the modern daisy-wheel typewriters can be fitted with an extra large typeface, and this can help a speaker to read under pressure on stage, particularly if he or she is short-sighted.

The third method of delivery is to use some form of teleprompting system. Two versions are currently available in the UK – Autocue and QTV. This method involves having the script typed on to a roll of paper which is fed through a machine backstage by an operator who is hired with the equipment. The paper is 'seen' by a small television camera which then sends the image to a television monitor in the base of the lectern. A small glass screen is positioned at eye level and the script is reflected in this. As the speaker delivers the script, the operator behind the scenes feeds the roll through the machine at the speaker's pace.

The advantage of this system is that the speaker can maintain eye contact with the audience throughout. It may sound very simple, but this can have a dramatic effect on the performance. When Margaret Thatcher first used this system at a conference, she received twice as long a standing ovation as she had received before. Added to that, the system is still unknown to many audiences and they will be convinced that the speaker has learnt a script by heart. That always impresses them.

There are variations of the system involving monitors placed out on the stage so that the speaker can wander around, but the principle is still the same. The system does cost a considerable amount of money to hire but, for important conferences, it is well worth the cost.

The commonest fear expressed by speakers expected to use this system for the first time is that the operator will feed the script through the machine too slowly or so fast that the speaker cannot keep up. In practice, the operator will vary the speed to match the speaker's delivery. If the script is going too fast, then all the speaker has to do is to pause or slow down.

The other fear is what happens if the system breaks down? Every speaker venturing on stage must have a typed script to hand. This may be on the lectern or in a pocket. Either way, if the comforting image on the screen disappears, it will be possible to fall back on the typed words.

Concentrating on speaking
Whatever system is used, it must be chosen because it will help the speaker to do a good job. When the speaker is out on stage, he or she should have to concentrate only on delivering the script as well as possible. No speaker should have to be concerned with technicalities like worrying about whether or not the sound system is working, and no speaker should ever be asked to control the slide changes.

Ad libs
Speakers must be careful where they *ad lib*. Some speakers seem unable to avoid this habit, which can detract from their presentation if it is done in the wrong place. The slide on screen may bear no relevance to what the speaker is saying.

Another danger is that the speaker will lose track of the subject and have difficulty in picking up the flow again.

Rehearsing

Every speaker owes it to the audience to rehearse. There are two stages to this. First, he or she should become thoroughly familiar with the script before arriving on-site. Then he or she must rehearse on the set to get a feel for what is going to happen. This will also help all the other people involved in the show to make themselves familiar with what he or she is going to do.

Part of the rehearsal period should be taken up with marking the speech for pauses. This will help with breathing. Marks can also be made on the script for emphasis. As an example, the following extract from a script has been marked.

Good morning ladies and gentlemen/ and welcome to this,/ our <u>third</u> annual conference./ During the next hour/ we will explain to you/ the effect of market fluctuations on our business,/ our competitors' activities/ and the actions that we are taking/ to ensure/ that we not only <u>retain</u>/ our market position/ but improve it.

Each individual speaker will find his or her own method of marking the script. The only point to remember is that the marks must be comprehensible when the speaker is on the stage. There is no time for decoding obscure scribbles when an audience is hanging on every word.

Using television

At some stage in the preparation of a conference it may be advisable to have the speakers deliver their scripts in front of a television camera. The performance can be recorded and played back so that the speakers can see themselves. This can be a traumatic experience and so it is best not to do it at the dress rehearsal of the conference. By then, it is almost certainly too late to make any but the most superficial changes to speaking style, and a less than good speaker can be so demoralized by seeing himself on screen that his performance actually gets worse.

Rehearsing problems

Some organizers also like to rehearse gremlins. This should only be done when a good rehearsal has been completed. Letting the speakers get used to the teleprompter going down or a film projector refusing to work at the right moment can help to give them more confidence. This type of rehearsal is not vital but individuals may want to do it.

Using nerves

As he or she goes on stage, any speaker will feel nervous. Within reason, this is to be welcomed. The flow of adrenalin will help to ensure alertness and any physical manifestations of nervousness like shaking legs will quickly disappear. On the other hand, too bad a bout of stage fright can be detrimental, and so speakers have to learn to control their nerves at a level that will help them to give a good performance without making the whole business of speaking painful both for them and their audience.

The organizer may have to wind-up a speaker who is obviously too relaxed to do a good job under the stage lights. This is a fairly controversial suggestion, but it has been known to save a speaker from making a fool of himself on stage because he was too relaxed.

Speakers who do not need this sort of wind-up should be left well alone in the minutes before going on stage. Some speakers resent anyone saying anything to them at this time and their wishes must be respected. They are about to do a very important job and they should be given all the help they need to do it.

For many speakers, the practice of having them sit in the front row of the audience prior to standing up to speak is a particularly unpleasant form of torture. They may prefer to pace the floor while waiting for their cue or read through their script one last time. This can also be irritating if they are taking part in a conference which is being run several times. Having to sit through the whole show over and over again can be very wearing. For these reasons, it is best if speakers can enter from a backstage area where they can use their own preparation techniques out of sight of the audience.

On-stage

Once on-stage there are various factors to remember. Many people's voices rise an octave or so when they are addressing an audience. This is probably one of the many physical signs of nerves. However, current research suggests that a deep voice carries more authority and so speakers should make a conscious effort to make sure that their voices are pitched in a fairly low register.

A voice needs to be projected too. This is just as much the case with microphones as without. A sound engineer will be able to deal with too much volume from a presenter far more easily than with too little. So the volume of the voice needs to be raised without it seeming like a shout. This is a fine line to draw, but it can be done.

This technique is very difficult to describe on paper; but if the speaker takes a deep breath, filling the lungs so that the area of the lower ribs is expanded, it should then be possible to speak as if the voice was coming from this area rather than from the throat. In the most extreme example, this method of delivery will sound like one of the old-time Shakespearean actors enunciating every syllable with great emphasis. Obviously, the average company chairman using this style of delivery will sound a little odd, but it can be used sparingly.

Along with this the speaker must have good, clear diction. The tendency to run words one into another, although acceptable in everyday speech, is no use on stage.

These are some of the techniques of the actor and they are what are needed to make a good conference speaker. Emphasizing a word will have to be done to the point where the speaker feels that he or she is really going over the top before the audience notices anything at all. The same is true of enthusiasm. If the speaker wishes to communicate enthusiasm for the subject, then it must be emphasized to the point where it begins to feel embarrassing: by then the audience will just about be able to discern it.

Finishing a speech

An audience usually begins to applaud when the speaker says 'Thank you'. That is the time to get off. It will also be the cue for the crew to go on to the next part of the show.

At one conference a speaker came to the end of his speech and said 'Thank you'. The audience began to applaud and the crew, thinking that he had finished, began the sequence of slides and music to introduce the next element. As the applause died away, the speaker could be seen mouthing words into a microphone that had been turned off while music began to play and a slide sequence ran behind him.

It is worth nominating a few people in the audience to start off the applause. Everyone else will follow and the applause will sound spontaneous. Apart from making the audience feel that they have heard something to be appreciated, it makes the speaker happier and avoids him having to walk off to the sound of his own footsteps.

Further advice

Drinks for the presenter
The remaining rules for speakers are very simple. The first is not to drink alcohol before going on stage. Microphones have a disconcerting habit of picking up the slightest slurring of words and making it sound worse. Nor will a speaker with a hangover give a good performance.

Cold drinking water should be available on-stage, and it is useful to have it backstage too, unless the speakers prefer orange juice or some other innocuous beverage. Some do need to be used with care, though, because they thicken the throat and make speaking difficult: that is why tea may be better than coffee. Iced water should not be used because it numbs the vocal chords.

Avoiding reflections

If the speaker has a large ring or a watch, these can catch the light and flash or create distracting reflections. Jewellery like this should be removed and left with someone else. Pockets should be emptied if possible so as to avoid bulges in jackets.

Working with the crew

Bigger shows will have a crew of some sort to operate them. Even a show that uses only a simple set, a couple of projectors and sound and light will have people operating the equipment. A speaker on-stage is entirely in their hands so it is as well to keep on good terms with them.

In reality they will do everything they can to make the show a success, and they should be thanked for a job well done. It takes only a minute or so for the speakers to find the crew and thank them after the show, and the benefit is out of all proportion to the time taken.

Gremlins and glitches

Speakers should also remember that they will have the sympathy of the audience when they are out on the stage. The last place any of the audience will want to be is up there in the speaker's place — especially if something goes wrong — and so they will want to appreciate what the speaker is doing. If the speaker gives a reasonable performance, therefore, he or she will be regarded as a success.

This audience sympathy can be played upon when something goes wrong. Gremlins can creep into even the best planned shows and, if they do not prevent the speaker from carrying on, they should be ignored. If the show does have to come to a grinding halt, the best policy is to admit that there is a technical hitch and explain that it will be necessary to wait for it to be corrected. Similarly, if the speaker's throat goes dry the audience will wait for a few seconds while a sip of water cures the problem.

While it is true that brilliant speakers are born, not trained, most people can become reasonably accomplished on the stage. It will take time and hard work, but it is worth the effort because a good speaker can enhance his or her own reputation at a conference in less time than is possible in any other area of business activity.

• CHECKLIST •

- Choose the best method of presentation:
  a read from cue cards?
  b read from a fully written script?
  c use a teleprompting system?

- Make sure the script is written for each speaker

- Rehearse each speaker

- Arrange for applause leaders

- Provide soft drinks for presenters

- Establish a rapport with the crew

10

Cabarets
and other diversions

The rising popularity of cabarets at conferences in recent years has been welcomed by the entertainment industry. With nightclubs failing all over the country and both the BBC and independent television companies cutting back on programme production, company cabarets have provided a very useful alternative source of work. But if the organizing of a conference is fraught with pitfalls, they can be as nothing compared with organizing a cabaret. Very often, this meeting of entertainment with industry or commerce can be traumatic for both sides. With care, the problems can be limited.

As with a conference, the first question an organizer should ask is whether or not a cabaret is really needed. The cost of even the simplest cabaret will run into four figures and it is very easy for it to cost more than £10 000. So the reason for having a cabaret in the first place has to be established. Very often it is used simply to provide a highly entertaining end to a conference. For some organizers it is a matter of providing an evening activity for the delegates rather than leaving them to their own devices.

Whatever the reason, a cabaret has to be as good as possible within the budget allowed, and it has to be chosen to appeal to the audience.

Selecting a suitable cabaret

The biggest problem facing the organizer is that he or she is setting out to please as many of the audience as possible. The first manifestation of this difficulty will be in choosing the cabaret. Many people in companies lose sight of the fact that they are going to entertain their delegates, not themselves. This leads them to choose acts which they will want to watch rather then choosing those that will appeal to their audience.

In fact, it can be more difficult to organize a successful company

157

cabaret because the audience differs markedly from an audience in a nightclub. The organizer's audience has not chosen to pay to see the cabaret. People who are given a free show are widely recognized as being much harder to entertain than those who have paid for their seats.

The effect of the venue
One of the factors that needs to be considered in selecting the cabaret is the room in which it is to be held.

It is usually inadvisable to hold a cabaret in a room other than the one in which the delegates have dinner because the mood that has been built up over the meal can be destroyed in the move to another room. So the banqueting room will have to be big enough for all of the audience to sit down and be able to see the stage from where they are sitting.

From the artists' point of view, hotel function rooms lack atmosphere and this can mean that they have to work much harder in order to entertain.

Duration of the cabaret
As with a conference, no cabaret should last for more than one hour. However, artistes will tend to overrun their alloted time if they and the audience are enjoying themselves, and so it is best to plan for fifty minutes. That will probably end up at an hour on the night. Some organizers will want to get what they regard as value for money by planning for a longer cabaret. In fact, the aim should be to leave the audience wanting more.

Choosing the acts
In selecting acts for the cabaret, the organizer should consider the characteristics of the audience. For example, if the audience is drawn entirely from the south-east of England, they are less likely to appreciate a northern comic. Similarly, a northern audience is less likely to enjoy an effeminate or 'camp' performer.

Wherever they are from, it is likely that they will be less sophisticated as a group than they would be as individuals. Some may like to go to the ballet when they are at home. When they are at a conference they are much more likely to enjoy broad humour.

Once the main characteristics of the audience have been established, the organizer needs to select acts that will appeal to them and provide a balanced cabaret. This will often be a mix of a singer, a comedian who will also act as MC, dancers, and a speciality act like a magician or illusionist.

Some organizers prefer to choose an act that will be able to cover fifty minutes on their own. Most of the best known comedians can do this, particularly if they can sing as well. Obviously, using one person in this way will simplify matters.

There are also some singing acts that can fill a one-hour cabaret very effectively, especially if their act includes some dancing.

Approving the acts
The real problem with the acts, though, is to choose them. This is particularly difficult if there is to be more than one person in the organizer's company who will have a say in which acts are booked. Getting approval for a cabaret line-up becomes progressively more difficult as more people are involved. Inevitably there will be comments that certain acts are not liked. Ideally, one person should be given the responsibility for the job and left to get on with it.

Can the acts do a cabaret?
Selecting acts is made more difficult by the fact that people who are seen and are successful on television will not necessarily be as good in a live show. Others may not have a cabaret act which involves more than stringing a few songs or jokes together. Some comedians are unable to produce a clean act for live audiences. Many organizers work on the principle that they will not allow blue material in their shows, and there is much to recommend this view, even with all-male audiences.

Some well-known performers will not agree to appear in company cabarets.

Seeing the acts work
The best recommendation for an act is for the organizer to have personally seen it. Most of the likely acts will work the nightclub and summer-season circuit. The organizer must make an effort to see anyone that he or she is seriously thinking of booking. An alternative is to ask the agent for a video tape of the act working in a cabaret. It is important that a tape of them working on television is not used as a basis for choosing because of the different conditions. If neither of these courses is possible the organizer should try to get a view from someone who *has* seen the act. This may involve asking the act's agent to tell the organizer what companies have booked the

act recently. Those companies can then be contacted for their comments.

The business side

Finding agents
The names and telephone numbers of agents can be obtained from various publications or, as a last resort, from the television companies.

Bands
So far as the band is concerned, there are organizations that will provide bands of varying sizes for company cabarets. They will be able to get virtually any band that the organizer wants.

Alternatively, some of the major bands have their own agents and the comments about finding the acts' agents hold good for bands too.

When booking a band it is necessary to remember that they will often need a piano to be supplied on-site. Some will use an electronic keyboard, but others still prefer to use a piano. This needs to be properly tuned before the show.

If the cabaret is to take place abroad, the organizer must remember that they will need transport for more than just the members of the band. Drum kits and double basses, in particular, take up a great deal of space, and the bass player will almost certainly insist that his instrument goes in the cabin and not in the luggage hold. This is because the atmospheric conditions in the hold can have a catastrophic effect on a bass.

Availability
When an organizer finds that a suitable act is available, a quick decision is required on whether to make a firm booking. Situations in the entertainment world change very quickly. If the organizer establishes on Monday that an act is available and does not confirm a booking until the following week, someone else may have stepped in during the days that have passed, and so the act is no longer available.

Contracts

Every cabaret act and band must be confirmed with a contract. Very often the agent will send a standardized contract which is in use throughout the industry. These are very comprehensive and there will be two clauses that need to be carefully noted. The first is the one dealing with availability on the day of the event. What this amounts to is that if the act is offered television or film work that conflicts with the dates of the conference, the organizer agrees to release them for it.

The chances of this happening are fairly remote, but the organizer must be aware of the possibility. If this does happen, a responsible agent will undertake to find a suitable alternative act. There is usually no possibility of trying to get this clause deleted. Any act that is likely to get television work would rather turn down a company cabaret than run the risk of missing a television date.

The other clause that has to be especially noted deals with payment terms. Many companies today work on the basis of delaying payment of all invoices by as much as ninety days. Most cabaret contracts will stipulate payment in less than fourteen days. This is particularly important with bands. The Musicians' Union is very powerful and can give and enforce an instruction to its members not to work for a particular client. This could make life very difficult on subsequent occasions.

All dealings with agents must be confirmed in writing. Unfortunately, some of the best-known acts are less than completely professional in their approach, and the organizer will be in a much stronger position to enforce his agreement if he has it in writing and agreed.

Space and equipment

Stage dimensions

In the hotel function room, in addition to the room for tables, there has to be sufficient space for the cabaret stage. The size of this will vary, depending on the type of show to be produced. If dancers are to be involved then it will need to be bigger. However, the size of the stage should be related to the size of the room. A small room will look wrong if it is dominated by a huge stage. Similarly, a small stage occupying a corner of a large function room will look foolish.

The stage needs to be at least one metre above the floor of the room so that everyone will be able to see the cabaret. Obviously this will create problems if the room is less than five metres high.

Cabaret equipment

While it is not vital that the stage be fitted with curtains, it is preferable since that will allow scene changes or props setting while an artiste is performing in front of the curtains.

The stage can, of course, be a prefabricated structure if there is not already a stage within the room. Many hotels have rostra that can be linked together to form a stage. What cannot be changed is the acoustic character of the room.

If there are large areas of glass around, then it will be difficult to provide a sound level that is comfortable without excessive echo. Similarly, if there are windows it must be possible to black them out. Cabarets commonly happen at around 10 p.m., and in northern Europe in summer there can still be a considerable amount of natural light around at that time. Cabarets held in a room where the stage lights are defeated by the rays of the setting sun tend not to be very successful.

Cabaret sound

A cabaret will need a sound system. This may be more complex than the system used in the conference since parts of the band may need microphones and there may be several artistes on stage who will also need microphones.

So far as the band is concerned, drums and brass are not likely to need amplification unless the room is very big. Piano, electronic keyboard and woodwind probably will need to be amplified in order to balance their sounds against the higher levels from the drums and brass.

So far as microphones on stage are concerned, it is a matter of establishing the greatest number of singers on stage at any one time and providing a microphone for each, along with one other which can be used for emergencies or for an artiste following the singers.

The other type of sound equipment that will be needed if singers are in the cabaret will be foldback. This is a system of speakers, often three or more, placed on the stage and facing the singer. The sound from the band and the singer is fed through these and they enable the singer to hear the sound being produced. It is difficult to sing in tune if you cannot hear your own voice. It is also difficult to keep up with the band if they cannot be heard properly.

Lighting

Lighting will be needed for the cabaret, and this will again depend on the style of cabaret. Generally speaking there needs to be enough to light the whole of the stage area well, along with at least one and preferably two follow spots. These are spotlights that can be swung around so that the light beam follows the person on stage.

Some venues will have all this equipment available, although it is much less common than basic conference equipment.

Dressing rooms

The number and style of dressing rooms needed will depend on the acts in the cabaret. Some will be able to cope by using their hotel bedrooms. However, if any of the acts use spectacular costumes it may not be advisable to have them walking through the hotel ready to go on stage. Other acts will need quick-change facilities near to the stage. This needs to be established with the agent when booking the acts.

The ideal is to have one dressing room for each act. These should be close to the stage and should be well lit with a table and a mirror for make-up. There should also be a full-length mirror backstage so that the acts can make a final check of their appearance before going on the stage. If an act involves more than one person, then they can usually be put into one dressing room so long as they are all of the same sex. Even girl and boy dancers should not be expected to share dressing rooms.

Production matters

Briefing

It is worth explaining to everyone involved in a cabaret exactly what the event is about. Some singing acts are prepared to perform a song about the company or its product. Comedians generally want to know if there is anyone well-known to the audience who can be used as the butt of some jokes. Others will want to know if there is any trade jargon that can be used to good effect. It is all part of making

163

it obvious that this is a show put together especially for that audience. The work put into briefing will usually pay off.

Rehearsals

Rehearsals or 'band calls' are needed for several reasons. The acts need to get to know the shape and size of the stage. This is particularly important for dancers who will need to rehearse all of their routines on the stage itself.

The singers and bands have often not worked together before and so the musical director needs to find out precisely what the singer wants from the band.

The technicians need to find out what is going to happen. The lighting engineer will need to know where light is needed, and to see the costumes so that an appropriate choice of coloured lights can be made.

The sound engineer will want to know what microphones are needed and where they should be. He or she will also need to hear all of the people who are using microphones in order to set up the sound system for them. Singers' voices need to be balanced against the band so that the singer can be heard.

In addition, everyone needs to know the running order of the show, who follows whom and where they enter and exit.

Ideally, all of this should be done in the cabaret room when it is free of all other activities. A one-hour cabaret is likely to need, at the very least, half a day's rehearsal. Sadly, cabarets are often neglected by organizers in the rehearsal schedule and the final show suffers as a result.

Outside organizers

As with conference production, there are companies and individuals who will undertake the organization of a cabaret. They will assemble a short-list of acts for the organizer's approval, book the acts, arrange the technical side of things, handle the rehearsal and make sure that the show is exactly as it should be.

Their services cost money but, for the organizer who has had no dealings with the world of light entertainment, this can be money well spent. It has to be admitted, however, that there are some people around who will charge an exorbitant fee for their services. Some will also inflate the fees being demanded by an act and take the extra for themselves. The only way around this is for the organizer to insist on paying the acts' agents directly and then pay the intermediary his fee separately. No reputable cabaret producer should object to this.

One alternative is that some agents who handle acts capable of carrying a whole cabaret can provide a complete package of act and equipment. This will certainly simplify matters for the organizer.

Some difficulties

In reality, the only difficulties that the organizer is likely to experience will stem from inexperience of the entertainment business, its customs and practices.

One problem that is becoming more common is brought about by the fact that many companies are using video recorders to make a video tape of their conferences. For most, this is purely for internal use and will never be broadcast. Even so, it is television and many musicians will expect to be paid more money when a camera is present. Some musicians have been known to leave the stage when a camera appeared, while others have refused to begin the show unless the camera was removed or more money paid. Once again, given the power of the Musicians' Union, the organizer has no choice but to agree to one or other course of action.

Some performers also react badly to being asked not to do something. They sometimes claim that they are reacting against censorship. Others may say that they do not like anyone telling them what they should do on-stage. There is no easy way around this problem. If the organizer tries to say that some areas are taboo, it could be too much of a temptation to an act and he will cheerfully wade in once he is on stage. If his actions are truly offensive to the organizer, then the best that can be done is to complain to the agent. There may be a case for refusing to pay the fee, but, in truth, an artist has to step a long way over the mark for this to be a realistic possibility.

Looking after the artists

It is well worth making sure that the artists are happy on-site: they will then do a better job for the organizer. This may involve nothing more than providing a few drinks before and after the show, or a decent meal. In relation to the cost of the event, such actions are inexpensive and the benefits will be enormous. When considering eating arrangements, the organizer has to recognize that some artists cannot eat before performing, and so a meal should be provided once the show is finished. On occasion, too, the band call will have meant that no one on the cabaret bill has eaten. Once again, food should be provided at an appropriate time.

After-dinner speakers

In considering entertainment, the organizer should remember that a good after-dinner speaker will often be more successful than a cheap cabaret. Indeed, there comes a point on the price scale where a cabaret is not possible.

Choosing a speaker depends on what is wanted. Politicians are available to talk about a variety of subjects and humorous speakers are available from many sources. Alternatively, the organizer may want someone who can talk about his company's industry from an outside expert's viewpoint. It is a question of deciding whether entertainment or edification is wanted.

Most senior people in companies go to dinners where people speak and their views on who is good or bad can be sought. There are some agencies that specialize in finding suitable speakers, but the difference between booking a speaker and a cabaret artist is that the organizer is unlikely to be able to see a speaker in action before the event.

Briefing
As with cabaret artists, it is necessary to brief an after-dinner speaker on the event, the company and the people who are present. They will often then build references to all of these into their speech.

Microphone
An after-dinner speech is best done from the table. This will involve providing a microphone standing on the table or a floor-standing mike close to it. The important thing is to hear the sound system before the event to make sure that it is good enough. Many hotel sound systems are woefully inadequate and if there is any doubt about its effectiveness a separate system must be hired in.

Lighting
It will be an advantage if there are spotlights that can be trained on the speaker. If this is the case, he should be warned in advance so that he knows that he has to stand in the light. A pool of light with the speaker standing to one side of it looks distinctly odd.

Other speakers
It is likely that someone from the company will speak before the guest, if only to make an introduction. The organizer should try to make sure that the company person does not drone on for thirty minutes and thus kill any interest in the guest. Even the funniest after-dinner speaker will be fighting against insuperable odds if the managing director has just told the audience that they are failing to perform. This sort of speech has no place at what should be a celebratory dinner and should be avoided at all costs.

Overall, the key to a good entertaining finish to a dinner is to plan it as carefully as the conference. If enough attention is paid to getting it right, then it will provide the successful finish that the organizer wants.

• CHECKLIST •

- Establish if a cabaret is needed

- Establish style of cabaret wanted

- Establish stage area available

- Book suitable acts

- Source sound and lighting equipment

- Arrange dressing rooms

- Brief the acts

- Arrange rehearsals

- If there is insufficient budget for a cabaret source suitable after-dinner speakers

- Provide a microphone and sound system

- Brief the speaker

11

On-site

Once all of the planning has been completed, all that remains is to install the show on-site and to run it.

Confirmations and checks

Confirming the conference room
It is worth making a telephone call to the venue a few days before the get-in is due to start in order to confirm that the conference is still expected. Although the organizer should have confirmed all of the arrangements in writing, and these should have been acknowledged, venues have been known to get their wires crossed and double book conference rooms. If the organizer has confirmed all of his requirements in writing it will be up to the venue to sort out any mistakes to the organizer's satisfaction.

Confirming equipment
At the same time, if the organizer is hiring all the equipment, a telephone call to the suppliers will ensure that they will arrive with the equipment on the agreed day. Once again, this should be merely a matter of making sure that the written instructions and acknowledgement have been remembered correctly.

Checking the conference room
It is worth arriving on-site the day before the get-in is due to start. The organizer will have the opportunity to make sure that the conference room is in the condition that is expected and that the access for equipment is available. This will save time on the following day.

Checking for damage in the venue

One of the tasks that the organizer should carry out before the set and equipment arrives is a check on the premises, noting any damage that is already there. If damage is done to the venue as a result of the conference being held, the venue will expect the client to pay for repairs. This is only fair, but the organizer must make sure that he is not being charged for someone else's negligence.

Establishing the organizer's office

This early stage of the get-in is also the time to get the organizer's office installed and running. This will provide a focus for everyone involved in the conference and a link with the home office. Having to keep going to a bedroom to make or receive telephone calls will be a severe irritation.

As soon as possible, someone should be selected to stay in the office at all times. There should be no risk of messages not getting through because there is no one to answer the telephone. Similarly, any offices or meeting rooms that are to be provided for the organizer's directors should be identified and set up. It is worth divorcing directors from the organizer because they can have a habit of holding confidential meetings in the organizer's office, requiring him to vacate it at crucial times.

Installing the equipment

If an outside production company is being used, when they arrive they can be pointed at the conference room and told to get on with the job of bringing in all of the equipment and installing it. On the other hand, if the organizer is handling the event it will be necessary to become involved in positioning the set, hoisting loudspeakers and stage lights into position and running cables around the room.

To help with this, an inexperienced organizer should make sure that a technician comes with all of the equipment. Nevertheless it is worth understanding some of the principles involved with the commonest equipment that is likely to be used.

Positioning the set

The biggest and most unwieldy item to be placed will be the set. Even if it is a prefabricated item, once it is in position it is best if it does not have to be moved. When the room was booked the organizer will have made the decision on where the set is to be placed. Generally speaking it should be at the end of the room furthest from the doors through which the audience will enter. It is best for them not to see the cables that will be strewn all over the floor and the equipment boxes stacked behind the screen. Added to that, latecomers should not be seen entering the room from doors alongside the set.

Assuming that back-projection is to be used, there needs to be enough space behind the set for the projectors (see Chapter 5). Having decided the precise position for the set and begun the building of it, it is then necessary to consider the sound system.

Rigging the sound system
This will be made up of three elements: the sound source, the amplification equipment and the loudspeakers. The sources will probably be microphones, a tape recorder and a film projector or video recorder.

Microphones
Obviously the microphones will need to be on the stage, near to the people who will be using them. There are two types of microphone in use, lead mikes and radio mikes. Within those two types there are many different variations, but this is moving into technicalities that need not worry the organizer too much. A good equipment supplier will make sure that the right type of microphone is provided so long as the organizer tells him what it is needed for. Generally speaking this is a matter of explaining which microphones will be needed for conference speakers and which for musical instruments. The characteristics of each can be different.

Lead mikes
A lead mike is the traditional type that most people have seen in use. The sound signal is sent along a cable to the amplifier, and so allowances will have to be made for those cables. This is particularly important for the lectern mikes. The organizer may want to take the lead through the stage and then out from underneath. This may have to be done before the building of the stage has been completed.

Radio mikes
A radio mike is a completely free unit since the signals are sent from it by radio to a receiver that then feeds them into the amplifier. This

is the type that will often be used by a speaker who has to move around the stage. Radio mikes are available as either the traditional hand-held type or the small microphone that can be pinned to a lapel or tie. A lapel mike will be connected by a thin wire to a small transmitter which has to be placed in a pocket or fixed to a belt.

Positioning microphones

Whichever type of microphone is used, they usually have to be positioned behind the line of the loudspeakers. The reason for this is that if they are in front they will pick up sound from the loud-speakers, and this will appear as a howl, known in the trade as 'feedback'.

Loudspeakers

The loudspeakers will have to be on the audience side of a line drawn across the front of the stage. In addition, because people are soft and soak up sound, the loudspeakers have to be lifted up above their heads. The sound will then carry across the room. Most reputable sound systems include stands to do this.

The amplifier

Finally, the amplifier and its associated mixer should be positioned at the back of the audience. Here, the sound engineer will be able to hear the results of his labours.

Tape recorders

Tape recorders can be used for three purposes in a conference. A cassette player will often be used to provide music as the audience walks into the conference room. A reel-to-reel tape recorder will be used to provide the sound for audio-visual modules and another may be used to record the conference as it is happening. Because the sound engineer will operate all of these, they need to be alongside the mixing desk at the back of the audience.

Lighting systems

Lighting is simpler in that it involves only two elements: the lights themselves, and their control gear, known as the control or dimmer board which will be linked to the power packs that actually control the lights. This system allows lights to be adjusted in intensity rather than being simply on or off.

The lights also have to be lifted up in the air and, once again, there are stands available to do this. The organizer will need at least two spotlights. This will enable light to be shone on a speaker from each side of the room. If the light is shone from only one side of the room, then the opposite side of the speaker's face will be in deep shadow which is not very flattering.

However, two lights will not allow for the lighting of the rest of the set, and so more will be needed, again on each side of the room. The control board for these will have to be at the back of the room too, but the associated dimmer racks can set up electronic interference which can play havoc with the sound system, so these need to be set away from the sound desk.

Communications ring
It follows, then, that two of the individuals controlling equipment will be at the back of the room. It is likely that there will also be a projectionist who will be behind the set. It is necessary that they can converse so that they all know what is happening and what they are all doing. To do this a communications system has to be installed, which will take the form of a series of headsets with headphones and a small microphone. Using this equipment they can all be in touch with each other and will also be able to hear the sound in the auditorium. This can be particularly important behind the set, where the sound is often at a low level.

In its simplest form, then, the layout can be determined to give the best position for all those involved in the conference. More complex shows will need more people and more equipment; but this type of show will usually be handled by a specialist production company who will have worked all of this out before arriving on-site.

Setting up the exhibition
While all the equipment is being set up in the conference room, any exhibition that is being set up to coincide with the conference will also have to be installed. Once again, this has to be laid out in order to provide all of the facilities needed. Tea and coffee or the bar should be at the far end of the room from the entrance. This will ensure that all of the delegates get into the room rather than crowding round the door to get their drinks.

Cables may need to be run across the floor in the exhibition; these must be covered over to avoid people tripping over them. They can be either taped to the floor or, better still, plastic covers can be obtained to form a reasonably smooth surface.

Coping with changes to the venue

When supervising the get-in of both the conference and the exhibition, the organizer must be aware of any changes that have taken place since the venue was last visited. For example, if the conference room has been redecorated with new mirrors hung around it, they will have to be neatly covered over in order to avoid unwanted reflections.

Tipping

It may be, too, that 'extras' will have to be paid for. These may vary from genuine gratuities to more doubtful payments that are demanded to ensure that a particular piece of equipment is installed. If such payments are demanded the organizer will have to estimate how serious the demand is. It may be possible to stall in the hope that the work is done anyway, but the chances are that the organizer will have to pay up.

Crew *per diems*

Per diems for the crew should be paid out when they arrive. These are the subsistence payments that are made in addition to the fees for hiring the individuals. Some crew members make a habit of arriving on-site with virtually no money and they cannot be allowed to starve until the organizer goes to the bank.

The pre-rehearsal period

Checking the venue

This period before the rehearsal is also the time for touring the venue to make sure that is is clean and tidy. If work needs to be done or message boards need to be placed, a written list should be given to the person who is the main contact with the venue.

Rooming lists

If accommodation is to be provided, then the hotel needs to be given the rooming lists at this time. Many hotels prefer to be able to allocate rooms themselves, working from a list of names marked for single, double or superior rooms and suites. For most organizers this will be acceptable, since there will be more than enough other tasks to be completed without bothering about the technicalities of who sleeps where. This may be the point at which the registration cards that formed part of the invitation can be handed over.

Final confirmations for the hotel
The delegate list should by now be complete, the only deviation being 'no shows'. All of the details of the conference can now be confirmed with the venue: meal times, coffee times and so on finally agreed so that everyone knows what is going to happen, and when.

Table plans
If the organizer has to draw up a table plan for meals, then it is likely that this will have to be done at this time too, since he or she will probably not know who is attending until shortly before arriving on-site. There should be a contingency plan for 'no shows' so that, if a person from table A does not arrive, then that place can be taken by another delegate. This will avoid the situation where arguments are going on behind the scenes about who sits where as the delegates are arriving at the conference.

Confirming ground-agent arrangements
If the event is being staged overseas, a ground agent will be used and a meeting must be held with him in order to make sure that he has made all the arrangements that were agreed. All special arrangements with Customs, transport, baggage handling and everything else has to be checked.

Technical rehearsal
The final stage of preparation before the conference speakers arrive on-site is the technical rehearsal. This will involve stepping slowly through the show and making sure that everyone knows what their cues are. It will be possible to make sure that all the equipment does what it should at the right time and that the whole show looks right.

This rehearsal is best done before the speakers arrive. If they do appear before the technical rehearsal they should be kept out of the conference room until they are needed. A technical rehearsal can appear to be a very scrappy affair to an outsider, with the crew going back over cues several times in order to make sure that everyone can be in the right position at the right time. Speakers who are aware of the importance of their show can very easily get the impression that it is falling apart around them, simply because they do not understand the complexities of the show.

174

Coping with the speakers

The organizer is now ready for the conference speakers to arrive. It is worth keeping them in a good humour and so, if possible they should be met. This is particularly important if the conference is being held overseas. Under these circumstances, a tactful individual who can reassure the speakers that everything is going to plan should be sent to the airport to meet them and take them to their hotels.

Before they arrive, the organizer should personally check their rooms and make sure that everything is as it should be. On arrival, they should be reminded of the time at which they should be in the conference room for rehearsals, and told how to find it.

Rehearsals

Separate teleprompter rehearsals
If a teleprompting system is being used and any of the speakers have either not used it before or have not marked up their scripts, it should be set up in a separate meeting room so that they can go through their scripts.

Coping with script changes
The organizer should make sure that the scripts in his or her possession are the same as the ones that the speakers are going to use. If last-minute changes have been made there is a danger that slides will not appear in the right places or film inserts will appear while the speaker is still in full flow. If the changes affect the order of the slides or films, the organizer should try to ensure that the original order is reinstated. Shuffling slides and film around at this stage of the production process is asking for confusion.

The organizer must then make sure that everyone on the crew knows about major script changes. Alteration of the odd word here and there should not matter much unless it is a cue word. The operator of the teleprompter should also be warned to keep the organizer abreast of any script changes that speakers make without telling the organizer.

First rehearsal
Once all of this has been done, it will be possible to hold a first rehearsal. Once again, this should be a slow stepping through of the show.

The organizer should begin by explaining to the individual speakers where they are to sit before they speak, where they enter the stage area, where they leave it, and what they do after they have left. They should then be talked through the show as a group, starting from the point at which the audience walk into the room, and finishing with the audience leaving at the end.

Now is the time for the first rehearsal proper to begin. It is likely that this will include mistakes since it will be the first time that the show has been put together properly. The organizer should sit through the rehearsal, timing the speeches and making notes about what goes wrong.

Dress rehearsal

After the first rehearsal, time should be allowed for mistakes to be put right before starting the dress rehearsal. This should run exactly as the final conference, with no mistakes. In effect, it should be an extra performance without an audience.

The speakers can then be told what time they have to be in the conference room for the show proper. This must be at least half an hour before the audience comes into the conference room.

Once the rehearsal has been finished, all those people not directly involved in the running of the show should be despatched to another part of the building. The crew will still have work to do – tidying the set, adjusting lamps, cleaning slides and so on – and the last thing they need is a management meeting taking place when they need to turn the lights out.

Discipline in rehearsals

In all rehearsals an element of discipline is needed from everyone. Speakers should recognize that, by the time they arrive on-site, it is too late to change slides. Everyone should also recognize that nothing should be changed after the dress rehearsal. Introducing changes at this time without a further opportunity to check them out will create opportunities for mistakes in the conference proper and that has to be avoided.

Similarly, speakers must be discouraged from changing their scripts at this point, other than the odd word here and there.

The individual that the organizer must be wary of is the one who claims that he does not need to rehearse. Even if he has delivered the same script many times before, entrances and exits will be different; and even if it is only a matter of him reading through his script an hour before the conference is due to start, every effort must be made to make him rehearse. If anyone genuinely cannot be present at the rehearsals, then someone else should read through the script so that the organizer can check that it fits properly into the show. The individual who is then going to deliver the script in the actual show must be walked through his or her performance before the audience arrives.

Cabaret rehearsal

If a cabaret forms a part of the programme, this will have to be rehearsed at some stage. Sound and lighting engineers have to know what is going to happen during the cabaret, and the artistes have to be given a chance to get the feel of the room. It is an unfortunate fact that this often has to be rushed and take place while the room is being set for dinner. While this is far from ideal, the difference between a cabaret and a conference is that cabaret artistes are professionals who have had to cope with much worse conditions in the past. If they can be allowed adequate time to rehearse in the cabaret room when nothing else is happening, so much the better.

As with the conference, microphones, loudspeakers and lights will be needed. If the cabaret is to take place on the same stage as the conference, time must be allowed to change the lights between the end of the conference and the beginning of the cabaret.

Meeting the delegates

When the delegates arrive there must be people on hand from the organizer's company. These people need to be briefed on their responsibilities. They will often be members of the sales team who may object to being used, as they see it, as commissionaires. The person handling the briefing should impress upon them the importance of their job. Part of their job will be to spot potential trouble. Outside help hired in to do the job of registration may not realize that they have insulted the company's most important customer and the company person will be able to step in and smooth any ruffled feathers.

Security

If people are to be given the job of checking that everyone who goes into the conference room has a badge, then their instructions have to be made crystal clear. By the same token, if such instructions are issued, then the organizer must do everything possible to make sure that everyone *does wear* a security badge.

Ushers
The people who will act as ushers in the conference room have to be identified and instructed to be there at least half an hour before the audience comes in.

Meeting delegates at the airport

For overseas conferences there must be a company person at the check-in desk at the departure airport in order to provide a personal welcome. The travel agent should also have someone present in order to sort out any problems that may occur. Obviously, these people will be in addition to and will not substitute for the airline staff.

On the aircraft a senior member of staff should be appointed 'flight director', whose role will be to represent the company on the aircraft and to be available for consultation by the airline cabin crew when necessary.

At the destination airport there should be a company person on hand to make sure that everything goes smoothly. At many airports it is possible for staff to be allowed into the Customs Hall provided the arrangements are made well in advance. Their job is principally one of PR, greeting delegates as they come in from the Immigration desk and telling them what they have to do next. The ground agent should also be on duty here to deal with any problems – like people who arrive with goods that should be on a carnet but who have forgotten to arrange one.

Meeting delegates at the hotel

At the registration area there should be someone from the hotel or the venue and the organizer or one of his staff. Their job will be to make sure that everyone is registered quickly and that they are all sent on to their next event smoothly.

The gathering area

Once the audience begins to arrive at the conference room, the organizer should have made sure that the doors are closed and that there is someone on duty who will politely explain that delegates cannot go in yet. The doors to the conference should be opened ten to fifteen minutes before the conference is due to start to allow everyone to be seated.

The ushers should be instructed to fill the conference room from the front so as to leave space away from the stage for latecomers. The last thing the organizer wants is people wandering across in front of the stage looking for an empty seat while the chairman is speaking.

Starting the show

When the audience is in place, then one person must have the responsibility of giving the signal to start the conference. Everyone involved in running it should know who this is in order to avoid confusion. Even the chairman should not be allowed to override this individual, who should make sure that the audience are all in and that the speakers are in position and ready to go. Only then should the show be started.

During the show

Once the show is up and running, if all of the preparation has been done properly the organizer should be able to concentrate completely on making sure that everything goes as smoothly as possible. If the show is to be run more than once, a note should be made of anything that goes wrong so that it can be corrected before the next performance. While the show is running, the organizer should keep an eye on the time so as to be able to slip out and warn the venue when the show is within about fifteen minutes of finishing. This will allow them to be ready for the members of the audience as they leave the conference room.

After the show

At the end of the show the doors to the conference room should be thrown wide so that the members of the audience know that they should leave. From here, most audiences will go to coffee, the bar or a meal. If well-known personalities have been used as guest speakers or presenters, they should be asked to mix with the audience so that at least some of them have the opportunity to meet a famous person.

Handling meals

During meals the organizer should be the last to sit down in order to be sure that all the delegates have seats. When the meal is being served it is necessary to watch to make sure that the service is up to scratch. If tables are being missed, this should be drawn to the attention of the banqueting head waiter who should make sure that the oversight is put right as soon as possible. In short, at mealtimes the organizer's job is to make sure that everyone else is doing what they should.

Speeches

If speeches are to be made, a microphone must be provided. This may be placed on the top table or be a floor-standing microphone near the stage. Whoever is speaking must be told to speak directly into the mike, otherwise their words may not be heard.

Starting the cabaret

There should be time for people to go to the toilets before the cabaret starts and for drinks to be served. The organizer should again be the only one who gives the signal for the cabaret to begin. The artistes should be told roughly when they will be needed, but the organizer must check that they are all present before giving the signal to begin. Guidance on the length of time needed for the meal can be got from the banqueting head waiter. Once the meal is finished an announcement can be made about a fifteen-minute break before the cabaret.

Delegates 'at leisure'

When the time comes for the delegates to amuse themselves, the organizer is best advised to keep clear of them. A peculiar change seems to take place when normally sober individuals attend a conference. Some will get drunk, others will demand female company. If any of them are stupid enough to get themselves arrested, then, in Britain, the chances are that they can safely be left to sort themselves out. If this happens abroad, then the ground agent must be prevailed upon to get them out of jail as soon as possible. If they have genuinely contravened the laws of the country in which the conference is taking place, then the organizer has no option but to cooperate with the police. This may mean that the delegate has to stay behind after his colleagues go home.

Under those circumstances the organizer must help the delegate to make the necessary arrangements, and then the ground agent will probably have to be left to sort things out.

The organizer's overall aim must be to make sure that every delegate returns to his or her office or home, having enjoyed the event. At the same time, the objectives must have been fulfilled. Part of the key to this is to make sure that the whole conference runs like clockwork. Detailed planning that steps carefully through every aspect of the conference will ensure that nothing important goes wrong. If that is achieved, then the audience will be satisfied and will have a better opinion of the organizer's company.

• CHECKLIST •

- Before travelling to the venue, check again that the conference is expected

- Check again that any equipment being hired will be on-site on time

- On arrival, check that the venue is clear and tidy

- Check the venue for damage before any equipment arrives

- Establish an organizer's office with a telephone

- Lay out the positions of equipment and set

- Install the set and equipment

- Set up the exhibition

- Provide room lists for hotel(s)

- Confirm catering numbers

- Draw up table plans

- Check through ground handling arrangements

- Allow time for technical rehearsals

- Allow time for speaker rehearsals

- Allow time for cabaret rehearsal

- Check security arrangements

- Brief all staff to be used for delegate control

- Agree sequence of events to start the show

- Provide a microphone and sound system for after-dinner speeches

- Agree signal to start the cabaret

12

Thank God it's over

When a conference is finally finished there is a tendency for everyone to heave a sigh of relief and relax. Some even go on holiday in order to recover from the rigours of the preceding months or weeks. In fact, the work is far from complete when the last delegate has gone home.

Clearing the venue

If the organizer has personally handled all the arrangements, his or her first priority will be to clear the venue as soon as the event has finished. All the equipment that has been hired has to be returned. It is worth checking all the equipment carefully as it is packed up, since the company will be charged for anything that is missing. So every projector, stage light, loudspeaker, nut, bolt and length of cable has to be accounted for and returned.

Some venues require the organizer to clean up after an event. If this is the case then someone will have to be provided with the necessary equipment to do this. He will be the unfortunate who discovers that self-adhesive tape usually leaves a mark when it is pulled off.

Once the clean-up has been completed the organizer should make a tour of the venue with the contact person to agree that no damage has been done. It must be admitted that some venues without a refurbishment budget seem to look to organizers to pay for redecoration and make good damage which existed before the conference moved in. The organizer must watch for such tactics and, if asked to pay for serious damage that was not noticed before the get-in, should try to find out how it happened or if anyone saw it as they moved in. If there is evidence that the damage had been done before the conference arrived, then the organizer should refuse to pay for it. This is where the survey that should have been carried out before the event will pay off.

Sometimes accidents do happen and damage is caused. Under these circumstances the bill should be paid. How it is dealt with by the organizer's company depends on their policy. Some will have insurance to cover such occurrences as a matter of course. Others may have taken out an insurance policy that will cover such events. Otherwise, it has to be set against the conference budget.

Settling the bills

Many of the bills will come in after the conference has finished. These can be surprisingly high and the secret here is to keep a record of unplanned expenditure as it is authorized. Much of this expense will have been incurred when things were happening fast, and it can be very difficult to remember months later what was agreed and how much it was supposed to cost. A proper budget control system will overcome this difficulty.

This applies both to the catering and accommodation and the production sides of the budget.

So far as catering and accommodation are concerned, much of it should be straightforward. The organizer will know what he agreed to pay for and will know how many delegates and staff were on-site.

Room bills may include extras which individuals should have paid for themselves. Once again, individual companies will decide to handle these in different ways. It may be uneconomic to try to recoup a £5.00 bill from a delegate, for example. If this is the case, then all the organizer can do is to grin and bear it.

Food and drink is often more difficult because a director may have been carried away in the euphoria of the moment and ordered more drinks without thinking about the effect of his actions on the budget. So far as the hotel is concerned such expenditure was duly authorized by a director and they will expect to be paid. However, if the organizer made it clear in writing that only one person could authorize extra costs, then there may be a case for refusing to pay if that authorization was not obtained.

This is one of the reasons that many venues will only meet such demands if a signature is given. The only question then is, whose signature was it and was it the right one?

So far as the production is concerned, there will probably be what is called a budget reconciliation meeting some weeks after the conference if an outside production company is used. By this time the production company should know precisely how much it spent and be able to give details supported by appropriate documentation.

For out-of-pocket expenses this documentation is important. If the production company is claiming anything it should be possible for them to provide supporting receipts. Going through all of this will take an enormous amount of time for a complex show, but it should be done.

Researching the conference

The one question that is very rarely asked after a conference is whether or not it was all worth while. Did the company reach its objectives?

Very few conferences can provide the opportunity for a quantifiable assessment of the event. It is very rare for any organizer to be able to say that sales were increased by a certain percentage that would not have been achieved without the conference. So other methods have to be used to make a judgement as to the effectiveness of the conference.

Some companies do make an attempt to answer this question but many do it informally, in the bar at the end of the conference. This will inevitably give a false result. People will still be riding on an emotional high and will almost certainly say that it has all been wonderful.

Other companies issue a questionnaire at the end of the conference. This is little better except that it formalizes the procedure. The results will be just as inaccurate.

The only real way to assess the effectiveness of a conference is to send out a questionnaire after the event, perhaps as much as a month later. By this time it will be possible to assess how much of the message stuck. In deciding what to include in the questionnaire it is necessary to look at the objectives of the conference and phrase questions that will show whether or not these have been met.

In addition, it may be desirable to find out whether or not the transport, hotel, meals and cabaret were to a standard that met with approval.

Obviously, there is a risk that the respondents to the questionnaire will give the answers that they think the organizer wants. If this

185

is likely to be the case, then an established research company should be asked to undertake the research in such a way as to make it difficult to guess who is asking the questions. This will cost money; but the company should be as concerned with establishing how well it spent the money for a conference as it would be in finding out how well its advertising budget was spent. Many major companies undertake extensive research into the effectiveness of their advertising and the same discipline should be applied to conferences.

The post mortem

The final part of the post-event activities should be a post mortem. This should involve all the people involved in organizing and running the conference and should be aimed at establishing what was done right and what went wrong: both are just as important. Knowing what went wrong, and why, will help to make sure that those mistakes are not repeated next time. Recognizing what was right will help to establish what aspects of the organization were done well, and these lessons can again be incorporated into the next conference.

Armed with that knowledge the organizer can confidently look forward to approaching the next conference even more professionally. That will improve his or her standing within the company. More important, it will help to improve the company's image with its audiences.

• CHECKLIST •

- Ensure that all equipment is removed from the venue

- Check that no damage has been done to the venue

- Check all bills in detail before paying

- Carry out research to establish whether or not objectives have been met

- Hold a meeting with operational staff to identify shortcomings and successes

PART 2
Where to find the information

Introduction

One of the major problems facing a conference organizer is that of tracking down information relevant to the task of staging an event. This section of the book is aimed at helping to overcome that difficulty.

In general terms, there are two types of information: that which has already been gathered together into book form and that which has never been published as a complete list before. An example of the former is the collection of guides to conference venues. These are often published annually and it would be pointless to try to duplicate their work here. As a result, where comprehensive guides already exist, they are shown along with the addresses from which they can be obtained.

However, where a central source of information does not exist, for example in the form of lists of production companies or convention bureaux, as many as possible are listed here.

Inevitably, these lists can never be complete. Some companies operating in the conference industry are not known to me, although a great deal of effort has been expended in tracking down as many as possible. However, if anyone knows of companies or organizations that they feel should be included, I would be grateful if they would let me know.

In addition, production companies, in particular, tend to rise and fall very quickly. For this reason, no guarantee can be given about the accuracy of the lists. Even so, they should provide a useful initial source of information.

Finally, the fact that a company or organization is listed should not be taken to imply any sort of recommendation on the part of either the author or the publisher.

Sources of information on venues and ground agents

The following publications provide information on venues and travel services. In addition, many of the convention bureaux listed elsewhere publish their own directories.

ABC Worldwide Hotel Guide
5/11 Worship Street, London EC2A 2AV
Tel.   01-402 6171
(International hotel guide)

BACT Conference Compendium
British Association of Conference Towns, International House, 36, Dudley Road, Royal Tunbridge Wells, Kent TN1 1LB
Tel.   0892 33442
(Directory of members of the BACT)

British Theatre Directory
John Offord (Publications) Ltd, P.O. Box 64, Eastbourne, East Sussex BN21 3LW
Tel.   0323 37841
(Directory of theatres in Britain)

British Universities
British Universities Accommodation Consortium, Box 287, University Park, Nottingham NG7 2RD
Tel.   0602 50471
(Directory of members of the BUAC — Universities offering conference facilities)

Conference Blue Book
Spectrum Publications, 183 Askew Road, London W12 9AX
Tel. 01-749 3061
(Directory of conference venues within the UK)

Conference Green Book
Spectrum Publications, 183 Askew Road, London W12 9AX
Tel. 01-749 3061
(Directory of venues with features of special interest, mainly
those with sports and leisure facilities)

Euromic Meetings Incentives Conventions
c/o Spectra Travel, 12–15 Hanger Green, London W5 3EL
Tel. 01-998 1021
(Directory published by a consortium of ground operators which
gives some information on meeting facilities in Europe, Egypt
and Israel along with addresses of ground agents)

Exhibitions and Conferences
64 Brunswick Centre, Marchmont Street, Bloomsbury, London
WC1N 1AE
Tel. 01-278 4299
(Directory of conference venues within the UK)

Expotel Insider's Guide
Expotel Conference Desk, Banda House, Cambridge Grove,
Hammersmith, London W6 0LE
Tel. 01-568 8765
(Directory of conference venues within the UK)

Higher Education Accommodation Consortium Brochure
HEAC, 36 Collegiate Crescent, Sheffield S10 2BP
Tel. 0742 683759
(Directory of HEAC members — colleges offering conference
facilities)

*Incentive Marketing and Sales Promotion — annual review and
buyer's guide*
Maclaren Publishers Ltd, P.O. Box 109, Maclaren House,
19 Scarbrook Road, Croydon CR9 1HQ
Tel. 01-688 7788
(Guide which includes information of use to meeting planners)

Meeting Point International Conference Directory
Meeting Point, Trusthouse Forte Hotels, 24/30 New Street,
Aylesbury, Bucks HP20 2NW
Tel. 01-567 3444
(Guide to Trusthouse Forte hotels with conference facilities in
several countries)

Meetings – Finding somewhere different
ACE International, Riverside House, High Street, Huntingdon,
Cambs PE18 6SG
Tel. 0480 57595
(Directory of unusual venues within the UK)

Official Meeting Facilities Guide
Murdoch Magazines, West Heath House, 32 North End Road,
London NW11 7PT
Tel. 01-458 7322
(Directory of conference facilities, mainly in the USA, but with
sections covering Canada, the Caribbean and Europe)

The Top Venue Guide
Suite 25/30, 12–13 Henrietta Street, London WC2E 8LH
Tel. 01-836 2916
(Directory of selected venues within the UK)

Travel Contacts
4 Christ Church Avenue, Royal Tunbridge Wells, Kent TN1 1UW
Tel. 0892 27737
(International directory of ground handling agents)

UK regional and city convention offices

Members of the British Association of Conference Towns (BACT) are marked with a *. In order to avoid having to contact all members individually, a brief can be sent to the BACT who will then circulate it to members. Those towns that can meet the brief will respond direct to the client. The BACT address is:

British Association of Conference Towns, International House, 36 Dudley Road, Royal Tunbridge Wells, Kent TN1 1LB Tel. 0892 33442

Aberdeen
Aberdeen Conference Team, St. Nicholas House, Broad Street, Aberdeen AB9 1DE
Tel.   0224 632727

Aviemore
Aviemore Centre, Aviemore, Inverness-shire, Scotland PH22 1PF
Tel.   0479 75601

Ayr
Kyle and Carrick District Council, Burns House, Burns Statue Square, Ayr KA7 1UP
Tel.   0292 281511

Bath
Conference and Retail Services, Bath City Council, The Pump Room, Bath BA1 1LZ
Tel.   0225 61111

* Indicates member of BACT (see note at head of list).

Berkshire
Beautiful Berkshire, Shire Hall, Shinfield Park, Reading
RG2 9XD
Tel.   0734 875444

*Belfast
Belfast City Council, City Hall, Belfast BT1 5GS
Tel.   0232 220202

*Birmingham
Birmingham Convention and Visitor Bureau, 1, Duchess Place,
Hagley Road, Edgbaston, Birmingham B16 8ND
Tel.   021-235 2051/4358
(*See also*, Heart of England)

Blackpool
Conference Blackpool, Tourism and Attractions Department,
1 Clifton Street, Blackpool FY1 1JD
Tel.   0253 25212

*Bournemouth
Bournemouth Convention Bureau, Westover Road, Bournemouth,
Dorset BH1 2BU
Tel.   0202 291715

Bradford
City Hall, Bradford BD1 1HY
Tel.   0274 753787

*Bridlington
East Yorkshire Borough Council Department of Tourism and
Resort Activities, The Spa, South Marine Drive, Bridlington,
East Yorkshire YO15 3JH
Tel.   0262 78255

*Brighton
Brighton Borough Council, Resort Services Department,
Marlborough House, 54 Old Stein, Brighton BN1 1EQ
Tel.   0273 29801

*Bristol
Bristol City Council, Publicity and Information Office,
The Council House, College Green, Bristol BS1 5TR
Tel.   0272 26031

194

Buxton
Conference Buxton, Pavilion Gardens, St Johns Road, Buxton, Derbyshire
Tel.   0298 3114/3910

Cambridge
Cambridge Tourist Information Centre, Wheeler Street, Cambridge CB2 3QB
Tel.   0223 322640

Cardiff
Conference Executive, St David's Hall, P.O. Box 20, Cardiff CF1 2SH
Tel.   0222 42611
(*See also* South Glamorgan)

Carlisle
Tourism Officer, City of Carlisle, Civic Centre, Carlisle, Cumbria CA3 8QG
Tel.   0228 23411

Cheltenham Spa
Director of Entertainments and Tourism, Cheltenham Borough Council, Town Hall Imperial Square, Cheltenham, Gloucestershire GL50 1QA
Tel.   0242 521621

Chester
Chester Marketing Bureau Ltd, Chester Visitor Centre, 2 Vicars Lane, Chester CH1 1QX
Tel.   0244 313126

Coventry
Coventry and District Conference Association, Coventry City Council, Earl Street, Coventry CV1 5RR
Tel.   0203 25555

Derby
Derby City Council, Assembly Rooms, Market Place, Derby DE1 3AH
Tel.   0332 31111

Devon
(*see* North Devon)

Dover
Dover District Council, Leisure and Recreation Department,
5/11 King Street, Deal, Kent CT14 6HU
Tel.   0304 361161

Droitwich
Droitwich Town Council, Norbury House, Friar Street, Droitwich
Spa, Worcestershire WR9 8HE
Tel.   0905 775155

Dundee
City of Dundee District Council, City Chambers, Dundee
DD1 3BY
Tel.   0382 23141

Durham City
Conference Office, 80 Claypath, Durham City DH1 1QT
Tel.   0385 67131

Eastbourne
Eastbourne Conference Bureau, Winter Garden, Compton Street,
Eastbourne, East Sussex BN21 4BP
Tel.   0323 641212, 0323 25252

Edinburgh
City of Edinburgh, Department of Public Relations and Tourism,
9 Cockburn Street, Edinburgh EH1 1BR
Tel.   031-226 6591

Exeter
Exeter City Council, Civic Centre, Dix's Field, Exeter, Devon
EX1 1JN
Tel.   0392 72434

Felixstowe
Suffolk Coastal District Council, Tourism and Entertainment
Department, Melton Hill, Woodbridge, Suffolk IP12 1AU
Tel.   03943 3789

Folkestone/Hythe
Shepway District Council, Leisure and Tourism Department,
Civic Centre, Castle Hill Avenue, Folkestone, Kent CT20 2QY
Tel.   0303 57388

Galashiels
Ettrick and Lauderdale District Council, Council Chambers,
P.O. Box 4, Paton Street, Galashiels TD1 3AS
Tel.   0896 4751

Glasgow
Greater Glasgow Tourist Board, 39 St Vincent Place, Glasgow G1
2ER
Tel.   041-227 4892, 041-227 4885

Great Yarmouth
Great Yarmouth Borough Council, 14 Regent Street, Great
Yarmouth, Norfolk NR30 1RW
Tel.   0493 4313

Guernsey
States of Guernsey Conference Bureau, P.O. Box 23, States
Office, Guernsey, Channel Islands
Tel.   0481 24411

Harrogate
Harrogate Borough Council, Resort Services Department,
Harrogate Centre, Kings Road, Harrogate, North Yorkshire
Tel.   0423 68051

Hammersmith and Fulham
The Conference Department, The Mezzanine, Hammersmith
Town Hall, King Street, London W6 9JU
Tel.   01-748 3020 ext. 5407/ext. 333

Hartlepool
Hartlepool Borough Council, Leisure and Amenities Department,
Civic Centre, Hartlepool, Cleveland TS24 8AY
Tel.   0492 66522

Hastings
Hastings Borough Council, Tourism and Recreation Department,
4 Robertson Terrace, Hastings, East Sussex TN34 1EZ
Tel.   0424 424242

Heart of England Tourist Board
Old Bank House, Bank Street, Worcester WR1 2EW
Tel.   0905 29511

Hull
Hull Conference Bureau, 77 Lowgate, Hull, North Humberside
HU1 1HP
Tel. 0482 226258

*Inverness
Inverness District Council, Town House, Bishops Road, Inverness
IV1 1JJ
Tel. 0463 239111

*Ipswich
Ipswich Borough Council, Department of Recreation and
Amenities, Civic Centre, Civic Drive, Ipswich, Suffolk IP1 2EE
Tel. 0473 55851

*Isle of Man Tourist Board
Coneferencemann, 13 Victoria Street, Douglas, Isle of Man
Tel. 0642 74323

*Isle of Thanet
Thanet District Council, P.O. Box 9, Margate, Kent CT9 5AA
Tel. 0843 20241

*Isle of Wight
Isle of Wight Tourist Board, 21 High Street, Newport, Isle of
Wight PO30 1JS
Tel. 0983 524343

Jersey
Jersey Conference Bureau, 15 Broad Street, St Helier, Jersey,
Channel Islands
Tel. 0534 76512

Kensington and Chelsea
Royal Borough of Kensington and Chelsea, The Town Hall,
Hornton Street, London W8 7NX
Tel. 01-937 5464

Lancaster
(*see* Morecambe/Lancaster)

Leatherhead
Leatherhead Leisure Centre, Guildford Road, Leatherhead,
Surrey KT22 9BL
Tel. 0372 377674

Leicester
Public Relations Unit, Leicester City Council, New Walk Centre, Welford Place, Leicester LE1 6ZG
Tel. 0533 549922

Lincoln
Lincoln City Council, Recreation and Leisure Department, City Hall, Beaumont Fee, Lincoln LN1 1DD
Tel. 0522 32151

Liverpool
(*See* Merseyside)

Llandudno
Tourism and Amenities Department, Aberconwy Borough Council, 1/2 Chapel Street, Llandudno, North Wales LL30 2UY
Tel. 0492 78881

London
London Visitor and Convention Bureau, 26 Grosvenor Gardens, London SW1W 0DU
Tel. 01-730 3450

Lowestoft
Waveney District Council, The Esplanade, Lowestoft, Suffolk NR33 0QF
Tel. 0502 62111

Malvern
Malvern Hills District Council, The Winter Gardens, Grange Road, Malvern, Worcs WR14 3HB
Tel. 068 45 2700

City of Manchester
Town Hall, Manchester M60 2LA
Tel. 061-234 3160

Greater Manchester Conference Office
County Hall, Piccadilly Gardens, Manchester M60 3HP
Tel. 061-236 2862/6660

Merseyside
Merseyside Conference Bureau, 29 Lime Street, Liverpool, Merseyside L1 1JG
Tel. 051-227 5234

Middlesbrough
Middlesbrough District Council, P.O. Box 99A, Middlesbrough,
Cleveland TS1 2QQ
Tel. 0642 245432

Morecambe/Lancaster
Publicity and Amenities Department, Lancaster City Council,
Town Hall, Morecambe, Lancashire LA4 5AF
Tel. 0524 417120

Newark
Newark District Council, Recreation and Tourism Department,
Kelham Hall, Kelham, Newark, Nottinghamshire NG23 5QX
Tel. 0636 705111

Newcastle : County Down
Down District Council, The Newcastle Centre, Central
Promenade, Newcastle, County Down, Northern Ireland
BT33 0DT
Tel. 03967 22222

Newcastle upon Tyne
Civic Centre, Newcastle upon Tyne NE1 8QN
Tel. 0632 610773

Newquay
Tourism and Publicity Department, Borough of Restormel,
Municipal Offices, Newquay, Cornwall TR7 1AF
Tel. 06373 5171

North Devon
North Devon District Council, Queens Hall Theatre, Barnstaple,
Devon EX1 1SY
Tel. 0271 74128

Norwich
City of Norwich, Tourist Information Centre, 14 Tombland,
Norwich NR3 1HF
Tel. 0603 666071

Nottingham
Nottingham City Council, Conference Office, Royal Centre,
Theatre Square, Nottingham NG1 5ND
Tel. 0602 413060

Oxford
Oxford Information Centre, City of Oxford, St Aldate's, Oxford
OX1 1DX
Tel.   0865 249811

Peebles
Peebles Hotel Hydro, Innerleithen Road, Peebles EH45 8LX
Tel.   0721 20602

Penzance and St Ives
Penwith District Council, Resorts Office, St Clare, Penzance,
Cornwall TR18 3QW
Tel.   0736 2341

Plymouth
Plymouth Marketing Bureau, Royal Building, St Andrew's Court,
12 St Andrews Street, Plymouth, Devon PL1 2AH
Tel.   0752 261125

Poole
Poole Tourist Information Centre, Poole Borough Council,
The Quay, Poole, Dorset BH15 1HE
Tel.   0202 686290

Portsmouth
City of Portsmouth, Guildhall, Portsmouth PO1 2AD
Tel.   0705 834174

Runnymede
Runnymede Borough Council, Council Offices, Station Road,
Addlestone, Weybridge, Surrey KT15 2AH
Tel.   0932 45500

Salisbury
Salisbury District Council, Publicity Office, Bourne Hill, Salisbury
SP1 3UZ
Tel.   0722 336272

Scarborough
Scarborough Conference Bureau, Landesborough Lodge, The
Crescent, Scarborough YO11 2PW
Tel.   0723 369151

Scottish Tourist Board
23 Ravelston Terrace, Edinburgh EH4 3EU
Tel.   031-332 2433

*Sheffield
Sheffield Publicity Department, Town Hall, Sheffield S1 2HH
Tel.   0742 734130

*Shrewsbury
Shrewsbury and Atcham Borough Council, Information Centre,
The Square, Shrewsbury SY1 1LH
Tel.   0743 52019

*Skegness
East Lindsey District Council, Entertainments and Amenities
Department, Tedder Hall, Manby, Louth, Lincolnshire
LN11 8UP
Tel.   0507 601111

*Solihull
Town Clerk's Department, Council House, Solihull, West
Midlands B91 3QS
Tel.   021-705 6789

*South Glamorgan
Cardiff Conference Association, c/o South Glamorgan County
Council, Newport Road, Cardiff, South Glamorgan CF2 1XA
Tel.   0222 499022

South Pembrokeshire District Council
The Conference Office, The Croft, Tenby, Pembrokeshire SA70
8AP
Tel.   0834 2402/2404

*Southampton
Conference and Tourism Unit, Civic Centre, Southampton SO9
4XF
Tel.   0703 559122 ext 2832

*Southport
Sefton Metropolitan Borough Council, P.O. Box 25, Cambridge
Arcade, Southport PR8 1AS
Tel.   0704 33133

Stratford upon Avon
33, Lansdowne Road, Worcester WR1 1SP
Tel.   0905 22653

*Teignbridge
Teignbridge District Council, Recreation and Tourism
Department, 16/19 Devon Square, Newton Abbott, Devon
TQ12 2JF
Tel.   0626 61101

*Tenby
(*see* South Pembrokeshire District Council)

Thanet
(*see* Isle of Thanet)

Thames and Chilterns Tourist Board
8, The Market Place, Abington, Oxon OX14 3UD
Tel.   0235 22711

*Torbay
The English Riviera, Torbay Tourist Board, Carlton Chambers,
Vaughan Parade, Torquay, Devon TQ2 5JG
Tel.   0803 26244

Torquay
English Riviera Convention Bureau, Carlton Chambers, Vaughan
Parade, Torquay TQ2 5JG
Tel.   0803 26244

*Wakefield
Assistant Secretary's Department, City of Wakefield, Public Halls
Section, Town Hall, Wakefield WF1 2HQ
Tel.   0924 370211

Wales Tourist Board
Brunel House, 2 Fitzalan Road, Cardiff CF2 1UY
Tel.   0222 499909

*Warwick
Warwick District Council, Amenities Department, Regent Square
House, Regent Street, Leamington Spa, Warwickshire CV32 4UJ
Tel.   0926 27072

Weston-super-Mare
Woodspring District Council, Leisure and Tourism Department,
Town Hall, Weston-super-Mare, Avon BS23 1UJ
Tel.   0934 31701

Weymouth and Portland
Weymouth and Portland Borough Council, The Pavilion,
The Esplanade, Weymouth, Dorset DT4 8ED
Tel.   03057 72444

Winchester
City of Winchester, Amenity Services Department, City Offices,
Colebrook Street, Winchester, Hampshire SO23 9LT
Tel.   0962 68166

Woking
Woking Borough Council, Leisure Services Department, Civic
Offices, Gloucester Square, Woking, Surrey GU21 1YL
Tel.   04862 5931

Worthing
Worthing Borough Council, Amenities Department, Town Hall,
Worthing, West Sussex BN11 1HQ
Tel.   0903 39999

York
York City Council, Department of Tourism, De Grey Rooms,
Exhibition Square, York, North Yorkshire, YO1 2HB
Tel.   0904 28666

UK college and university venues

Universities that are members of the British Universities Accommodation Consortium are identified with a *. A directory of members and their facilities is available from:

British Universities Accommodation Consortium
Box No. 287, University Park, Nottingham NG7 2RD
Tel. 0602 504571

Colleges that are members of the Higher Education Accommodation Consortium are identified by a †. The Consortium will circulate enquiries among their members which will reply direct to the enquirer. A directory of members and their facilities is available from:

Higher Education Accommodation Consortium
36 Collegiate Crescent, Sheffield, South Yorkshire S10 2BP
Tel. 0742 683759

The Scottish Universities Accommodation Consortium will circulate enquiries among their members which will respond direct to the enquirer. Their address is as follows:

Scottish Universities Accommodation Consortium
P.O. Box 808, Edinburgh EH14 4AS
Tel. 031-449 4034

Individual Universities and Colleges

Aberdeen
Conference Officer, University of Aberdeen, Aberdeen AB9 1FX
Tel. 0224 40241

* Indicates member of BUAC.
† Indicates member of HEAC (see notes at beginning of list)

Aberystwyth
University College of Wales, Penbryn, Penglais, Aberystwyth,
Dyfed SY23 3BY
Tel.   0970 3757

Aberystwyth
College of Librarianship Wales, Llanbadarn Fawr, Aberystwyth,
Dyfed SY23 3AS
Tel.   0970 3181

†*Ambleside*
Charlotte Mason College of Education, Rydal Road, Ambleside,
Cumbria LA22 9BB
Tel.   0966 33066 (ext. 205)

Bangor
Conference Office, University College of North Wales, Bangor,
Gwynedd LL57 2DG
Tel.   0248 351151

Bath
Accommodation and Conference Office, University of Bath,
Claverton Down, Bath BA2 7AY
Tel.   0225 61244

†*Bedford*
Bedford College of Higher Education, Mander Site, Cauldwell
Street, Bedford MK42 9AH
Tel.   0234 45151 (ext. 244)

Birmingham
P.O. Box 363, University of Birmingham, Birmingham B15 2TT
Tel.   021-472 1301

Birmingham
University of Aston, Gosta Green, Birmingham B4 7ET
Tel.   021-359 3611

Bradford
Administrative Assistant, Student Services, University of
Bradford, Bradford BD7 1DP
Tel.   0274 733466

†*Bradford*
Bradford and Ilkley Community College, Margaret McMillan
Hall of Residence, Easby Road, Bradford BD7 1QZ
Tel. 0274 733291

*Brighton
Conference Officer, Refectory Building, University of Sussex,
Falmer, Brighton BN1 9QU
Tel. 0273 678678

†*Brighton*
Brighton Polytechnic, Mithras House, Lewes Road,
Moulsecoomb, Brighton, East Sussex BN2 4AT
Tel. 0273 693655

*Bristol
Conference Secretary, Goldney House, University of Bristol,
Lower Clifton Hill, Bristol BS8 1BH
Tel. 0272 213181

†*Bristol*
Bristol Polytechnic, Coldharbour Lane, Frenchay, Bristol
BS16 1QY
Tel. 0272 656261 (ext. 568)

†*Broadstairs*
Kingsgate House of Thanet Technical College, Kingsgate House,
Convent Road, Broadstairs, Kent CT10 3PX
Tel. 0843 61903

†*Burton* (Wirral)
Burton Manor College, Burton, South Wirral L64 5SJ
Tel. 051-336 5172

*Canterbury
Conference Office, The University, Canterbury, Kent CT2 7NZ
Tel. 0227 69186

†*Canterbury*
Christ Church College, North Holmes Road, Canterbury
CT1 1QU
Tel. 0227 65548

Cambridge
The Conference Office, Churchill College, Cambridge CB3 0DS
Tel.   0223 61200

Cambridge
Robinson College, Grange Road, Cambridge CB3 9AN
Tel.   0223 311431

*Cardiff
Conference Office, University College Cardiff, P.O. Box 78,
Cardiff CF1 1XL
Tel.   0222 44211

†*Cardiff*
Cyncoed Conference Centre, Cyncoed Road, Cardiff CF2 6XD
Tel.   0222 551111 (ext. 3349)

†*Chalfont St Giles*
Buckinghamshire College of Higher Education, Newlands Park,
Gorelands Lane, Chalfont St Giles, Bucks HP8 4AB
Tel.   0240 74441

†*Chelmsford*
Danbury Park Management Centre, Danbury, Chelmsford, Essex
CM3 4AT
Tel.   0245 412141

†*Chichester*
West Sussex Institute of Higher Education, Bishop Otter College,
College Lane, Chichester, West Sussex PO19 4PE
Tel.   0243 787911

*Cirencester
Domestic Bursar, Royal Agricultural College, Cirencester, Glos
GL7 6JS
Tel.   0258 2531

*Colchester
Conference Manager, University of Essex, Wivenhoe Park,
Colchester CO4 3SQ
Tel.   0206 868510

Coleraine
Head of Student Services, The New University of Ulster,
Coleraine, Northern Ireland BT52 1SA
Tel.   0265 4141

Coventry
Manager Residences and Conferences, University of Warwick,
Coventry CV4 7AL
Tel.   0203 523279

†*Coventry*
Coventry (Lanchester) Polytechnic, Priory Street, Coventry, West
Midlands CV1 5FB
Tel.   0203 24166 (ext. 442)

†*Crewe*
Crewe and Alsager College of Higher Education, Crewe Road,
Crewe, Cheshire CW1 1DU
Tel.   0270 583661

†*Dalkeith*
Newbattle Abbey College, Dalkeith, Mid Lothian EH22 3LL
Tel.   031-663 1921

†*Doncaster*
Doncaster Metropolitan Institute of Higher Education, High
Melton, Doncaster DN5 7SZ
Tel.   0709 582427

Dundee
Residences Office, University of Dundee, Dundee DD1 4HN
Tel.   0382 23181

†*Dundee*
Dundee College of Further Education, Gardyne Road, Broughty
Ferry, Dundee DD5 1NY
Tel.   0382 453433

Durham
Senior Bursar, University of Durham, Old Shire Hall, Durham
DH1 3HP
Tel.   0385 64466

Edinburgh
Steward to the Halls and Houses, Box C85 UED, Pollock Halls,
18 Holyrood Park Road, Edinburgh EH16 5AY
Tel. 031-667 1971

Edinburgh
Heriot-Watt University, Riccarton Campus, Edinburgh EH14 4AS
Tel. 031-449 5111

Exeter
University of Exeter, Conference Office, Devonshire House,
Stocker Road, Exeter, EX4 4PZ
Tel. 0392 215566

†*Galashiels*
Scottish College of Textiles, Netherdale, Galashiels, Selkirkshire
TD1 3HF
Tel. 0896 3351

Glasgow
Conference and Vacation Office, University of Glasgow,
52 Hillhead Street, Glasgow G12
Tel. 041-339 8855

Glasgow
Controller Residence and Catering Services, University of
Strathclyde, 73 Rottenrow East, Glasgow G4 0NG
Tel. 041-552 4400

†*Glasgow*
Jordanhill College of Education, 76 Soutbrae Drive, Glasgow
G13 1PP
Tel. 041-959 1232 (ext. 292)

Guilford
Conference Manager, University of Surrey, Guildford, Surrey
GU2 5XH
Tel. 0483 579266

†*Harlech*
Coleg Harlech, Harlech, Gwynedd LL46 2PU
Tel. 0766 780363

†*Hatfield*
The Hatfield Polytechnic, P.O. Box 109, College Lane, Hatfield, Herts AL10 9AB
Tel. 07072 79060

†*Huddersfield*
Huddersfield Polytechnic, Queensgate, Huddersfield HD1 3DH
Tel. 0484 22288 (ext. 2339)

*Hull
Conference Office, Staff House, The University of Hull, Kingston upon Hull HU6 7RX
Tel. 0482 497947

†*Hull*
Cumberbirch Conference Centre, Humberside College of Education, Cottingham Road, Hull HU6 7RT
Tel. 0482 446707

*Keele
The University of Keele Conference Centre, Keele, Staffordshire ST5 5BG
Tel. 0782 621111

*Lancaster
Conference Officer, University of Lancaster, Bailrigg, Lancaster LA1 4YW
Tel. 0524 65201

*Leeds
Conference Office, University of Leeds, Leeds LS2 9JT
Tel. 0532 431751

†*Leeds*
Trinity and All Saints' College, Brownberrie Lane, Horsforth, Leeds LS18 5HD
Tel. 0532 584341

*Leicester
Conference Manager, University of Leicester, University Road, Leicester LE1 7RH
Tel. 0533 554455

†Leicester
Leicester Polytechnic, P.O. Box 143, Leicester LE1 9BH
Tel. 0533 551551

*Liverpool
The Conference Office, University of Liverpool, P.O. Box 147,
Liverpool L69 3BX
Tel. 051-709 6022

†Liverpool
Christ's and Notre Dame College, Woolton Road, Liverpool
L16 8ND
Tel. 051-722 7331 (ext. 222)

*London
Bloomsbury Conference Agency, University of London,
15, Woburn Square, London WC1H 0NS
Tel. 01-636 8000

London
London College and Polytechnic Accommodation, ILEA, Cedars
Hall, Welham Road, London SW17 9BU
Tel. 01-672 0134

†London
Polytechnic of Central London, 104–108 Bolsover Street, London
W1P 7HF
Tel. 01-636 4991

London
Conference Administrator, Chelsea College, 552 King's Road,
London SW10 0UA
Tel. 01-351 2488

London
City University, Northampton Square, London EC1V 0HB
Tel. 01-253 4399 ext 3003

†London
Digby Stuart College, Roehampton Lane, London SW15 5PH
Tel. 01-876 8273

London
Conference Officer, Goldsmith's College, University of London, New Cross, London SE14 6NW
Tel.   01-692 6672

London
Kings College, Strand, London WC2R 2LS
Tel.   01-836 5454

†*London*
Middlesex Polytechnic, Short Courses and Conference Centre, 60 Games Road, Barnet, Herts EN4 9HW
Tel.   01-440 4252

London
Queen Elizabeth College, Campden Hill Road, London W8 7AH
Tel.   01-937 5411

London
Halls Manager, Queen Mary College Halls of Residence, 98/110 High Road, South Woodford, London E18 2QJ
Tel.   01-504 9282

London
Conference Manager, Royal Holloway and Bedford New College, Egham Hill, Egham, Surrey TW20 0EX
Tel.   0784 34455

†*London*
Sir John Cass Hall, 150 Well Street, Hackney, London E9 7LQ
Tel.   01-533 2529

London
St Bartholomew's Hospital Medical College, The Robin Brook Centre, St Bartholomew's Hospital, West Smithfield, London EC1A 7BE
Tel.   01-606 0695

†*London*
Thames Polytechnic, Wellington Street, Woolwich, London SE18 6PF
Tel.   01-854 2030

†London
West London Institute of Higher Education, 300 St Margaret's
Road, Twickenham, Middlesex TW1 1PT
Tel. 01-891 0121

*Loughborough
Residential Organization, Loughborough University, Leicestershire
LE11 3TU
Tel. 0509 216162

*Manchester
Manchester Business School, Booth Street West, Manchester
M15 6PB
Tel. 061-273 8228

*Manchester
Conference Officer, The University of Manchester, Oxford Road,
Manchester M13 9PL
Tel. 061-273 3333

*Manchester
University of Manchester Institute of Science and Technology
(UMIST), P.O. Box 88, Sackville Street, Manchester M60 1QD
Tel. 061-236 3311

†Manchester
Manchester Polytechnic, All Saints Building, Oxford Road,
Manchester M15 6BH
Tel. 061-228-6171

*Newcastle upon Tyne
University of Newcastle, 3 Park Terrace, Newcastle upon Tyne,
NE1 7RU
Tel. 0632 616000

†Newcastle upon Tyne
Newcastle upon Tyne Polytechnic, Ellison Building, Ellison Place,
Newcastle upon Tyne NE1 8ST
Tel. 0632 326002

†Newport (Gwent)
Gwent College of Higher Education, College Crescent, Caerleon,
Gwent NP6 1XJ
Tel. 0633 421292

†Newton Abbot
Seale-Hayne College, Newton Abbot, Devon TQ12 6NQ
Tel.   0626 2323

†Northampton
Nene College, Park Campus, Boughton Green Road, Moulton
Park, Northampton NN2 7AL
Tel.   0604 715000 (ext. 275)

*Norwich
University of East Anglia, University Plain, Norwich, Norfolk
NR4 7JT
Tel.   0603 56161

*Nottingham
University of Nottingham, University Park, Nottingham
NG7 2RD
Tel.   0602 506101

†Ormskirk
Edge Hill College of Higher Education, St Helens Road,
Ormskirk, Lancashire L39 4QP
Tel.   0695 75171

Oxford
Information on all Oxford Colleges is available from:
The Domestic Bursar, St. Katherine's College, Manor Road,
Oxford OX1 3UJ
Tel.   0865 249541

†Oxford
Oxford Polytechnic, Gipsy Lane, Headington, Oxford OX3 0BP
Tel.   0865 64777

†Oxford
Ruskin College, Walton Street, Oxford OX1 2HE
Tel.   0865 54331

†Pontypridd
The Polytechnic of Wales, Pontypridd, Mid-Glamorgan
CF37 1DL
Tel.   0443 405133 (ext. 2040)

†*Portsmouth*
Portsmouth Polytechnic, The Nuffield Centre, St Michaels Road, Portsmouth PO1 2ED
Tel. 0705 827681

†*Preston*
Lancashire Polytechnic, Preston, Lancashire PR1 2TQ
Tel. 0772 22141 (ext. 2003)

*Reading
Whiteknights House, The University, Reading RG6 2AH
Tel. 0734 752334

†*Reading*
Bulmershe College of Higher Education, Woodlands Avenue, Early, Reading RG6 1HY
Tel. 0734 663387

Salford
University of Salford, Conference Office, Maxwell Building, Salford, M5 4WT
Tel. 061-736 5843 ext 650/449

*Sheffield
Octagon Centre, University of Sheffield, Sheffield S10 2TQ
Tel. 0742 78555

†*Sheffield*
Sheffield City Polytechnic, 36 Collegiate Crescent, Sheffield S10 2BP
Tel. 0742 665274

†*Silsoe*
Silsoe College, Silsoe, Bedfordshire MK45 4DT
Tel. 0525 60428 (ext. 288)

*Southampton
University of Southampton, Highfield, Southampton SO9 5NH
Tel. 0703 559122

†*St Albans*
Hertfordshire College of Agriculture, Oaklands, St Albans AL4 0JA
Tel. 0727 50651

St Andrews
College Gate, St Andrews, Fife, Scotland
Tel.   0334 76161

Stirling
Administration Building, University of Stirling, Stirling FK9 4LA
Tel.   0786 73171

†*Stoke on Trent*
North Staffordshire Polytechnic, College Road, Stoke on Trent
ST4 2DE
Tel.   0782 45531

Swansea
Accommodation and Conference Office, UCS, Singleton Park,
Swansea
Tel.   0792 5331

Uxbridge
Brunel University Conference Centre, The Conference Office,
Brunel University, Uxbridge, Middx UB8 3PH
Tel.   0895 37188

†*Winchester*
Hampshire College of Agriculture, Sparsholt, Winchester SO21
2NF
Tel.   0962 72441

†*Wokingham*
Easthampstead Park, Wokingham, Berkshire RG11 3DF
Tel.   0734 780686

†*Wolverhampton*
Wolverhampton Polytechnic, Randall Lines House, North Road,
Wolverhampton WV1 1RN
Tel.   0902 25936

York
University of York, Heslington, York YO1 5DD
Tel.   0904 411770

Venue finding services

The following organizations will assist conference planners to find suitable venues. In addition, National Convention Bureaux will suggest suitable venues within their own territories.

British Association of Conference Towns
International House, 36 Dudley Road, Royal Tunbridge Wells, Kent TN1 1LB
Tel.   0892 33442

British Universities Accommodation Consortium
Box No. 287, University Park, Nottingham NG7 2RD
Tel.   0602 504571

Conference Coordinates
70 Richmond Road, Twickenham, Middx TW1 3BE
Tel.   01-891 4951

Conference Clearway
Conference House, 9 Pavilion Parade, Brighton BN2 1RA
Tel.   0273 695811

Consort Hotels 'Venuefinder'
Ryedale Building, Piccadilly, York YO1 1PN
Tel.   0904 643151

Crest Meeting Places
20–26 Cursitor Street, London EC4A 1LT
Tel.   01-430 0991

Eaton Catering
Banda House, Cambridge Grove, Hammersmith, London W6 0LE
Tel.   01-568 8765

Expotel Conference Desk
Banda House, Cambridge Grove, Hammersmith, London W6 0LE
Tel.   01-568 8765

Higher Education Accommodation Consortium
36 Collegiate Crescent, Sheffield, South Yorkshire S10 2BP
Tel.   0742 683759

Manor Promotion Services
Peerland House, 40–42 Chapel Street, Marlow on Thames,
Buckinghamshire SL7 1DD
Tel.   062 84 75721

Meeting Point
(Trusthouse Forte Hotels)
24/30 New Street, Aylesbury, Bucks HT20 2NW
(All of the following telephone numbers link to the central
computer at Aylesbury)

Belfast	0232 628378
Birmingham	021-236 3951
Cardiff	0222 371889
Dublin	764401
Durham	0385 62561
Edinburgh	031-226 4346
Glasgow	041-221 6164
Leeds	0532 431261
Liverpool	051-236 0841
London	01-567 3444
Manchester	061-969 6111

Peter Rand Conference Placements
10 The Quadrant, Coventry CV1 2EL
Tel.   0203 555383

Room Centre (UK) Ltd
Kingsgate House, Kingsgate Place, London NW6 4MG
Tel.   01-328 1790

Scottish Universities Accommodation Consortium
P.O. Box 808, Edinburgh EH14 4AS
Tel.   031-449 4034

T.V.O. France
Building B – Quai Gambetta, BP52, 62200 Boulougne Sur-Mer,
France
Tel.   (21)87 00 69
Tel.   01-630 9161

Overseas national/city convention offices

The following is by no means an exhaustive list of Convention Offices, although it is as complete as I could make it. Many countries, regions and cities do not yet have an official Convention Bureau and so many of the addresses shown are for Tourist Offices. In these cases, the relevant Tourist Office claims to be able to supply information about conference and incentive facilities in their area. It has to be admitted that they vary enormously in their ability to provide relevant information. Some are worse than useless, others are extremely efficient. However, I hope that these addresses will provide a useful starting point in the search for an overseas venue.

Antigua and Barbuda

Antigua, Barbuda and Redonda National Tourist Office
15, Thayer Street, London, W1M 5LD
Tel.   01-486 7073

Australia

Australian Tourist Commission
Heathcoat House, 20 Savile Row, London W1X 1AE
Tel.   01-434 4371

Adelaide
Adelaide Convention and Visitors Bureau, 4th Floor, 12 Pierce Street, Adelaide 5000, South Australia, Australia
Tel.   010 61 8 212 4794

Brisbane
Brisbane Visitor and Convention Bureau, Brisbane City Hall,
King George Square, Brisbane 4000, Queensland, Australia
Tel. 010 61 7 221 8411

Canberra
Canberra Visitor and Convention Bureau, Jolimont Building,
Northbourne Avenue, Canberra, A.C.T. 2601, Australia
Tel. 010 61 62 47 4730

Gold Coast
Gold Coast Visitor Bureau, Suite 12, Regent Street Offices,
Pacific Fair, Surfers Paradise, 4217 Queensland, Australia
Tel. 010 61 75 38 4688

Melbourne
Melbourne Convention Bureau, 20th Level, Nauru House,
80 Collins Street, Melbourne, Australia 3000
Tel. 010 61 3 654 2288

Northern Territories
Northern Territories Convention Bureau, 31 Smith Street Mall,
Darwin, 7594 Northern Territories, Australia
Tel. 010 61 89 817532

Perth
Perth Convention Bureau, 10th Floor, 16 St George's Terrace,
Perth, 6000 Western Australia, Australia
Tel. 010 61 9 325 9400

Sydney
Sydney Convention and Visitors Bureau, Suite 2, Level 1, The
Centrepoint, 100 Market Street, Sydney 2000, Australia
Tel. 010 61 2 232 1377

Tasmania
Tasmanian Visitor Corporation, 40 Murray Street, Hobart,
7000 Tasmania, Australia
Tel. 010 61 02 30055

Austria

Austrian National Tourist Office
30, St George Street, London W1R 0AL
Tel. 01-629 0461

Graz
Graz Convention Bureau, Herrengasse 16, 8010 Graz, Austria
Tel.   010 43 316 70 52 41

Salzburg
Salzburg Convention and Visitors Bureau, Kongressbetriebe der
Stadt Salzburg, Auerspergstrasse 7, Salzburg, Austria A-5020
Tel.   010 43 662 76 51 10

Tyrol
Tourist Board Tyrol, Bozner Platz 6, A-6010 Innsbruck,
Austria
Tel.   010 43 5222 36521

Vienna
Vienna Convention Bureau, Kinderspitelgasse 5, A-1095 Vienna,
Austria
Tel.   010 43 222 43 16 08

Bahamas

Bahamas Ministry of Tourism
23 Old Bond Street, London W1X 4PQ
Tel.   01-629 5238

Nassau and Paradise Island Promotion Board
79 Dean Street, London W1V 6HY
Tel.   01-437 8766

Barbados

Barbados Board of Tourism
6, Upper Belgrave Street, London SW1X 8AZ
Tel.   01-235 2449

Bermuda

Bermuda Department of Tourism
9/10, Saville Row, London W1X 2BL
Tel.   01-734 8813

Belgium

38 Dover Street, London W1X 3RB
Tel. 01-499 5379

Antwerp
Antwerp Convention Bureau, 102 Desguinlei, Antwerp B-2018,
Belgium
Tel. 010 32 31 237 0698

Bruges
Provinciale Westvlaamse Vereniging Voor Toerisme,
Vlamingstraat 55, B-8000 Brugge, Belgium
Tel. 010 32 50 33 73 44

Brussels
Brussels Congress FIB, Parc des Expositions, Place de
Belgique, 1010 Brussels, Belgium
Tel. 010 32 2 217 8012

Liege
Liege Convention Bureau, Palais de Congres, Esplanade de
l'Europe, B-4000 Liege, Belgium
Tel. 010 32 41 43 90 50

Brazil

Brazilian National Tourist Office
c/o Varig Brazilian Airlines, 16/17 Hanover Street, London
W1R 9HG
Tel. 01-629 9408

Brazil
Brazilian Tourism Authority, Rua Mariz e Barros, 13–4/14,
CEP. 20270, Rio de Janeiro, Brazil
Tel. 010 55 21 273 2212

Bahia
Bahiatursa, Rua da Graca 411, 4000 Salvador, Bahia, Brazil
Tel. 010 55 71 245 8433

Rio de Janeiro
Rio De Janeiro Convention Bureau, Rua Visconde de Piraja,
547/610 a 617, 22410, Rio de Janeiro, Brazil
Tel.   010 55 21 259 6165

Sao Paulo
Sao Paulo Convention Bureau, Parque Anhembi, 02012,
Sao Paulo SP, Brazil
Tel.   010 55 11 267 2122

Canada

Tourism Canada
Canadian High Commission, Canada House, Trafalgar Square,
London SW1Y 5BJ
Tel.   01-629 9492

London Offices for Provincial Tourist Authorities
Alberta
Travel Alberta, 1 Mount Street, London W1Y 5AA
Tel.   01-491 3430
(*See also* listings for Banff, Calgary, Edmonton)

British Columbia
Tourism British Columbia, 1 Regent Street, London
SW1Y 4NS
Tel. 01-930 6857
(*See also* listings for Prince George, Vancouver and Victoria)

Nova Scotia
Tourism Nova Scotia, 14 Pall Mall, London SW1Y 5LV
Tel.   01-930 6864
(*See also* listings for Dartmouth and Halifax)

Ontario
Government of Ontario, Ontario House, 13 Charles II Street,
London SW1Y 4QS
Tel.   01-930 6404
(*See also* listings for Brantford, Cambridge, Collingwood,
Cornwall, Hamilton, Kingston, London, Niagara Falls, Niagara
on the Lake, North Bay, Ottawa, Peterborough, Sarnia,
Stratford, Thunder Bay, Toronto, Windsor)

Quebec
Tourism Quebec, 59 Pall Mall, London SW1Y 5JH
Tel.   01-930 8314
(*See also* listings for Hull, Montreal and Quebec City)

Saskatchewan
Saskatchewan Tourism, 21 Pall Mall, London SW1
Tel.   01-930 7491
(*See also* listing for Saskatoon)

Local Convention Bureaux in Canada

Alberta
Travel Alberta, 10065 Jasper Avenue, 14th Floor, Capitol
Square, Edmonton, Alberta, Canada
Tel.   010 1 403 427 4323
(*See also* Banff, Calgary and Edmonton)

Bannff (Alberta)
Banff/Lake Louise Chamber of Commerce, P.O. Box 1298,
Banff, Alberta T0L 0C0, Canada
Tel.   010 1 403 762 3777

Brandon (Manitoba)
Brandon Visitors and Convention Bureau, c/o Chamber of
Commerce, P.O. Box 1417, 907 Princess Avenue, Brandon,
Manitoba R7A 6N2, Canada

Brantford (Ontario)
Visitors and Convention Bureau, 77 Charlotte Street,
Box 1294, Brantford, Ontario N3T 5T6, Canada

British Columbia
(*See Prince George, Vancouver and Victoria*)

Calgary (Alberta)
Calgary Tourist and Convention Bureau, 237 8th Avenue SE,
Calgary, Alberta T2G 0K8, Canada
Tel.   010 1 403 263 8510

Cambridge (Ontario)
Visitor and Convention Bureau, 531 King Street East,
Cambridge, Ontario N3H 3N4, Canada

Charlottetown (Prince Edward Island)
PEI Convention Bureau, P. O. Box 2077, Charlottetown,
Prince Edward Island C1A 7N7, Canada
Tel.   010 1 902 892 5900

Collingwood (Ontario)
Tourist Association and Convention Bureau, 601 First Street,
Collingwood, Ontario L9Y 4L2, Canada

Cornwall (Ontario)
Convention Bureau, 100 Water Street East, Cornwall, Ontario
K6H 6G4, Canada

Dartmouth (Nova Scotia)
Dartmouth Convention Bureau, City Hall, P.O. Box 817,
Dartmouth, Nova Scotia B2Y 3Z3, Canada

Edmonton (Alberta)
Edmonton Convention and Tourism Authority, 9797 Jasper
Avenue, Edmonton, Alberta T5J 1N9, Canada
Tel.   010 1 403 426 4715

Fredericton (New Brunswick)
Visitors and Convention Bureau, City Hall, Queen Street,
P.O. Box 130, Fredericton, New Brunswick E3B 4Y7, Canada

Halifax (Nova Scotia)
Tourism Halifax, P.O. Box 1749, Halifax, Nova Scotia
B3J 3A5, Canada
Tel.   010 1 902 421 8736

Hamilton (Ontario)
Visitors and Convention Services, P.O. Box 910, 119 King
Street W, Hamilton, Ontario L8N 3V9, Canada
Tel.   010 1 416 526 4222

Hull (Province of Quebec)
Regional Tourist and Convention Bureau, Maison des
Citoyens, 25 Laurier Street, Hull, Province of Quebec
J8X 4C8, Canada
Tel.   010 1 819 778 2222

Kingston (Ontario)
Visitors and Convention Bureau, 209 Ontario Street, Kingston,
Ontario K7L 2Z1, Canada

London (Ontario)
Visitors and Convention Services, 300 Dufferin Avenue,
P.O. Box 5035, London, Ontario N6A 4L9, Canada

Manitoba
(*See* Brandon and Winnipeg)

Montreal (Province of Quebec)
Greater Montreal Convention and Tourism Bureau, MARTF,
1 Frontenac, Montreal, Province of Quebec H5A 1E6, Canada
Tel.   010 1 514 871 1129

New Brunswick
(*See* Fredericton and Saint John)

Newfoundland
(*See* St John's)

Niagara Falls (Ontario)
Visitors and Convention Bureau, 4610 Ontario Avenue,
Niagara Falls, Ontario L2E 3P9, Canada

Niagara on the Lake (Ontario)
Visitor and Convention Bureau, P.O. Box 1045, Niagara on
the Lake, Ontario L0S 1J0, Canada

North Bay (Ontario)
Tourist and Convention Department, P.O. Box 360, North
Bay, Ontario P1B 8H8, Canada

Nova Scotia
(*See* Dartmouth and Halifax)

Ontario
(*See* Brantford, Cambridge, Collingwood, Cornwall, Hamilton,
Kingston, London, Niagara Falls, Niagara on the Lake, North
Bay, Ottawa, Peterborough, Sarnia, Stratford, Thunder Bay,
Toronto, Windsor)

Ottawa (Ontario)
Canada's Capital Visitors and Convention Bureau, 222 Queen Street, 7th Floor, Ottawa, Ontario K1P 5V9, Canada
Tel. 010 1 613 237 5150

Peterborough (Ontario)
Kawartha Tourism and Convention Bureau, 135 George Street North, Peterborough, Ontario K9J 3G6, Canada

Prince Edward Island
(*See* Charlottetown)

Prince George (British Columbia)
Visitors and Convention Bureau, P.O. Box 909, Station A, Prince George, British Columbia V2L 4T9, Canada

Quebec
(*See* Hull, Montreal and Quebec City)

Quebec City
Tourism and Convention Bureau of the Quebec Urban Community, 53 Rue D'Auteuil, Quebec, Province of Quebec G1R 4C2, Canada
Tel. 010 1 418 692 2471

Sarnia (Ontario)
Visitors and Convention Bureau, 224 North Vidal Street, Sarnia, Ontario N7T 5Y3, Canada

Saskatchewan
(*See* Saskatoon)

Saskatoon (Saskatchewan)
Tourist and Convention Bureau, 308 24th Street East, Saskatoon, Saskatchewan S7K 4R2, Canada

Saint John (New Brunswick)
Saint John Visitors and Convention Bureau, P.O. Box 1971, City Hall, Saint John, New Brunswick E2L 4L1, Canada
Tel. 010 1 506 658 2990

St John's (Newfoundland)
St John's Tourist Commission and Convention Bureau, P.O.
Box 1567, City Hall, St John's, Newfoundland A1C 5P3,
Canada
Tel.   010 1 709 722 7080

Stratford (Ontario)
Visitors and Convention Bureau, 38 Albert Street, Stratford,
Ontario N5A 3K3, Canada

Thunder Bay (Ontario)
Visitors and Convention Department, 520 Leith Street,
Thunder Bay, Ontario P7C 1M9, Canada

Toronto (Ontario)
Metropolitan Toronto Convention and Visitors Association,
Toronto Eaton Centre Galleria, P.O. Box 510, 220 Yonge
Street, Toronto, Ontario M5B 2H1, Canada
Tel.   010 1 416 979 3133

Vancouver (British Columbia)
Greater Vancouver Convention and Visitors Bureau, Suite
1625, 1055 W Georgia Street, P.O. Box 11142, Royal Centre,
Vancouver, British Columbia V6E 4C8, Canada
Tel.   010 1 604 682 2222

Victoria
Greater Victoria Convention and Visitors Bureau, 812 Wharf
Street, Victoria, British Columbia V8W 1T3, Canada
Tel.   010 1 604 382 2127

Windsor (Ontario)
Tourist and Convention Bureau, 80 Chatham Street East,
Windsor, Ontario N9A 2W1, Canada

Winnipeg (Manitoba)
Winnipeg Convention and Visitors Bureau, 232/375 York
Avenue, Winnipeg, Manitoba R3C 3J3, Canada
Tel.   010 1 204 943 1970

Cyprus

Cyprus Tourism Organization
213, Regent Street, London W1R 8DA
Tel.   01-734 9822

North Cyprus

North Cyprus Tourist Office
28 Cockspur Street, London SW1Y 5BN
Tel. 01-839 5530

Denmark

Danish Tourist Board
169/173, Regent Street, London W1R 8PY
Tel.   01-734 2637

> *Danish Convention Bureau*
> Vestebrogarde 6D, DK-1620 Copenhagen V, Denmark
> Tel.   010 45 1 11 14 15

> *Copenhagen*
> Copenhagen Tourist Association, 7A Norregade, DK-1165
> Copenhagen K, Denmark
> Tel.   010 45 1 13 70 07

Dubai

Dnata World Travel
125 Pall Mall, London SW1Y 5AE
Tel. 01-930 5356

Egypt

Egyptian State Tourist Office
168 Piccadilly, London W1V 9DE
Tel.   01-493 5282

El Salvador

San Salvador Convention and Visitors Bureau, 9a Avenida Norte
406, Apartado Postal 2124, San Salvador, El Salvador, CA
Tel.   010 503 22 4044

Finland

Finnish Tourist Board
66, Haymarket, London
Tel.   01-839 4048

Helsinki-Finland Congress Bureau
Rikhardinkatu 4 B 22, 00130 Helsinki 13, Finland
Tel.   010 358 0 170 688

France

French National Tourist Office
178 Piccadilly, London W1V 0AL
Tel.   01-629 1272

Bordeaux Congress
33 300 Bordeaux, France
Tel.   010 33 56 50 84 49

Cannes Tourist and Convention Bureau
Esplanade President George Pompidou, La Croisette, 06400
Cannes, France
Tel.   010 33 93 39 01 01

Courchevel Tourist Office
73120 Courchevel 1850, Savoie, France
Tel.   010 33 79 08 00 29

Deauville Office du Tourisme
Place de la Marie, BP 79, 14800 Deauville, France
Tel.   010 33 31 88 21 43

France-Congres (French Ass. of Convention City Mayors)
24 Avenue de l'Opera, F-75001 Paris, France
Tel.   010 33 1 42 96 03 61

Lille Office du Tourisme
Palais Rihour, BP205, F-59002 Lille-Cedex, France
Tel.   010 33 20 30 81 00

Marseille (Provence Riviera Congres)
Palais de la Bourse, 13001 Marseille, France
Tel.   010 33 91 37 91 22

Mulhouse (Office de Tourism)
9 Avenue Foch, 68100 Mulhouse, France
Tel.   010 33 89 45 68 31

Nice Convention Bureau
1 Esplanade Kennedy, 06300 Nice, France
Tel.   010 33 93 92 80 74

Paris Convention Bureau
127 Avenue des Champs Elysees, 75008, Paris, France
Tel.   010 33 1 47 23 61 72

Promotoulouse
Donjon du Capitole, Square Charles de Gaulle, 3100 Toulouse,
France
Tel.   010 33 61 21 92 32

Germany (Federal Republic of)

German National Tourist Office
61, Conduit Street, London W1R 0EN
Tel.   01-734 2600

German Convention Bureau
Lyoner Str. 20, D 6000 Frankfurt/M, Federal Republic of
Germany
Tel.   010 49 69 666 70 83

Dusseldorf
Office for City Promotion and Tourism, Muhlenstrasse 29,
D-4000 Dusseldorf 1, Federal Republic of Germany
Tel.   010 49 211 899 3828

Frankfurt am Main
Frankfurt Tourist Office, Gutleutstrasse 7–9, D-6000 Frankfurt am Main 1, Federal Republic of Germany
Tel.   010 49 611 212 85 51

Hamburg
Tourism Marketing Department, Hamburg-Information GmbH, Neuer Jungfernsteig 5, D-2000 Hamburg 36, Federal Republic of Germany
Tel.   010 49 40 35 00 10

Hannover
City of Hannover Tourist Promotion Board, Nyumbani, Lynwick Street, Rudgwick, Sussex
Tel.   0403 722837

Munich
Tourist Information Office of the City of Munich, Rindermarkt 5, D-8000 Munchen 2, Federal Republic of Germany
Tel.   010 49 89 239 12 46

Gibraltar

Gibraltar Government Tourist Office, Arundel Great Court, 179 The Strand, London WC2R 1EH
Tel.   01-836 0777

Gibraltar
Gibraltar Government Tourist Office, Cathedral Square, Gibraltar
Tel.   010 350 76400

Greece

Greek National Tourist Office
195/7 Regent Street, London W1R 8DL
Tel.   01-734 5997

Guatemala

Gautemala Convention and Visitors Bureau, 7a Avenida 1–17, Zona 4, 5°. Nivel, Edificio Inguat, Apartado Postal 2573, Guatemala City, Guatemala, C.A.
Tel.   010 502 2 31 29 85

Holland

(*See* Netherlands)

Hong Kong

Hong Kong Tourist Association
125 Pall Mall, London SW1Y 5EA
Tel.   01-930 4775

Hong Kong Tourist Association, 35th Floor, Connaught Centre, Connaught Road, Central, Hong Kong
Tel.   010 852 5 24 41 91

Hungary

Danube Travel
6, Conduit Street, London W1
Tel.   01-493 0263

India

Government of India Tourist Office
7, Cork Street, London W1X 2AB
Tel.   01-437 3677

Indonesia

Embassy of Indonesia
Grosvenor Square, London W1
Tel.   01-499 7661

234

Indonesian Tourist Promotion Office
Geoffrey Gray-Forton Associates Ltd, 16 Hanover Square,
London W1R 0AU
Tel.   01-629 4917

Indonesian Tourist Promotion Office
Jalan Kramat Raya 81, Jakarta 10045, Indonesia
Tel.   010 62 21 359001

Ireland

Irish Tourist Board
150, New Bond Street, London W1Y 0AQ
Tel.   01-493 3201

Israel

Israel Government Tourist Office
18, Great Marlborough Street, London W1V 1AF
Tel.   01-434 3651

Italy

Italian State Tourist Office
1, Prince Street, London W1R 7RA
Tel.   01-408 1254

Italcongressi
Piazza della Liberta 21, 00192 Roma, Italy
Tel.   010 39 6 32 25 58

Jamaica

Jamaica Tourist Board
50, St. James's Street, London SW1A 1JT
Tel.   01-493 3647

Japan

Japanese National Tourist Office
167, Regent Street, London W1R 7ED
Tel. 01-734 9638

Osaka Convention Bureau
Osaka Chamber of Commerce and Industry, 58–7
Uchihommachi-Hashizume-Cho, Higashi-Ku, Osaka, 540 Japan
Tel. 010 81 6 944 6485

Korea

Korea National Tourism Corporation
Vogue House, 1 Hanover Square, London W1R 9RD
Tel. 01-408 1591

Korea National Tourism Corporation, 10 Ta-dong, Chung-ku,
C.P.O. Box 903, Seoul 100, Korea
Tel. 010 82 2 757 3988

Malaysia

Malaysia Tourist Development Corporation
17 Curzon Street, Mayfair, London W1Y 7FE
Tel. 01-499 7388

Malaysia Tourist Development Corporation
Tourist Development Corporation Malaysia, Wisma MP1,
PO Box 10328, Jalan Raja Chulan, Kuala Lumpur, Malaysia
Tel. 010 60 3 423033

Madeira

(*See* Portugal)

Malta

Malta Government Tourist Office
Suite 207, College House, Wrights Lane, London W8
Tel. 01-938 1140

Mexico

Mexican Government Tourist Office
7, Cork Street, London W1X 1PB
Tel. 01-734 1058

Mexico City
Mexico City Convention and Visitors Council, Emerson 316,
3rd Floor, 11560 Mexico City, Mexico
Tel. 010 52 5 250 5449

Monaco

Monaco Government Tourist and Convention Office
Graigs Court House, 25 Whitehall, London SW1A 2BS
Tel. 01-930 4699

Monaco Government Tourist and Convention Office
2a Boulevard des Moulins, MC 98030 Monaco, CEDEX
Tel. 010 33 93 30 87 01

Morocco

Moroccan National Tourist Office
174 Regent Street, London W1R 6HB
Tel. 01-437 0073

Netherlands

Netherlands Convention Bureau
143 New Bond Street, London W1Y 9FD
Tel. 01-499 9367

Amsterdam
Amsterdam Tourist Office, P.O. Box 3901, 1001 AS
Amsterdam, Netherlands
Tel. 010 31 20 22 10 16

Maastricht
Maastricht Convention and Visitors Bureau, Kleine Staat,
6211 ED Maastricht, Netherlands
Tel.   010 43 25 21 21

Netherlands Convention Bureau
Rivierstaete, Amsteldijk 166, 1079 LH Amsterdam, Netherlands
Tel.   010 31 20 46 25 80

Rotterdam
Rotterdam Tourist and Congress Office, Stadhuisplan 19,
3012 AR Rotterdam, Netherlands
Tel.   010 31 10 14 14 00

New Zealand

New Zealand Tourist Office
New Zealand House, Haymarket, London SW1Y 4TQ
Tel.   01-930 8422

Auckland
Auckland Convention Bureau, P.O. Box 7048
Auckland, New Zealand

Christchurch
Christchurch Convention Bureau, P.O. Box 2600,
Christchurch, New Zealand

Dunedin
Dunedin Convention Bureau, P.O. Box 5375, Dunedin,
New Zealand

West Coast
West Coast Public Relations and Information Centre Inc.,
P.O. Box 95, Greymouth, New Zealand

Far North
Far North Convention Centre, P.O. Box 303, Kaitaia,
New Zealand

Gisborne
Gisborne Convention Bureau, P.O. Box 170, Gisborne,
New Zealand

Hastings
Hastings Convention Bureau, Private Bag, Hastings,
New Zealand

Invercargill
Invercargill Convention Bureau, P.O. Box 311, Invercargill,
New Zealand

Napier
Napier Convention Bureau, P.O. Box 722, Napier,
New Zealand

Nelson
Nelson Convention Bureau, P.O. Box 194, Nelson,
New Zealand

New Plymouth
New Plymouth Convention Bureau, Private Bag,
New Plymouth, New Zealand

Palmerstone North
Palmerstone North Convention Bureau, Civic Complex,
The Square, Palmerstone North, New Zealand

Rotorua
Rotorua Convention Bureau, Private Bag, Rotorua,
New Zealand

South Canterbury
South Canterbury Convention Bureau P.O. Box 194, Timaru,
New Zealand

Taupo
Taupo Convention Bureau, P.O. Box 142, Taupo,
New Zealand

Tauranga
City of Tauranga Convention Bureau, P.O. Box 1070,
Tauranga, New Zealand

Wairarapa
Wairarapa Convention Bureau, P.O. Box 814, Masterton,
New Zealand

Wanganui
Wanganui Convention Bureau, P.O. Box 637, Wanganui,
New Zealand

Wellington
Wellington Convention Bureau, P.O. Box 28–046, Wellington,
New Zealand

Wellington
Greater Wellington Convention Bureau, P.O. Box 1590,
Wellington, New Zealand

Whangarei
Whangarei Convention Bureau, P.O. Box 1133, Whangarei,
New Zealand

Norway

Norwegian Tourist Board
20 Pall Mall, London SW1Y 5NE
Tel. 01-839 2650

Bergen
Bergen Tourist Board, Slottsgt. 1, 5000 Bergen, Norway
Tel. 010 47 5 31 38 60

Stavanger Forum
P.O. Box 410, N-4001 Stavanger, Norway
Tel. 010 47 4 55 81 00

Oslo Convention Bureau
Raadhusgaten 19, 0158 Oslo 1, Norway
Tel. 010 047 2 42 71 70

Philippines

Philippine Tourist Office
199, Piccadilly, London W1V 9LE
Tel. 01-439 3481

Philippine Convention Bureau (European Office)
Ambassade des Philippines, Services Culturels, 39 Avenue
Georges Mandel, Paris, France 75116
Tel. 010 33 4553-3492

Philippine Convention Bureau
4th Floor, Suite 7, 10–17 Legaspi Towers, 300 Roxas
Boulevard, Metro Manila, Philippines
Tel.   010 63 2 57 50 31

Portugal (including Madeira)

Portugese National Tourist Office
New Bond Street House, 1–5 New Bond Street, London
W1Y 0NP
Tel.   01-493 3873

Singapore

Singapore Tourist Board
33, Heddon Street, London W1R 7LB
Tel.   01-437 0033

Singapore Tourist Promotion Board
131 Tanglin Road, Tudor Court, Singapore 1024, Republic of
Singapore
Tel.   010 65 2356611

South Africa

South African Tourist Corporation
Regency House, 1/4, Warwick Street, London W1R 5WB
Tel.   01-439 9661

South African Tourist Association
254 Regent Street, London W1R 7AD
Tel.   01-437 9621

Spain

Spanish National Tourist Office
57/58 St. James's Street, London SW1A 1LD
Tel.   01-499 0901

Andalucia
Junta de Andalucia Direccion General de Ordenacion y
Promocion del Tourismo, P.O. Box 120.000, Avenida Rep.
Argentina 23–5, 41011 Sevilla, Spain
Tel.   010 34 54 27 01 39

Barcelona
Promotion and Convention Sales, Avenida Paral lel 202, 08015
Barcelona, Spain
Tel.   010 34 3 224 42 06

Costa Del Sol Tourist Promotion Board
Palacio de Congresos, P.O. Box 298, Torremolinos, Malaga,
Spain
Tel.   010 34 52 38 57 31

Granada
Patronato Provincial de Tourismo de Granada, Plaza Mariana
Pineda 8-3, 18009 Granada, Spain
Tel.   010 34 58 22 35 27

Madrid
Madrid Convention Bureau, C/Senores de Luzon 10-2, 28013
Madrid, Spain
Tel.   010 1 34 1 266 39 00

Malaga
(*See* Costa del Sol)

Seville
Tourist Promotion Board of Sevilla, Avda. de la Constitucion
24, 41001 Sevilla, Spain
Tel.   010 34 54 21 10 91

Torremolinos
(*See* Costa del Sol)

Sri Lanka

Sri Lankan Tourist Board
Suite 433, High Holborn House, 52, High Holborn, London
WC1V 6RL
Tel.   01-405 1194

Sweden

Swedish National Tourist Office
3, Cork Street, London W1X 1HA
Tel. 01-437 5816

Gothenburg
Gothenburg Convention Bureau, Kungsportsplazen 2, S-411 10
Gothenburg, Sweden
Tel. 010 46 31 13 60 32

Stockholm
Stockholm Convention Bureau, Jakobs Torg 3, S-111 52
Stockholm, Sweden
Tel. 010 46 8 230 990

Switzerland

Swiss National Tourist Office
1, New Coventry Street, London W1V 8EE
Tel. 01-734 1921

Basel
Basel Tourist Board, Blumenrain 2, CH-4001 Basel,
Switzerland
Tel. 010 41 61 25 50 50

Geneva
Convention Department, Geneva Tourist Office, 1 Rue de la
Tour-de-L'ile, CH-1211 Geneva 11, Switzerland
Tel. 010 41 22 28 72 33

Interlaken
Interlaken Tourist Office, Hoheweg 37, 3800 Interlaken,
Switzerland
Tel. 010 41 36 22 21 21

Lausanne
Lausanne Tourist Office and Convention Bureau, 60 Avenue
d'Ouchy, P.O. Box 248, CH-1000 Lausanne 6, Switzerland
Tel. 010 41 21 27 73 21

Luzern
Luzern Tourist Promotion Board, Haldenstrasse 6, 6002
Luzern, Switzerland
Tel.   010 41 41 51 71 71

Montreux
Montreux Official Tourist Office, Rue du Theatre 5, P.O. Box
97, CH-1820 Montreux, Switzerland
Tel.   010 41 21 63 12 12

Zurich
Zurich Tourist Association, Bahnhofbrucke 1, CH-8023 Zurich,
Switzerland
Tel.   010 41 1 211 12 56

Thailand

Tourism Authority of Thailand
9, Stafford Street, London W1X 3FE
Tel.   01-499 7679

Thailand Convention Promotion Association
THA Building, Third Floor, 1 Soi Prachane, Wireless Road,
Bangkok 10500, Thailand
Tel.   010 66 2 251 3017

Trinidad and Tobago

Trinidad and Tobago Tourist Board
20 Lower Regent Street, London SW1Y 4PH
Tel.   01-930 6566

Tunisia

Tunisian National Tourist Office
33 Dover Street, London W1
Tel.   01-629 0858

Turkey

Turkish Tourism and Information Office
170/173 Piccadilly, London W1V 9DD
Tel. 01-734 8681

United Arab Emirates (*Northern*)

Dnata World Travel
125 Pall Mall, London SW1Y 5AE
Tel. 01-930 5356

United States of America

United States Travel and Tourist Administration
22, Sackville Street, London W1X 2EA
Tel. 01-439 7433

Quick reference guide by State
Alabama
See Decatur, Birmingham, Mobile, Huntsville and Montgomery.

Alaska
See Anchorage, Janeau, Fairbanks and Valdez.

Arizona
See Arizona, Mesa, Phoenix, Scottsdale, Tucson and
Yuma.

Arkansas
See Hot Springs, and Little Rock

California
See Anaheim, Beverly Hills, Buena Park, California, Concord,
Destination Marketing, Eureka, Fresno, Long Beach, Los
Angeles, Monterey, Oakland, Oxnard, Palm Springs, Pasadena,
Riverside, Sacramento, Salinas, San Diego, San Francisco, San Jose,
San Mateo, Santa Barbara, Santa Clara, Santa Cruz, Santa Monica,
Stockton, Sonoma, Tahoe and Ventura.

Colorado
See Colorado, Denver, Motivators and Vail.

Connecticut
See Hartford and Milford

Delaware
See Wilmington

District of Columbia
See Washington.

Florida
See Broward County, Daytona, Florida, Florida's Lee Island
Coast, Fort Lauderdale, Fort Myers, Jacksonville, Kissimmee,
Miami Beach, Miami, Motivators (for Lee County), Orlando,
Palm Beach, Tallahassee and Tampa.

Georgia
See Atlanta, Augusta, Brunswick, Columbus, DeKalb, Jekyll
Island and Savannah.

Hawaii
See Hawaii and Maui.

Idaho
See Boise

Illinois
See Bloomington, Carbondale, Champaign, Chicago, Collinsville,
Danville, Decatur, Kankakee County, Mount Vernon, Peoria,
Quincy, Rockford, Rock Island, Rosemont, Springfield and
Motivators (for Chicago).

Indiana
See Bloomington, Evansville, Fort Wayne, Indianapolis,
Jeffersonville, Lafayette, South Bend and Terre Haute.

Iowa
See Cedar Rapids, Des Moines, Dubuque, Iowa City and
Waterloo.

Kansas
See Overland Park, Topeka and Wichita.

Kentucky
See Bowling Green, Covington, Lexington, Louisville and
Northern Kentucky.

Louisiana
See Alexandria, Baton Rouge, Lafayette, Lake Charles, Monroe,
Motivators, New Orleans, Rapides Parish, Shreveport, Slidell,
St Tammany and Southwest Louisiana.

Maine
See Portland.

Maryland
See Baltimore and Ocean City.

Massachusetts
See Boston and Worcester.

Michigan
See Ann Arbor, Battle Creek, Detroit, Flint, Grand Rapids,
Lansing, Traverse City and Saginaw.

Minnesota
See Bloomington, Duluth, Minneapolis, Minnesota, Rochester
and St Paul.

Mississippi
See Jackson, Mississippi and Natchez.

Missouri
See Coloumbia, Independence, Kansas City, Springfield and
St Louis.

Montana
See Bozeman, Great Falls, Kalispell and Missoula.

Nebraska
See Grand Island, Lincoln and Omaha.

Nevada
See Elko, Las Vegas and Reno.

New Jersey
See Atlantic City.

New Mexico
See Albuquerque, Carlsbad, Las Cruces, Santa Fe and Roswell.

New York State
See Albany, Buffalo, Destination Marketing, Glen Falls, Long
Island, New York, Niagara Falls, Oneida County, Poughkeepsie,
Rochester, Saratoga and Syracuse.

North Carolina
See Asheville, Charlotte, Greensboro, High Point and
Winston-Salem.

North Dakota
See North Dakota.

Ohio
See Akron, Canton, Cincinnati, Cleveland, Columbus, Dayton,
Lima, Marietta Niles, Toledo and Trumbull County.

Oklahoma
See Oklahoma, Motivators (also for Oklahoma), Oklahoma City
and Tulsa.

Oregon
See Eugene and Portland.

Pennsylvania
See Lancaster, Norristown, Pennsylvania, Philadelphia, Pittsburg
and Valley Forge.

Peurto Rico
See San Juan.

Rhode Island
See Providence.

South Carolina
See Charleston, Columbia, Greenville, Hilton Head Island and
Myrtle Beach.

South Dakota
See Rapid City and Sioux Falls.

Tennessee
See Chattanooga, Gatlinburg, Johnson City, Knoxville, Memphis
and Nashville.

Texas
See Abilene, Amarillo, Arlington, Austin, Beaumont, Corpus
Christi, Dallas, Denton, El Paso, Fort Worth, Galveston,
Grapevine, Houston, Irving City, Laredo, Lubbock, McAllen,
Odessa, San Angelo City, San Antonio, Texas, Victoria and
Waco.

US Virgin Islands
See Destination Marketing.

Utah
See Motivators and Salt Lake City.

Virginia
See Alexandria, Norfolk, Richmond, Roanoke, Virginia Beach
and Williamsburg.

Washington State
See Seattle and Spokane.

West Virginia
See Huntington, Charleston, and Wheeling.

Wisconsin
See Eau Claire, Fond du Lac, Green Bay, LaCrosse, Lake
Geneva, Madison, Milwaukee, Racine and Sheboygan.

Wyoming
See Motivators and Wyoming.

Individual convention bureaux
Abilene (Texas)
Abilene Convention and Visitors Council, Abilene Chamber of
Commerce, 325 Hickory, P.O. Box 2281, Abilene, Texas 79604,
USA
Tel.   010 1 915 677 7241

Akron (Ohio)
Akron Convention and Visitors Bureau, 1 Cascade Plaza, Akron,
Ohio 44308, USA
Tel.   010 1 216 376 4254

Albany (New York)
Albany County Convention and Visitors Bureau, 600 Broadway,
Albany, New York 12207, USA
Tel.   010 1 518 434 1217

Albuquerque (New Mexico)
Albuquerque Convention and Visitors Bureau Inc., Suite 301, 202
Central Southeast, P.O. Box 26866, Albuquerque, New Mexico
87102, USA
Tel.   010 1 505 243 3696

Alexandria (Louisiana)
Alexandria-Pineville Convention and Tourist Bureau, P.O. Box
992, Alexandria, Louisiana 71301, USA
Tel.   010 1 318 442 6671

Alexandria (Virginia)
Alexandria Tourist Council, 221 King Street, Alexandria, Virginia
22314, USA
Tel.   010 1 703 549 0205

Amarillo (Texas)
Convention and Visitors Board, 1000 South Polk Street, P.O.
Box 9480, Amarillo, Texas 79101, USA
Tel.   010 1 806 373 7800

Anaheim (California)
Anaheim Area Visitor and Convention Bureau, 800 West Katella
Avenue, Anaheim, California 9413, USA
Tel.   010 1 714 999 8999

Anchorage (Alaska)
Anchorage Convention and Visitors Bureau, 201 East Third
Avenue, Anchorage, Alaska 99501, USA
Tel.   010 1 970 276 4118

Ann Arbor (Michigan)
Ann Arbor Conference and Visitors Bureau, 207 East Washington
Street, Ann Arbor, Michigan 48104-2072, USA
Tel.   010 1 313 995 7281

Arizona
Arizona Office of Tourism, Office of the Governor, 1480 East
Bethany Home Road, Phoenix, Arizona 85014 USA
Tel.   010 1 602 255 3618

Arlington (Texas)
Arlington Convention and Visitors Bureau, P.O. Box A,
Arlington, Texas 76010, USA
Tel.   010 1 817 265 7721

Asheville (North Carolina)
Asheville Area Convention and Visitors Bureau, 151 Haywood
Street, P.O. Box 1011, Asheville, North Carolina 28802, USA
Tel.   010 1 704 258 3916

Atlanta (Georgia)
Atlanta Convention and Visitors Bureau, 233 Peachtree Street
NE, Suite 200, Atlanta, Georgia 30043, USA
Tel.   010 1 404 521 6600

Atlantic City (New Jersey)
Atlantic City Convention and Visitors Bureau, 16 Central Pier,
Atlantic City, New Jersey 08401, USA
Tel.   010 1 609 345 7536

Augusta (Georgia)
Augusta Convention and Visitors Bureau, P.O. Box 657,
Augusta, Georgia 30913, USA
Tel.   010 1 404 722 0421

Austin (Texas)
Austin Convention and Visitors Council, P.O. Box 1967, Austin,
Texas 78767, USA
Tel.   010 1 512 478 9383

Baltimore (Maryland)
Baltimore Convention Bureau, 1 East Pratt Street, Suite 14, Plaza
Level, Baltimore, Maryland 21202, USA
Tel.   010 1 301 659 7300

Baton Rouge (Louisiana)
Baton Rouge Area Convention and Visitors Bureau, P.O. Drawer
4149, Baton Rouge, Lousiana 70821, USA
Tel.   010 1 504 383 1825

Battle Creek (Michigan)
Greater Battle Creek/Calhoun County Visitor and Convention
Bureau, 172 West Van Buren Street, Battle Creek, Michigan
49017, USA
Tel.   010 1 616 962 2240

Beaumont (Texas)
Beaumont Convention and Visitors Bureau, 595 Orleans Street,
P.O. Box 3150, Beaumont, Texas 77704, USA
Tel.   010 1 409 838 1424

Beverly Hills (California)
Beverly Hills Visitors and Convention Bureau, 239 South Beverly
Drive, Beverly Hills, California 90212, USA
Tel.   010 1 213 271 8174

Birmingham (*Alabama*)
Greater Birmingham Convention and Visitors Bureau, 2027 First
Avenue North, 300 Commerce Center, Birmingham, Alabama
35203, USA
Tel.   010 1 205 252 9825

Bloomington (*Illinois*)
Bloomington-Normal Area Convention and Visitors Bureau,
210 South East Street, Bloomington, Illinois 61701, USA
Tel.   010 1 309 829 1641

Bloomington (*Indiana*)
Bloomington/Monroe County Convention and Visitors Bureau,
441 Gourley Pike, Bloomington, Indiana 47401, USA
Tel.   010 1 812 334 8900

Bloomington (*Minnesota*)
Bloomington Convention and Visitors Bureau, 9801 Dupont
Avenue South, Suite 440, Bloomington, Minnesota 55431, USA
Tel.   010 1 612 888 8810

Boise (*Idaho*)
Boise Convention and Visitors Bureau, P.O. Box 2106, Boise,
Idaho 83701, USA
Tel.   010 1 208 344 7777

Boston (*Massachusetts*)
Greater Boston Convention and Visitors Bureau, Prudential Plaza,
P.O. Box 490, Boston, Massachusetts 02199, USA
Tel.   010 1 617 536 4100

Bowling Green (*Kentucky*)
Bowling Green Tourist and Convention Commission, 1755–D
Scottsville Road, P.O. Box 1040, Bowling Green, Kentucky
42102, USA
Tel.   010 1 502 782 0800

Bozeman (*Montana*)
Bozeman Convention and Visitors Bureau, P.O. Box B,
Bozeman, Montana 59715, USA
Tel.   010 1 406 586 5421

Broward County (*Florida*)
Broward County Tourist Development Council, 201 SE 8th
Avenue, Fort Lauderdale, Florida 33301, USA
Tel.   010 1 305 765 5508

Brunswick (*Georgia*)
Golden Isles Tourist and Convention Bureau, 4 Glynn Avenue,
Brunswick, Georgia 31520, USA
Tel.   010 1 912 265 0620

Buena Park (*California*)
Buena Park Visitors and Convention Bureau, 6696 Beach
Boulevard, P.O. Box 5308, Buena Park, California 90622, USA
Tel.   010 1 714 994 1511

Buffalo (*New York*)
Buffalo Area Convention and Visitors Bureau, 107 Delaware
Avenue, Buffalo, New York 14202, USA
Tel.   010 1 716 849 6609

California
California Office of Tourism, 1030 13th Street, Suite 200,
Sacramento, California 95814, USA
Tel.   010 1 916 322 1396

California
Western Association of Convention and Visitors Bureau, 2580
Sierra Boulevard, Suite E, Sacramento, California 95825, USA
Tel.   010 1 916 481 4170

California Cities
(*See* Destination Marketing)

Canton (*Ohio*)
Canton/Stark County Convention and Visitors Bureau, 229 Wells
Avenue NW, Canton, Ohio 44703, USA
Tel.   010 1 216 454 1439

Carbondale (*Illinois*)
Carbondale Convention and Tourism Bureau, 714 East Walnut
Street, Carbondale, Illinois 62901-3103, USA
Tel.   010 1 618 529 4451

Carlsbad (New Mexico)
Carlsbad Convention and Visitors Bureau, P.O. Box 910,
Carlsbad, New Mexico 88220, USA
Tel.   010 1 505 887 6516

Cedar Rapids (Iowa)
Cedar Rapids Area Convention and Visitors Bureau, P.O. Box
4860, Cedar Rapids, Iowa 52407, USA
Tel.   010 1 319 364 2591

Champaign (Illinois)
Champaign-Urbana Convention and Visitors Bureau, P.O. Box
1626, Champaign, Illinois 61820, USA
Tel.   010 1 217 351 4133

Charlotte (North Carolina)
Charlotte Convention and Visitors Bureau Inc., One
Independence Center, Suite 1290, Charlotte, North Carolina
28246, USA
Tel.   010 1 704 334 2282

Charleston (South Carolina)
Charleston/Trident Convention and Visitors Bureau, P.O. Box
975, Charleston, South Carolina 29402, USA
Tel.   010 1 803 723 7641

Charleston (West Virginia)
Charleston Convention and Visitors Bureau, 200 Civic Center
Drive, Suite 002, Charleston, West Virginia 25301, USA
Tel.   010 1 304 344 5075

Chattanooga (Tennessee)
Chattanooga Area Convention and Visitors Bureau, 1001 Market
Street, Tennessee 37402, USA
Tel.   010 1 615 756 2121

Chicago (Illinois)
(*See* Motivators)

Chicago (Illinois)
Chicago Convention and Tourism Bureau Inc., McCormick Place
on the Lake, Chicago, Illinois 60616, USA
Tel.   010 1 312 225 5000

Cincinnati (Ohio)
Greater Cincinnati Convention and Visitors Bureau, 200 West
Fifth Street, Cincinnati, Ohio 45202, USA
Tel.   010 1 513 621 2142

Cleveland (Ohio)
Convention and Visitors Bureau of Greater Cleveland, 1301 East
Sixth Street, Cleveland, Ohio 44114, USA
Tel.   010 1 216 621 4110

Collinsville (Illinois)
Collinsville Convention and Tourism Bureau, 125 South Center
Street, Collinsville, Illinois 62234, USA
Tel.   010 1 618 344 5252

Colorado
(*See* Motivators)

Colorado Springs (Colorado)
Colorado Springs Convention and Visitors Bureau, 801 South
Tejon, Colorado Springs, Colorado 80903, USA
Tel.   010 1 303 635 7506

Columbia (Missouri)
Columbia Convention and Visitors Bureau, 32 North 8th Street,
P.O. Box N, Columbia, Missouri 65205, USA
Tel.   010 1 314 875 1231

Columbia (South Carolina)
Greater Columbia Convention and Visitors Bureau, 1527 Senate
Street, Columbia, South Carolina 29201, USA
Tel.   010 1 803 254 0479

Columbus (Georgia)
Columbus Convention and Visitors Bureau, 801 Front Avenue,
P.O. Box 2768, Columbus, Georgia 31902, USA
Tel.   010 1 404 322 1613

Columbus (Ohio)
Greater Columbus Convention and Visitors Bureau, 50 West
Broad Street, Suite 1600, Columbus, Ohio 43215, USA
Tel.   010 1 614 221 6623

Concord (California)
Concord Convention and Visitors Bureau, Salvio Pacheo Square,
2151 Salvio Street, Suite N, Concord, California 94520, USA
Tel.   010 1 415 685 1184

Corpus Christi (Texas)
Corpus Christi Area Convention and Visitors Bureau, 1201 North
Shoreline, P.O. Box 2664, Corpus Christi, Texas 78403, USA
Tel.   010 1 512 882 5603

Covington (Kentucky)
Covington/North Kentucky Convention and Visitors Bureau, 605
Philadelphia Street, Covington, Kentucky 41011, USA
Tel.   010 1 606 261 4677

Danville (Illinois)
Danville Area Convention and Visitors Bureau, P.O. Box 992,
Danville, Illinois 61832, USA
Tel.   010 1 217 442 1887

Dallas (Texas)
Dallas Convention and Visitors Bureau, Dallas Chamber of
Commerce, 1507 Pacific Avenue, Dallas, Texas 75201, USA
Tel.   010 1 214 954 1450

Dayton (Ohio)
Dayton/Montgomery County Convention and Visitors Bureau,
1880 Kettering Tower, Dayton, Ohio 45423-1880, USA
Tel.   010 1 513 226 8248

Daytona (Florida)
Convention and Tourism, Daytona Beach Area Chamber of
Commerce, P.O. Box 2775, Daytona Beach, Florida 32015, USA
Tel.   010 1 904 255 0981

Decatur (Illinois)
Decatur Area Convention and Visitors Bureau, One Central Park
East, Decatur, Illinois 62523 USA
Tel.   010 1 217 423 7000

DeKalb (Georgia)
DeKalb Convention and Visitors Bureau, 750 Commerce Drive,
Suite 201, Decatur, Georgia 30030, USA
Tel.   010 1 404 378 2525

Denton (Texas)
Denton Convention and Visitors Bureau, 414 Parkway, P.O.
Drawer P, Denton, Texas 76202, USA
Tel.   010 1 817 382 7895

Denver (Colorado)
Denver Metro Convention and Visitors Bureau, 225 West Colfax
Avenue, Denver, Colorado 80202, USA
Tel.   010 1 303 892 1112

Des Moines (Iowa)
Des Moines Convention and Visitors Bureau, 800 High Street,
Des Moines, Iowa 50307, USA
Tel.   010 1 515 286 4960

*Destination Marketing (For New York, California and US Virgin
Islands)*
25, Bedford Square, London WC1B 3HG
Tel.   01-637 9761

Detroit (Michigan)
Metropolitan Detroit Convention and Visitors Bureau, 100
Renaissance Center, Suite 1950, Detroit, Michigan 48243, USA
Tel.   010 1 313 259 4333

Dubuque (Iowa)
Dubuque Area Chamber of Commerce, Convention and Visitors
Division, 880 Locust-Fischer Arcade Building, Dubuque, Iowa
52201, USA
Tel.   010 1 319 557 9200

Duluth (Minnesota)
Duluth Convention and Visitors Bureau, 1731 London Road,
Duluth, Minnesota 55812, USA
Tel.   010 1 218 728 4285

Dutchess (New York)
Dutchess County Visitors and Convention Bureau, 80 Washington
Street, P.O. Box 964, Poughkeepsie, New York 12601, USA
Tel.   010 1 914 454 1702

Eau Claire (Wisconsin)
Eau Claire Area Convention and Tourism Bureau, Wagner's
Complex, 2127 Brackett Avenue, Eau Claire, Wisconsin 54701, USA
Tel.   010 1 715 836 7680

Elko (Nevada)
Elko Convention and Visitors Authority, 700 Festival Way, Elko, Nevada 89801, USA
Tel.   010 1 702 738 4091

El Paso (Texas)
Greater El Paso Tourist and Convention Bureau, 5 Civic Centre Plaza, El Paso, Texas 79999, USA
Tel.   010 1 915 534 0600

Eugene (Oregon)
Eugene/Springfield Convention and Visitors Bureau Inc., P.O. Box 10286, Eugene, Oregon 97440, USA
Tel.   010 1 503 484 5307

Eureka (California)
Eureka/Humboldt County Convention and Visitors Bureau, 1034 Second Street, Eureka, California 95501, USA
Tel.   010 1 707 443 5097

Evansville (Indiana)
Evansville Convention Bureau, 715 Locust Street, Evansville, Indiana 47708, USA
Tel.   010 1 812 425 5402

Fairbanks (Alaska)
Fairbanks Convention and Visitors Bureau, 550 First Avenue, Fairbanks, Alaska 99501, USA
Tel.   010 1 907 456 5774

Flint (Michigan)
Flint Convention and Visitors Bureau, 400 North Saginaw Street, Suite 101A, Flint, Michigan 48502, USA
Tel.   010 1 313 232 8900

Florida Division of Tourism
55, Park Lane, Suite 1, Mayfair, London W1Y 3DH
Tel.   01-493 1343

Florida's Lee Island Coast
9 Longbridge Walk, Horley, Surrey, RH6 7GQ
Tel.   0293 786755

Fond du Lac (*Wisconsin*)
Fond du Lac Convention and Visitors Bureau, 207 North Main
Street, Fond du Lac, Wisconsin 54935, USA
Tel. 010 1 414 923 3010

Fort Lauderdale (*Florida*)
Tourism/Convention Department, Fort Lauderdale Area Chamber
of Commerce, P.O. Box 14516, Fort Lauderdale, Florida 33302,
USA
Tel. 010 1 305 462 6000

Fort Lauderdale (*Florida*)
Broward County Tourist Development Council, 201 SE 8th
Avenue, Fort Lauderdale, Florida 33301, USA
Tel. 010 1 305 765 5508

Fort Myers (*Florida*)
Fort Myers Convention and Visitors Bureau, P.O. Box CC,
Fort Myers, Florida 33902, USA
Tel. 010 1 813 334 1133
(*See also* Lee County)

Fort Wayne (*Indiana*)
Fort Wayne Convention and Visitors Bureau, 826 Ewing Street,
Fort Wayne, Indiana 46802, USA
Tel. 010 1 219 424 1435

Fort Worth (*Texas*)
Fort Worth Convention and Visitors' Bureau, 700 Throckmorton
Street, Fort Worth, Texas 76102, USA
Tel. 010 1 817 336 8791

Fresno (*California*)
Fresno Convention Bureau, 700 M Street, Fresno, California
93721, USA
Tel. 010 1 209 233 0836

Galveston (*Texas*)
Galveston Convention and Visitors Bureau, 2106 Seawall
Boulevard, Moody Civic Center, Galveston, Texas 77550, USA
Tel. 010 1 713 763 4311

Gatlinburg (*Tennessee*)
Gatlinburg Tourist and Convention Bureau, 520 Parkway, P.O.
Box 527, Gatlinburg, Tennessee 37738, USA
Tel. 010 1 615 436 4178

Glen Falls (New York)
Glen Falls-Adirondack Regional Convention and Visitors Bureau,
169 Warren Street, Glen Falls, New York 12801, USA
Tel.   010 1 518 798 1761

Grand Island (Nebraska)
Grand Island/Hall County Convention and Visitors Bureau, 309
West 2nd Street, Box 1486, Grand Island, Nebraska 68802, USA
Tel.   010 1 308 382 9210

Grand Rapids (Michigan)
Greater Grand Rapids Convention and Visitors Bureau, 245
Monroe, NW Grand Rapids, Michigan 49503, USA
Tel.   010 1 616 459 8287

Grapevine (Texas)
Grapevine Tourist and Convention Bureau, 909 South Main
Street, Grapevine, Texas 76051, USA
Tel.   010 1 817 481 0454

Great Falls (Montana)
Great Falls Convention and Visitors Bureau, P.O. Box 2127,
Great Falls, Montana 59403, USA
Tel.   010 1 406 761 4434

Green Bay (Wisconsin)
Green Bay Area Visitor and Convention Bureau Inc., 1901 South
Oneida Street, P.O. Box 10596, Green Bay, Wisconsin
54307-0596, USA
Tel.   010 1 414 494 9507

Greensboro (North Carolina)
Greensboro Area Convention and Visitors Bureau, 220 South
Eugene Street, P.O. Box 1588, Greensboro, North Carolina
27402, USA
Tel.   010 1 919 274 2282

Greenville (South Carolina)
Greater Greenville Convention and Visitors Bureau, P.O. Box
10527, Greenville, South Carolina 29603, USA
Tel.   010 1 803 233 0461

Hartford (*Connecticut*)
Greater Hartford Convention and Visitors Bureau Inc., One Civic
Center Plaza, Hartford, Connecticut 06103, USA
Tel.   010 1 203 728 6789

Hawaii
Hawaii Visitors Bureau, 16 Bedford Square, London WC1B 3JH
Tel.   01-580 4392
also at:

Hawaii Visitors Bureau, 2270 Kalakaua Avenue, Suite 801,
Honolulu, Hawaii 96815
Tel.   010 1 808 923 1811

High Point (*North Carolina*)
High Point Convention and Visitors Bureau, 100 West Green
Drive, P.O. Box 2273, High Point, North Carolina 27261, USA
Tel.   010 1 919 884 5255

Hilton Head Island (*South Carolina*)
Hilton Head Island Visitors and Convention Bureau, P.O. Box
5647, Hilton Head Island, South Carolina 29938, USA
Tel.   010 1 803 785 3673

Hot Springs (*Arkansas*)
Convention and Visitors Division, Hot Springs Chamber of
Commerce, P.O. Box 1500, Hot Springs, Arkansas 71901, USA
Tel.   010 1 501 321 1700

Houston (*Texas*)
Greater Houston Convention and Visitors Council, 3300 Main
Street, Houston, Texas 77002, USA
Tel.   010 1 713 523 5050

Huntington (*West Virginia*)
Cabell-Huntington Convention and Visitors Bureau Inc., P.O.
Box 347, Huntington, West Virginia 25708, USA
Tel.   010 1 304 525 7333

Huntsville (*Alabama*)
Huntsville Convention and Visitors Bureau, 700 Monroe Street,
Huntsville, Alabama 36101, USA
Tel.   010 1 205 533 0125

Independence (Missouri)
Independence Visitors and Convention Bureau, 111 East Maple
Street, Independence, Missouri 64050, USA
Tel.   010 1 816 836 7111

Indianapolis (Indiana)
Indianapolis Convention and Visitors Bureau, One Hoosier
Dome, Suite 100, 200 South Capitol Avenue, Indianapolis,
Indiana 46225, USA
Tel.   010 1 317 639 4282

Iowa City (Iowa)
Iowa City/Coralville Convention and Visitors Bureau, 109 East
Burlington Street, P.O. Box 2358, Iowa City, Iowa 52244, USA
Tel.   010 1 319 337 9637

Irving City (Texas)
Irving Convention and Visitors Bureau, 2121 West Airport
Freeway, Suite 555, Irving, Texas 75062, USA
Tel.   010 1 214 252 7476

Jackson (Mississippi)
Jackson Convention and Visitors Bureau, P.O. Box 1450,
Jackson, Mississippi 39205, USA
Tel.   010 1 601 960 1891

Jacksonville (Florida)
Convention and Visitors Bureau of Jacksonville and Its Beaches,
33 South Hogan Street, Jacksonville, Florida 32202, USA
Tel.   010 1 904 353 9736

Jeffersonville (Indiana)
Clark-Floyd Counties Convention and Tourism Bureau, P.O. Box
608, Jeffersonville, Indiana 47131, USA
Tel.   010 1 812 282 6654

Jekyll Island (Georgia)
Jekyll Island Convention and Visitors Bureau, One Beachview
Drive, Jekyll Island, Georgia 31520, USA
Tel.   010 1 912 635 3400

Johnson City (Tennessee)
Johnson City Conventions and Visitors Bureau, 603 East Market
Street, P.O. Box 1674, Johnson City, Tennessee 37601, USA
Tel.   010 1 615 926 2141

Juneau (Alaska)
Juneau Convention and Visitors Bureau, 76 Egan Drive, Suite
140, Juneau, Alaska 99801, USA
Tel.   010 1 907 586 1737

Kankakee County (Illinois)
Kankakee County Convention and Visitors Association, 701
South Harrison, P.O. Box 1967, Kankakee, Illinois 60901, USA
Tel.   010 1 815 935 7390

Kalispell (Montana)
Kalispell Convention and Visitors Bureau, P.O. Box 978,
Kalispell, Montana 59901, USA
Tel.   010 1 406 755 6166

Kansas City (Missouri)
Convention and Visitors Bureau of Greater Kansas City, City
Center Square, Suite 2550, 1100 Main Street, Kansas City,
Missouri 64105, USA
Tel.   010 1 816 221 5242

Kissimmee (Florida)
Kissimmee-St Cloud Convention and Visitors Bureau, P.O. Box
2007, 1925 E Space Coast Parkway, Kissimmee, Florida 32742,
USA
Tel.   010 1 305 847 5000

Knoxville (Tennessee)
Knoxville Convention and Visitors Bureau, P.O. Box 15012, 500
Henley Street, Knoxville, Tennessee 37901, USA
Tel.   010 1 615 523 7263

LaCrosse (Wisconsin)
LaCrosse Area Convention and Visitors Bureau, P.O. Box 1895,
Riverside Park, LaCrosse, Wisconsin 54601, USA
Tel.   010 1 608 782 2366

Lafayette (Indiana)
Greater Lafayette Convention and Visitors Bureau Inc., South
Road 26 East, P.O. Box 5547, Lafayette, Indiana 47903, USA
Tel.   010 1 317 447 5061

Lafayette (Louisiana)
Lafayette Parish Convention and Visitors Commission, P.O.
Drawer 52066, Lafayette, Louisiana 70505 USA
Tel.   010 1 318 232 3737

Lake Charles (Louisiana)
Lake Charles-Calcasien Parish Convention and Tourist
Commission, P.O. Box 1912, 1211 North Lakeshore, Lake
Charles, Louisiana 70602, USA
Tel.   010 1 318 346 9588

Lake Geneva (Wisconsin)
Lake Geneva Convention and Visitors Bureau, 201 Wrigley Drive,
Lake Geneva, Wisconsin 53147, USA
Tel.   010 1 414 248 4416

Lancaster (Pennsylvania)
Pennsylvania Dutch Visitors Bureau, 1799 Hempstead Road,
Lancaster, Pennsylvania 17601, USA
Tel.   010 1 717 299 8901

Lansing (Michigan)
Greater Lansing Convention and Visitors Bureau, Civic Center,
Suite 302, Lansing, Michigan 48933, USA
Tel.   010 1 517 487 6800

Laredo (Texas)
Laredo Convention and Visitors Council, P.O. Box 790, Laredo,
Texas 78042, USA
Tel.   010 1 512 722 9895

Las Cruces (New Mexico)
Las Cruces Visitors and Convention Bureau, 311 North
Downtown Mall, Las Cruces, New Mexico 88001, USA
Tel.   010 1 505 524 8521

Las Vegas (Nevada)
Las Vegas Convention and Visitors Authority, 3150 Paradise
Road, Nevada 89109-2323, USA
Tel.   010 1 702 733 2323

Lee County (*Florida*)
Lee County Tourist Development Council, P.O. Box 2445, Fort
Myers, Florida 33902-2445, USA
Tel.   010 1 813 355 2631
(*See also* Motivators)

Lexington (*Kentucky*)
Greater Lexington Convention and Visitors Bureau, Suite 363,
430 West Vine Street, Lexington, Kentucky 40507, USA
Tel.   010 1 606 233 1221

Lima (*Ohio*)
Lima/Allen County Convention and Visitors Bureau, 53 Town
Square, Lima, Ohio 45801, USA
Tel.   010 1 419 222 6045

Lincoln (*Nebraska*)
Convention and Visitors Bureau, Lincoln Chamber of Commerce,
1221 North Street, Suite 606, Lincoln, Nebraska 68508, USA
Tel.   010 1 402 476 7511

Little Rock (*Arkansas*)
Little Rock Bureau for Conventions and Visitors, P.O. Box 3232,
Little Rock, Arkansas 72203, USA
Tel.   010 1 501 376 4781

Long Beach (*California*)
Long Beach Convention and Tourism Bureau, 180 East Ocean
Boulevard, Suite 150, Long Beach, California 90802, USA
Tel.   010 1 213 436 3645

Long Island (*New York*)
Long Island Tourism and Convention Commission, MacArthur
Airport, Main Terminal, Ronknokoma, New York 11779, USA
Tel.   010 1 516 585 6660

Los Angeles (*California*)
Greater Los Angeles Convention and Visitor Bureau, Arco Plaza,
Level B, 505 South Flower Street, Los Angeles, California 90071,
USA
Tel.   010 1 213 239 0200
also   010 1 213 488 9100

Louisiana
(*See* Motivators)

Louisville (Kentucky)
Louisville Convention and Visitors Bureau, P.O. Box 1258, 501
South Third Street, Louisville, Kentucky 40202, USA
Tel. 010 1 502 584 2121

Lubbock (Texas)
Lubbock Visitors and Convention Bureau, P.O. Box 561,
Lubbock, Texas 79408, USA
Tel. 010 1 806 747 5232

Madison (Wisconsin)
Greater Madison Convention and Visitors Bureau Inc., 425 West
Washington Avenue, Madison, Wisconsin 53703, USA
Tel. 010 1 608 255 0701

Marietta (Ohio)
Marietta Tourist and Convention Bureau, 310 Front Street,
Marietta, Ohio 45750, USA
Tel. 010 1 614 373 5176

Maui (Hawaii)
Maui Convention and Visitors Association, 25 North Puunene
Avenue, P.O. Box 1738, Kahului, Hawaii 96732, USA
Tel. 010 1 808 877 7822

McAllen (Texas)
Convention and Visitors Bureau, P.O. Box 790, McAllen, Texas
78501, USA
Tel. 010 1 512 682 2871

Memphis (Tennessee)
Memphis Convention and Visitors Bureau, 203 Beale Street, Suite
305, Memphis, Tennessee 38103, USA
Tel. 010 1 901 526 1919

Mesa (Arizona)
Mesa Convention and Visitors Bureau, 10 West First Street,
Mesa, Arizona 85201, USA
Tel. 010 1 602 969 1307

Miami (Florida)
The Greater Miami Convention and Visitors Bureau,
4770 Biscayne Boulevard, Miami, Florida 33138, USA
Tel. 010 1 305 573 4300

Miami Beach (Florida)
Miami Beach Visitor and Convention Authority, 555 17th Street,
Miami Beach, Florida 33139, USA
Tel.   010 1 305 673 7080

Milford (Connecticut)
Hill and Harbor Convention and Visitors Bureau, 5 Broad Street,
Milford, Connecticut 06460, USA
Tel.   010 1 203 874 6789

Milwaukee (Wisconsin)
Greater Milwaukee Convention and Visitors Bureau, 756 North
Milwaukee Street, Milwaukee, Wisconsin 53202, USA
Tel.   010 1 414 273 3950

Minneapolis (Minnesota)
Minneapolis Convention and Tourism Commission, 15 South
Fifth Street, Minneapolis, Minnesota 55402, USA
Tel.   010 1 612 348 4313

Minnesota
Minnesota Office of Tourism, 240 Bremer Building, 419 North
Robert Street, St Paul, Minnesota 55101, USA
Tel.   010 1 612 297 2901

Mississippi
Mississippi Gulf Coast Convention Bureau, P.O. Box 4554, 3800
West Beach Boulevard, Biloxi, Mississippi 39531, USA
Tel.   010 1 601 388 8000

Missoula (Montana)
Missoula Convention and Visitors Bureau, P.O. Box 7577,
Missoula, Montana 59807, USA
Tel.   010 1 406 543 6623

Mobile (Alabama)
Convention and Visitors Bureau, Mobile Area Chamber of
Commerce, 451 Government Street, Mobile, Alabama 36602,
USA
Tel.   010 1 205 433 6951

Monroe (Louisiana)
Monroe/West Monroe Convention and Visitors Bureau,
141 DeSiard, Suite 114, Monroe, Louisiana 71201, USA
Tel.   010 1 318 387 5691

Monterey (California)
Monterey Peninsular Visitors and Convention Bureau, 380
Alvarado Street, P.O. Box 1770, Monterey, California 93940,
USA
Tel.   010 1 408 649 1771

Montgomery (Alabama)
Convention and Visitors Division, Montgomery Area Chamber of
Commerce, 41 Commerce Street, Montgomery, Alabama 36101,
USA
Tel.   010 1 205 834 5200

Motivators
2 Middleburg, B-1170 Brussels, Belgium
Tel.   010 32 2 660 47 47
(European Agents for Chicago, Colorado, Lee County (Florida),
Louisiana, Oklahoma, Utah, Wyoming)

Mount Vernon (Illinois)
Mount Vernon Convention and Visitors Bureau, 215 Potomac
Boulevard, P.O. Box 2580, Mount Vernon, Illinois 62864, USA
Tel.   010 1 618 242 3151

Myrtle Beach (South Carolina)
Myrtle Beach Area Convention Bureau, P.O. Box 2115, Myrtle
Beach, South Carolina 29577, USA
Tel.   010 1 803 448 1629

Nashville (Tennessee)
Convention and Visitors Division, Nashville Area Chamber of
Commerce, 161 Fourth Avenue North, Nashville, Tennessee
37219, USA
Tel.   010 1 615 259 3900

Natchez (Mississippi)
Natchez Convention and Visitors Commission, P.O. Box 794,
Natchez, Mississippi 39120-0794, USA
Tel.   010 1 601 446 6345

New Orleans (Louisiana)
Greater New Orleans Tourist and Convention Commission, 1520
Sugar Bowl Drive, New Orleans, Louisiana 70112, USA
Tel.   010 1 504 566 5011

New York City
New York Convention and Visitors Bureau, 2 Columbus Circle, New York, NY 10019, USA
Tel. 010 1 212 397 8200

New York City
See also Destination Marketing

Niagara Falls (New York)
Niagara Falls Convention and Visitors Bureau, Carborundum Center, Suite 101, 345 Third Street, Niagara Falls, New York 14303, USA
Tel. 010 1 716 278 8010

Niles (Ohio)
Trumbull County Convention and Visitors Bureau Inc., 650 Youngstown Warren Road, Niles, Ohio 44446, USA
Tel. 010 1 216 544 3468

Norfolk (Virginia)
Norfolk Convention and Visitors Bureau, Monticello Arcade, 208 East Plume Street, Norfolk, Virginia 23510, USA
Tel. 010 1 804 441 5266

Norristown (Pennsylvania)
Valley Forge County Convention and Visitors Bureau, P.O. Box 311, Norristown, Pennsylvania 19404, USA
Tel. 010 1 215 278 3558

North Dakota
North Dakota Tourism Promotion Division, 1050 E Interstate Avenue, Bismarck, North Dakota 58505, USA
Tel. 010 1 701 224 2525

Northern Kentucky (Kentucky)
Northern Kentucky Convention and Visitors Bureau, 605 Philadelphia Street, Covington, Kentucky 41011, USA
Tel. 010 1 606 261 4677

Oakland (California)
Oakland Convention and Visitors Bureau, Trans Pacific Center, 1000 Broadway, Suite 200, Oakland, California 94607, USA
Tel. 010 1 415 839 9000

Ocean City (Maryland)
Ocean City Convention and Visitors Bureau Inc., 4001 Coastal
Highway, Ocean City, Maryland 21842 USA
Tel.   010 1 301 289 8181

Odessa (Texas)
Odessa Convention and Visitors Bureau, 400 West 4th Street,
P.O. Box 3626, Odessa, Texas 79760, USA
Tel.   010 1 915 332 8189

Oklahoma
Oklahoma Tourism and Recreation Department, Marketing
Services Division, State of Oklahoma, 505 Will Rogers Building,
Oklahoma City, Okla 73105, USA
Tel.   010 1 405 521 2406

Oklahoma
(*See* Motivators)

Oklahoma City
Convention and Tourism Bureau, Oklahoma City Chamber of
Commerce, 4 Santa Fe Plaza, Oklahoma City, Oklahoma 73102,
USA
Tel.   010 1 405 278 8912

Omaha (Nebraska)
Omaha Convention and Visitors Bureau, Omaha/Douglas Civic
Center, 1819 Farnam Street, Suite 1200, Omaha, Nebraska 68183,
USA
Tel.   010 1 402 444 4660

Oneida County (New York)
Oneida County Convention and Visitors Bureau, P.O. Box AA,
Oriskany, New York 13424, USA
Tel.   010 1 315 736 2999

Orlando (Florida)
Orlando/Orange County Convention and Visitors Bureau, 7600
Dr Phillips Boulevard, Suite 6, Orlando, Florida 32819-8199,
USA
Tel.   010 1 305 345 8882

Overland Park (Kansas)
Overland Park Convention and Visitors Bureau, 9300 Metcalfe,
Suite 240, Overland Park, Kansas 66212, USA
Tel.   010 1 913 649 3309

Oxnard (California)
Oxnard Convention and Visitors Bureau, 325 Esplanada Drive,
Oxnard, California 93030, USA
Tel.   010 1 805 485 8833

Palm Beach (Florida)
Palm Beach County Tourist Development Council, 35 Piccadilly,
London W1V 9PB
Tel.   01-734 7282
Also at:

1555 Palm Beach Lakes Boulevard, Suite 204, West Palm Beach,
Florida 33401, USA
Tel.   010 1 305 471 3995

Palm Springs (California)
Palm Springs Convention and Visitors Bureau, Airport Park
Plaza, 225 El Cielo Road, Suite 315, Palm Springs, California
92262, USA
Tel.   010 1 619 327 8411

Pasadena (California)
Pasadena Convention and Visitors Bureau, 171 South Los Robles,
Pasadena, California 91101, USA
Tel.   010 1 213 795 9311

Pennsylvania
Bureau of Travel Development, Commonwealth of Pennsylvania
Department of Commerce, 416 Forum Building, Harrisburg, PA
17120, USA
Tel.   010 1 717 787 5453

Pennsylvania (Pennsylvania)
Pennsylvania Dutch Visitors Bureau, 1799 Hempstead Road,
Lancaster, Pennsylvania 17601, USA
Tel.   010 1 717 299 8901

Peoria (Illinois)
Peoria Convention and Visitors Bureau, 331 Fulton, Suite 625,
Peoria, Illinois 61602, USA
Tel.   010 1 309 676 0303

Philadelphia
Philadelphia Convention and Visitors Bureau, 3 Penn Center
Plaza, Philadelphia, Pennsylvania 19102, USA
Tel.   010 1 215 636 3300

Phoenix (Arizona)
Phoenix/Valley of the Sun Convention and Visitors Bureau, 505
North Second Street, Suite 300, Phoenix, Arizona 85004, USA
Tel.   010 1 602 254 6500

Pittsburgh (Pennsylvania)
Pittsburgh Convention and Visitors Bureau Inc., Four Gateway
Center, Pittsburgh, Pennsylvania 15222, USA
Tel.   010 1 412 281 7711

Portland (Maine)
Convention and Visitors Bureau of Greater Portland, 142 Free
Street, Portland, Maine 04101, USA
Tel.   010 1 207 772 4994

Portland (Oregon)
Greater Portland Convention and Visitors Association Inc.,
26 SW Salmon, Portland, Oregon 97204-3299, USA
Tel.   010 1 503 222 2223

Providence (Rhode Island)
Greater Providence Convention and Visitors Bureau, Commerce
Center, 30 Exchange Terrace, Providence, Rhode Island 02903,
USA
Tel.   010 1 401 274 1636

Quincy (Illinois)
Quincy Convention and Visitors Bureau Inc., 314 Maine Street,
Quincy, Illinois 62301, USA
Tel.   010 1 217 223 1000

Racine (Wisconsin)
Greater Racine Area Convention and Visitors Bureau, 300 Fifth
Street, Racine, Wisconsin 53403, USA
Tel.   010 1 414 634 3293

Raleigh (*North Carolina*)
Convention and Visitors Bureau, Raleigh Chamber of Commerce,
P.O. Box 2978, 335 South Salisbury Street, Raleigh, North
Carolina 27602, USA
Tel.   010 1 919 833 3005

Rapid City (*South Dakota*)
Convention and Visitors Bureau, Rapid City Chamber of
Commerce, Box 747, Rapid City, South Dakota 57709, USA
Tel.   010 1 605 343 1744

Rapides Parish (*Louisiana*)
Rapides Parish Convention and Visitors Bureau, P.O. Box 8110,
Alexandria, Louisiana 71306, USA
Tel.   010 1 318 443 7049

Reno (*Nevada*)
Reno/Sparks Convention Authority, P.O. Box 837, Reno,
Nevada 89504, USA
Tel.   010 1 702 827 7600

Richmond (*Virginia*)
Metropolitan Richmond Convention and Visitors Bureau, 300
East Main Street, Suite 100, Richmond, Virginia 23219, USA
Tel.   010 1 804 782 2777

Riverside (*California*)
Riverside Visitors and Convention Bureau, 3443 Orange Street,
Riverside, California 92501, USA
Tel.   010 1 714 787 7950

Roanoke (*Virginia*)
Roanoke Valley Convention and Visitors Bureau, 14 West Kirk
Avenue, Roanoke, Virginia 24011, USA
Tel.   010 1 703 342 6025

Rochester (*Minnesota*)
Rochester Convention and Visitors Bureau, 212 First Avenue,
S. W. Rochester, Minnesota 55902, USA
Tel.   010 1 507 288 1122

Rochester (*New York*)
Rochester/Monroe County Convention and Visitors Bureau Inc.,
120 East Main Street, Rochester, New York 14604, USA
Tel.   010 1 716 546 3070

Rockford (*Illinois*)
Rockford Area Convention and Visitors Bureau, 515 North Court Street, Rockford, Illinois 61103, USA
Tel.   010 1 815 987 8105

Rock Island (*Illinois*)
Illinois Quad-Cities Travel and Visitors Bureau, 329 18th Street, Rock Island, Illinois 61201, USA
Tel.   010 1 309 788 7800

Rosemont (*Illinois*)
Rosemont O'Hare Convention Bureau, 9291 West Bryn Mawr, Rosemont, Illinois 61103, USA
Tel.   010 1 312 823 2100

Roswell (*New Mexico*)
Roswell Convention and Visitors Bureau, P.O. Drawer 70, 131 West 2nd Street, Roswell, New Mexico 88201, USA
Tel.   010 1 505 624 6870

Sacramento (*California*)
Sacramento Visitors and Convention Bureau, 1311 'I' Street, Sacramento, California 95814, USA
Tel.   010 1 916 442 5542

Saginaw (*Michigan*)
Saginaw County Convention and Visitors Bureau, 901 South Washington Avenue, Saginaw, Michigan 48601, USA
Tel.   010 1 517 752 7164

Salinas (*California*)
Visitors and Convention Bureau, Salinas Chamber of Commerce, P.O. Box 1170, 119 East Alisal, Salinas, California 93902, USA
Tel.   010 1 408 424 7611

Salt Lake City (*Utah*)
Salt Lake Valley Convention and Visitors Bureau, 180 Southwest Temple, Salt Lake City, Utah 84101, USA
Tel.   010 1 801 521 2822

San Angelo City (*Texas*)
San Angelo Tourist and Convention Bureau, 500 Rio Concho Drive, San Angelo, Texas 76902, USA
Tel.   010 1 915 653 1206

San Antonio (*Texas*)
San Antonio Convention and Visitors Bureau, P.O. Box 2277,
San Antonio, Texas 78298, USA
Tel.   010 1 512 270 8700

San Diego (*California*)
San Diego Convention and Visitors Bureau, 1200 Third Avenue,
Suite 824, San Diego, California 92101, USA
Tel.   010 1 619 232 3101

San Francisco (*California*)
San Francisco Convention and Visitor Bureau, Convention Plaza,
201 Third Street, Suite 900, San Francisco, California 94103,
USA
Tel.   010 1 415 974 6900

San Jose (*California*)
San Jose Convention Bureau, One Paseo de San Antonio,
P.O. Box 6178, San Jose, California 95113, USA
Tel.   010 1 408 295 9600

San Juan (*Puerto Rico*)
San Juan-Puerto Rico Convention Bureau, 1120 Ashford Avenue,
San Juan, Puerto Rico 00907
Tel.   809 725 2110 (No direct dialling from the UK)

San Mateo (*California*)
San Mateo County Convention and Visitors Bureau, 601 Gateway
Boulevard, Suite 970, South San Francisco, California 94080,
USA
Tel.   010 1 415 952 7600

Santa Barbara (*California*)
Santa Barbara Conference and Visitors Bureau, 1301 Santa
Barbara Street, P.O. Box 299, Santa Barbara, California 93102,
USA
Tel.   010 1 805 965 3023

Santa Clara (*California*)
Santa Clara Convention and Visitors Bureau, 1515 El Camino
Real, P.O. Box 387, Santa Clara, California 95052, USA
Tel.   010 1 408 296 6863

Santa Cruz (California)
Santa Cruz County Convention and Visitors Bureau, P.O. Box 1476, Santa Cruz, California 95061, USA
Tel. 010 1 408 423 6927

Santa Fe (New Mexico)
Santa Fe Convention and Visitors Bureau, P.O. Box 909, Santa Fe, New Mexico 87504-0909, USA
Tel. 010 1 505 984 6760

Santa Monica (California)
Santa Monica Convention and Visitors Bureau, P.O. Box 5278, Santa Monica, California 90405, USA
Tel. 010 1 213 392 9631

Saratoga (New York)
Saratoga Convention and Visitors Bureau, 522 Broadway, Room 106, Saratoga Springs, New York 12866, USA
Tel. 010 1 518 584 1531

Savannah (Georgia)
Savannah Area Convention and Visitors Bureau, 301 West Broad Street, Savannah, Georgia 31499, USA
Tel. 010 1 912 233 6651

Scottsdale (Arizona)
Convention and Visitors Department, Scottsdale Chamber of Commerce, P.O. Box 129, Scottsdale, Arizona 85252, USA
Tel. 010 1 602 945 8481

Seattle (Washington State)
Seattle-King County Convention and Visitors Bureau, 1815 Seventh Avenue, Seattle, Washington 98101, USA
Tel. 010 1 206 447 4200

Scottsdale (Arizona)
Scottsdale Chamber of Commerce, Convention/Tourism Department, 7333 Scottsdale Mall, P.O. Box 130, Scottsdale, Arizona 85252, USA
Tel. 010 1 602 945 8481

Sheboygan (Wisconsin)
Sheboygan Area Convention and Visitors Bureau, 631 New York Avenue, P.O. Box 687, Sheboygan, Wisconsin 53082, USA
Tel. 010 1 414 457 9495

Shreveport (*Louisiana*)
Shreveport-Bossier Convention and Tourist Bureau, 629 Spring
Street, Shreveport, Louisiana 71101, USA
Tel.   010 1 318 222 9391

Sioux Falls (*South Dakota*)
Sioux Falls Convention and Visitors Bureau, P.O. Box 1425,
Sioux Falls, South Dakota 57101, USA
Tel.   010 1 605 336 1620

Slidell (*Louisiana*)
St Tammany Parish Tourist and Convention Commission,
P.O. Box 432, Slidell, Louisiana 70459, USA
Tel.   010 1 504 649 0730

Sonoma (*California*)
Sonoma County Convention and Visitors Bureau, 637 First
Street, Santa Rosa, California 95404, USA
Tel.   010 1 707 545 1420

South Bend (*Indiana*)
South Bend/Mishawaka Area Chamber of Commerce,
Convention and Tourism Division, P.O. Box 1677, South Bend,
Indiana 46634, USA
Tel.   010 1 219 234 0079

Southwest Louisiana (*Louisiana*)
Southwest Louisiana Convention and Visitors Bureau, 1211 North
Lakeshore Drive, P.O. Box 1912, Lake Charles, Louisiana 70602,
USA
Tel.   010 1 318 346 9588

Spokane (*Washington State*)
Spokane Regional Convention and Visitors Bureau, West 301
Main, Spokane, Washington 99201, USA
Tel.   010 1 509 624 1341

Springfield (*Illinois*)
Springfield Convention and Visitors Bureau, 624 East Adams
Street, Springfield, Illinois 62701, USA
Tel.   010 1 217 789 2360

Springfield (*Missouri*)
Springfield Convention and Visitors Bureau, P.O. Box 1687,
Springfield, Missouri 65805, USA
Tel.   010 1 417 862 5501

St Louis (*Missouri*)
St Louis Convention and Visitors Commission, 10, South
Broadway, Suite 300, St Louis, Missouri 63102, USA
Tel.   010 1 314 421 1023

Stockton (*California*)
Stockton Convention and Visitors Bureau, 46 West Fremont
Street, Stockton, California 95202, USA
Tel.   010 1 209 943 1987

St Paul (*Minnesota*)
St Paul Convention, Exhibition and Tourism Commission,
Landmark Center, B-100, St Paul, Minnesota 55102, USA
Tel.   010 1 612 292 4360

St Tammany (*Louisiana*)
St Tammany Tourist and Convention Commission, P.O. Box 432,
Slidell, Louisiana 70459, USA
Tel.   010 1 504 649 0730

Syracuse (*New York*)
Syracuse Convention and Visitors Bureau,100 East Onondaga
Street, Syracuse, New York 13202, USA
Tel.   010 1 315 470 1343

Tahoe (*California*)
Tahoe North Visitors and Convention Bureau, P.O. Box 5578,
Tahoe City, California 95730, USA
Tel.   010 1 916 583 3494

Tallahassee (*Florida*)
Tallahassee Convention and Visitors Bureau, P.O. Box 1639,
Tallahassee, Florida 32301, USA
Tel.   010 1 904 224 8116

Tampa (*Florida*)
Greater Tampa Convention and Visitors Bureau, P.O. Box 420,
801 East Kennedy Boulevard, Tampa, Florida 33601, USA
Tel.   010 1 813 228 7777

Terre Haute (*Indiana*)
Terre Haute Convention and Visitors Bureau of Vigo County,
Honey Creek Square Complex, P.O. Box 500, Terre Haute,
Indiana 47808, USA
Tel.   010 1 812 234 5555

Texas
Texas Tourist Development Agency, Employees Retirement
System Building, 18th and Brazos, Suite 513, Box 12008, Capitol
Station, Austin, Texas 78711, USA
Tel.   010 1 512 463 7400

Toledo (*Ohio*)
Greater Toledo Office of Tourism and Conventions Inc.,
218 Huron Street, Toledo, Ohio 43604, USA
Tel.   010 1 419 243 8191

Topeka (*Kansas*)
Topeka Convention and Visitors Bureau, 722 South Kansas
Avenue, Topeka, Kansas 66603, USA
Tel.   010 1 913 234 2644

Traverse City (*Michigan*)
Grand Traverse Area Convention and Visitors Bureau, 900 East
Front Street, Suite 100, Traverse City, Michigan 49684, USA
Tel.   010 1 616 947 1120

Trumbull County (*Ohio*)
Trumbull County Convention and Visitors Bureau Inc., 650
Youngstown Warren Road, Niles, Ohio 44446, USA
Tel.   010 1 216 544 3468

Tucson (*Arizona*)
Metro-Tucson Convention and Visitors Bureau, 450 West Paseo
Redondo, Suite 110, Tucson, Arizona 85705, USA
Tel.   010 1 602 624 1817

Tulsa (*Oklahoma*)
Tulsa Convention and Visitors Bureau, 616 South Boston
Avenue, Tulsa, Oklahoma 74119, USA
Tel.   010 1 918 585 1201

US Virgin Islands
See Destination Marketing.

Utah
(*See* Motivators)

Vail (*Colorado*)
Vail Resort Association, 241 East Meadow Drive, Vail, Colorado 81657, USA
Tel. 010 1 303 476 1000

Valdez (*Alaska*)
Valdez Convention and Visitors Bureau, P.O. Box 1603, Valdez, Alaska 99686, USA
Tel. 010 1 907 835 2984

Valley Forge (*Pennsylvania*)
Valley Forge County Convention and Visitors Bureau, P.O. Box 311, Norristown, Pennsylvania 19404, USA
Tel. 010 1 215 278 3558

Ventura (*California*)
Ventura Visitor and Convention Bureau, 785 South Seaward Avenue, Ventura, California 93001, USA
Tel. 010 1 805 648 2075

Victoria (*Texas*)
Victoria Convention and Visitors Bureau, 1106 East Rio Grande, P.O. Box 2465, Victoria, Texas 77902, USA
Tel. 010 1 512 573 5277

Virginia Beach (*Virginia*)
Virginia Beach Convention Bureau, P.O. Box 136, Virginia Beach, Virginia 23458, USA
Tel. 010 1 804 428 8000

Waco (*Texas*)
Waco Convention and Visitors Bureau, P.O. Box 123, Waco, Texas 76703, USA
Tel. 010 1 817 753 3621

Washington (*District of Columbia*)
Washington Convention and Visitors Bureau Inc., 1575 Eye Street, NW Washington, DC 20005, USA
Tel. 010 1 202 789 7000

Waterloo (Iowa)
Waterloo Convention and Visitors Bureau, 221 West Fifth Street,
P.O. Box 1587, Waterloo, Iowa 50704, USA
Tel.   010 1 319 233 8431

Wheeling (West Virginia)
Wheeling-Ohio County Convention and Visitors Bureau Inc., 607
Central Union Building, Wheeling, West Virginia 26003, USA
Tel.   010 1 304 233 7709

Wichita (Kansas)
Wichita Convention and Visitors Bureau, 111 West Douglas,
Suite 804, Wichita, Kansas 67202, USA
Tel.   010 1 316 265 2800

Williamsburg (Virginia)
Williamsburg Area Tourism and Conference Bureau,
P.O. Drawer GB, Williamsburg, Virginia 23187, USA
Tel.   010 1 804 253 0192

Wilmington (Delaware)
Greater Wilmington Convention and Visitors Bureau, 1300
Market Street, Suite 504, Wilmington, Delaware 19801, USA
Tel.   010 1 302 652 4088

Winston (North Carolina)
Winston-Salem Convention and Visitors Bureau, Greater
Winston-Salem Chamber of Commerce, 500 North Fifth Street,
P.O. Box 1408, Winston-Salem, North Carolina 27102-1408, USA
Tel.   010 1 919 725 2361

Worcester (Massachusetts)
Worcester County Convention and Visitors Bureau, 350
Mechanics Tower, Worcester, Massachusetts 01608, USA
Tel.   010 1 617 753 2920

Wyoming
Wyoming Travel Commission, I-25 at College Drive, Cheyenne,
WY 82002, USA
Tel.   010 1 307 777 7777

Wyoming
(*See* Motivators)

Yuma (Arizona)
Yuma Convention Bureau, P.O. Box 6468, Yuma, Arizona
85364, USA
Tel.   010 1 602 344 3800

Yugoslavia

Yugoslav Convention Bureau
Kaptol 5, 4100 Zagreb, Yugoslavia
Tel.   010 38 41 430 630

Major international hotel groups/agents

Abela Hotels
4–6 Savile Row, London W1X 1AF
Tel.   01-734 6700
(Properties in France, Jamaica, Spain and Sudan)

Anchor Hotels Ltd
Kew Bridge House, Kew Bridge Road, Brentford, Middx
TW8 0EJ
Tel.   01-847 3661
(Properties across the UK)

Astir Hotel Company Inc.
204/208 Tottenham Court Road, London W1P 9LA
Tel.   01-636 0817
(Properties across Greece)

Atahotels
199 Piccadilly, London W1
Tel.   01-439 0701
(Properties across Italy)

Best Western Hotels
Interchange House, 26, Kew Road, Richmond, Surrey TW9 2NA
Tel.   01-940 7566
(Properties across the UK)

Caledonian Hotel Management
Caledonian House, Crawley, West Sussex RH20 2XA
Tel.   0293 548571

Canadian Pacific (CP Hotels)
62/65 Trafalgar Square, London WC2N 5DT
01-839 1850
(Properties across the World)

Carotel
Brugata 1, N-0186 Oslo, Norway
Tel. 010 47 2 41 91 40
(Properties throughout Norway)

Celebrated Country Hotels
Oakley Court, Windsor Road, Near Windsor, Berks SL4 5UR
Tel. 0682 37230
(Properties in Southern England)

Chaine Lucien Barriere
Hotel Majestic, 14 La Croisette, 06400 Cannes, France
Tel. 010 33 93 68 91 00
(Properties across France)

Ciga Hotels
67 Jermyn Street, London SW1
Tel. 01-930 4147
Head Office:
Largo Donegni 2, 2121 Milan, Italy
Tel. 010 39 2 6266 432
(Properties in Italy, Paris and Miami)

Comfort Hotels International
Comfort House, 167 Queensway, London W2 4XG
Tel. 01-221 2626
(Properties across the UK)

Concorde Hotels
58 Boulevard Gouvion St Cyr – 75017 Paris
Tel. 010 33 1 758 12 84
(Properties in Egypt, France, Spain, Switzerland, United Arab Emirates and the UK)

Consort Hotels Ltd
Ryedale Buildings, Piccadilly, York YO1 1PN
Tel. 0904 643151
(Properties across the UK)

CP Hotels
(*see* Canadian Pacific)

Crest Hotels International
Spectrum House, 20/26 Cursitor Street, London EC4A 1LT
Tel.   01-430 0991
(Properties across Europe)

Crown Hotels (Management) Ltd
4th Floor, 35 Piccadilly, London W1
Tel.   01-439 6540

De Vere Hotels
P.O. Box 27, Loushers Lane, Warrington, Cheshire WA4 6RQ
Tel.   0925 35471
(Properties across the UK)

Distinctive Inns
The Bear Hotel, Park Street, Woodstock, Oxon
Tel.   0993 811511
(Properties across the UK)

Dunfey Hotels
c/o The London Tara Hotel, Scarsdale Place, Kensington,
London W8
Tel.   01-937 7211
(Properties in France, UK and USA)

Tom Eden Associates
13/14 Golden Square, London W1R 3A
Tel.   01-734 6446
(Represents properties in Bahamas, Barbados, Bora Bora, Crete,
Cook Islands, France, Hawaii, Italy, Madeira, Rarotonga, Spain,
Tahiti, USA)

Edwardian Hotels
Granville Place, London W1H 0EH
Tel.   01-408 0130
(Properties in Central London)

Embassy Hotels
34 Queen's Gate, London SW7 5JA
Tel.   01-584 8222
(Properties across the UK)

Four Seasons Hotels
Inn on the Park, Hamilton Place, Park Lane, London W1A 1AZ
Tel.   01-499 0888

Gleneagles Hotels
30 Rutland Square, Edinburgh EH1 2AB
Tel. 031-228 2881
(Properties in Perthshire, Edinburgh and Central London)

Grand Metropolitan Hotels
Grand Metropolitan House, Stratford Place, London W1A 4YU
Tel. 01-629 6611

HRI — the Leading Hotels of the World
15 New Bridge Street, London EC4
Tel. 01-583 1712
(Properties across the World)

Heritage Hotels
Enbrook House, Sandgate Hill, Folkestone, Kent CT20 3SG
Tel. 0303 39341
(Properties across the UK)

Hilton International Hotels
179–199 Holland Park Avenue, London W11 4UL
Tel. 01-603 5232
(Properties across the World)

Holiday Inn International Hotels
CPA House, 350A King Street, Hammersmith, London W6
Tel. 01-741 4311
(Properties across the World)

Hotel Promotion Services
228 The Linen Hall, 162/168 Regent Street, London W1R 5TB
Tel. 01-434 4431
(Represents hotels throughout Europe and Israel)

Hotel Reservation Service
Heumarkt 14, D-5000 Cologne, West Germany
Tel. 010 49 221 23 45 55
(Reservation service for hotels across the World)

Hotels of Distinction
288 Regent Street, London W1R 5HE
Tel. 01-580 8313
(Properties in the Caribbean, Portugal and Spain)

Hyatt Hotels
Hyatt Carlton Tower, 2 Cadogan Place, London SW1Z 9PY
Tel.   01-235 5411
(Properties across the World)

Inter-Continental and Forum Hotels
Dorland House, 14/16 Regent Street, London SW1Y 4PH
Tel.   01-930 5981
(Properties across the World)

Ladbroke Hotels
Millbuck House, Clarendon Road, Watford, Herts WD1 1DN
Tel.   0923 50222
(Properties across the UK)

Loews Representation International
89/91 Clarence Street, Kingston upon Thames, Surrey KT1 1QY
Tel.   01-541 1199
(Properties across the World)

Mandarin Oriental Group
99/101 Regent Street, London W1R 7HB
Tel.   01-734 6671
Head Office:
16th Floor, Swire House, Connaught Road, Central, Hong Kong
Tel.   010 852 5 842 8428
(Properties throughout the Far East and in Vancouver)

Marriott Hotels and Resorts
London International Sales Office, 80 Regent Street, London
W1R 6AQ
Tel.   01-434 2299
(Properties across the World)

Mercure Hotels
(*see* Novotel)

Metropole Hotels
London Metropole Hotel, Edgware Road, London W2 1JU
Tel.   01-402 4141
(Properties in Birmingham, Blackpool, Brighton and London)

MHS Marketing
110 Langdraget, DK-3250 Gilleleje, Denmark
Tel.   010 45 2 30 27 27
(Represents a group of conference hotels in Denmark)

Morris Kevan International Ltd
Chase Green House, 42 Chase Side, Enfield, Middlesex EN2 6NF
Tel.   01-367 5175
(Represents hotels across the World)

Movenpick Hotels International
Zurichstrasse 106, CH-8134, Adliswil-Zurich, Switzerland
Tel.   010 41 1 10 17 17
(Properties in Switzerland, Germany, Egypt and Saudi Arabia)

Norfolk Capital Hotels
c/o Royal Court Hotel, Sloane Square, London SW1W 8EG
Tel.   01-730 9191
(Properties across the UK)

Novotel Hotels
Sofitel Hotels
Mercure Hotels
1 Shortlands, Hammersmith, London W6 8DR
Tel.   01-741 1555
(Properties across the World)

PLM-ETAP Hotels
8 Rue d'Athenes, 75440 Paris, France
Tel.   010 33 1 268 2770

Pan Pacific Hotels
67/68 New Bond Street, London W1Y 1DF
Tel.   01-491 3812
(Properties throughout the Pacific)

The Peninsula Group
7 Apple Tree Yard, London SW1 6LD
Tel.   01-839 4593
(Properties in the Far East and China)

Penta Hotels
Room 9023, Heathrow Penta Hotel, Bath Road, Hounslow,
Middlesex TW6 2AQ
Tel.   01-897 0551
(Properties in France, Israel, Spain, Portugal, UK, USA, West
Germany)

Prestige Hotels
13/14 Golden Square, London W1
Tel.   01-734 4267
(Properties across the UK)

Ramada Hotel Group
50 Curzon Street, London W1
Tel.   01-493 0621
(Properties throughout the World)

Queens Moat Houses (Hotels) Ltd
St Edwards Way, Romford, Essex RM1 4DD
Tel.   0708 25814

Rank Hotels
4 Harrington Gardens, Kensington, London SW7 4LH
Tel.   01-373 8191
(Properties in London and the USA)

Seymour Hotels of Jersey
3 Taymount Grange, Taymount Rise, Forest Hill, London
SE23 3UH
Tel.   01-699 3979

Sheraton Hotels
Kiln House, 210 New Kings Road, London SW6 4NZ
Tel.   01-731 2387
(Properties across the World)

Shire Inns Ltd
P.O. Box 78, The Oaks Hotel, Colne Road, Reedley, Burnley
BB10 2NG
Tel.   0282 414141

Societe des Hotels Meridien
69 Boston Manor Road, Brentford, Middlesex
Tel.   01-847 2631
(Properties across the World)

Society Hotels (SBM Monte Carlo)
1 Sherwood Street, London W1V 7RA
Tel. 01-439 9751
(Properties in Monaco)

Sofitel
(*See* Novotel)

Stakis Hotels
244 Buchanan Street, Glasgow G1 2NB
Tel. 041 332 4343 01-222 4081
(Properties across the UK)

Steigenberger Reservation Service — SRS
123/125 Gloucester Place, London W1
Tel. 01-486 5754
(Represent hotels across the World)

Swallow Hotels
Swallow House, P.O. Box 8, Seaburn Terrace, Sunderland
SR6 8BB
Tel. 0783 194666

Thistle Hotels
5 Victoria Road, London W8 5RA
Tel. 01-937 6323
(Properties across the UK)

Trusthouse Forte Hotels
20 Queensmere, Slough, Berks SL1 1YY
Tel. 0753 73266
(Properties across the World)

Virani Group of Hotels
82–83 Ecclestone Square, London SW1V 1PS
Tel. 01-834 5787

Westin Hotels
7/8 Conduit Street, London W1R 9TG
Tel. 01-408 0636
(Properties throughout the World except Europe)

Windotel Ltd
Suite 19, College House, 29/31 Wrights Lane, Kensington,
London W8 5JH
Tel.   01-602 7181
(Properties in the Caribbean)

Travel companies

The following companies specialize in travel services for conferences.

The Air Charter Centre
Gatwick Airport, Gatwick RH6 0PG
Tel. 0293 549555
(Air charter brokers)

American Express Travel Service
Portland House, Stag Place, Victoria Street, London SW1
Tel. 01-834 5555

Business Travel Team Ltd
Suite D, The Priory, Syresham Gardens, Haywards Heath, West
Sussex RH16 3LB
Tel. 0444 417521

Compass Travel
46 Albemarle Street, London W1X 4EP
Tel. 01-408 4343
(Conference and incentive travel division of Thomas Cook)

Conference Connection (British Rail)
Ryedale Building, P.O. Box 12, York YO1 1YX
Tel. 0904 643101
(Arranges rail travel for conferences)

Design Travel (Birmingham) Ltd
205, Hagley Road, Edgbaston, Birmingham B16 9RE
Tel. 021-455 7011

Fishley Sebley Associates (Travel) Ltd
4 Lower Belgrave Street, London SW1W 0LJ
Tel. 01-730 2182

Fryer Travel
315 Oxford Street, London W1
Tel. 01-499 3651

Groups Unlimited Ltd
2 Lower Sloane Street, London SW1W 8BJ
Tel. 01-730 5203

Hallmark International
Sandbourne House, 302 Charminster Road, Bournemouth, Dorset
BH8 9RU
Tel. 0202 525167

Hogg Robinson
10 The Borough, Farnham, Surrey
Tel. 0252 711022

Kendall Travel
35 Alfred Place, Store Street, London WC1E 7DY
Tel. 01-637 2300

Len Wright Travel
3 Fleming Way, Worton Road, Isleworth, Middx TW7 6EU
Tel. 01-568 1734
(Coach hire)

Meon Group Travel
Meon House, Petersfield, Hampshire GU32 3JN
Tel. 0730 66561

Midas Aviation Ltd
Shenley Hall, Rectory Lane, Shenley, Radlett, Herts
Tel. 092 76 4797
(Helicopter and light aircraft charters)

OCCT
8 Dorset Square, London NW1 6PU
Tel. 01-723 6036

Opal Tours
Administration et Gestion du Voyage, Domaine de l'Hermitage,
BP28 62520 Le Touquet, France
Tel. (21)05 11 11

Page and Moy Ltd
136–140 London Road, Leicester LE2 1EN
Tel. 0533 542000

Pickfords Travel Service
Lawrence House, 238 City Road, London EC1V 2ND
Tel.   01-253 3305

Pressplan Travel Ltd
17 Verulam Road, St Albans, Herts AL3 4DA
Tel.   0727 33291

Reception International
39 Crawford Street, London W1H 1HA
Tel.   01-262 5511

Small World
850 Brighton Road, Purley, Surrey CR2 2BH
Tel.   01-660 3999

Spectra Travel
12–15 Hanger Green, London W5 3EL
Tel.   01-998 1021

Sportsworld Travel Ltd
88–92 Earls Court Road, London W8 6EH
Tel.   01-938 1877

Thomas Cook Ltd
(*See* Compass Travel)

Travel Awards
27A Sloane Square, London SW1W 8AB
Tel.   01-730 2261

Travel Contacts
4 Christchurch Avenue, Tunbridge Wells, Kent TN1 1UW
Tel.   0892 27737

The Travel Organization
The Old Market Hall, Creed Street, Wolverton, Milton Keynes
MK12 5RY
Tel.   0908 310866

Travel Strategy Ltd
4–5 Primrose Mews, Regents Park, London NW1 8YL
Tel.   01-586 4922

Two's Company
8 South Molton Street, London W1Y 1DG
Tel.   01-493 8391
(Executive diner coaches)

Wakefield Fortune
St George House, Station Approach, Cheam SM2 7AT
Tel.   01-661 0323

Warwick West Ltd
21/23 Chilworth Street, London W2
Tel.   01-402 7121

WGT Ltd
KMH House, Market Place, Yeadon, Leeds LS19 7PP
Tel.   0532 505321

Major international airlines

Aer Lingus
223, Regent Street, London W1
Tel.   01-734 1212

Air Canada
140 Regent Street, London W1R 6AT
Tel.   01-439 7941

Air France
158 New Bond Street, London W1Y 0AY
Tel.   01-499 8611

Air Jamaica
6 Bruton Street, London W1
Tel.   01-499 6802

Air Malta
23 Pall Mall, London SW1
Tel.   01-839 5872

Air New Zealand
15 Charles II Street, London SW1
Tel.   01-930 1088

Air Portugal
19 Regent Street, London SW1
Tel.   01-839 1031

Air UK
Berkeley House, High Street, Redhill, Surrey
Tel.   0737 65941

Alitalia
205 Holland Park Avenue, London W11 4XB
Tel.   01-759 2501

American Airlines
7 Albemarle Street, London W1X 3HF
Tel.   01-629 0195

Austrian Airlines
50 Conduit Street, London W1R 0NP
Tel.   01-439 1851

Britannia Airways
25 Tavistock Place, London WC1
Tel.   01-388 2881

British Airways plc
200 Buckingham Palace Road, London SW1Y 9TA
Tel.   01-821 4060

British Caledonian Airways
Caledonian House, Crawley, West Sussex RH10 2XA
Tel.   0293 27890, 01-668 9311

British Midland Airways
Donington Hall, Castle Donington, Derby
Tel.   0332 810741

British West Indian Airways (BWIA)
20 Lower Regent Street, London W1
Tel.   01-839 7155

Cathay Pacific Airways
7 Apple Tree Yard, Duke of York Street, London SW1Y 6LD
Tel.   01-930 4444

CP Air
62–65 Trafalgar Square, London WC2N 5DT
Tel.   01-930 3501

Dan-Air Services
36–38 New Broad Street, London EC2M 1NH
Tel.   01-638 1747

Delta Airlines
Room 3092, Terminal Building, Gatwick Airport, Sussex
Tel.   0293 502023

Eastern Airlines
Princes House, 36–40 Jermyn Street, London SW1Y 6DN
Tel.   01-734 7637

Egyptair
296 Regent Street, London W1
Tel.   01-580 5477

El Al Israel Airlines
185 Regent Street, London W1
Tel.   01-437 9277

Finnair
56 Haymarket, London SW1
Tel.   01-930 3941

Iberia
Venture House, 29 Glasshouse Street, London W1 5RG
Tel.   01-437 9822

Japan Airlines
Hanover Court, 5 Hanover Square, London W1R 0DR
Tel.   01-629 9244

KLM Royal Dutch Airlines
Time Life Building, New Bond Street, London W1Y 0AD
Tel.   01-493 1231

Lufthansa
10 Old Bond Street, London W1X 4EN
Tel.   01-408 0322

Luxair (Luxembourg Airlines)
British Airways Ticket Office, Lower Regent Street, London SW1
Tel.   01-370 5411

Northwest Orient Airlines
49 Albemarle Street, London W1X 3FE
Tel.   01-491 3270

Olympic Airways
141 New Bond Street, London W1Y 0BB
Tel.   01-493 7262

Pan American World Airways
193 Piccadilly, London W1V 0AD
Tel.   01-759 2595

Philippine Airlines
19th Floor, Centre Point, 103 New Oxford Street, London WC1
Tel.   01-409 1177

Quantas Airways
500 Chiswick High Road, London W4 5RW
Tel.   01-995 1361

Sabena
36 Piccadilly, London W1
Tel.   01-437 6950

Scandinavian Airlines System (SAS)
52 Conduit Street, London W1
Tel.   01-734 4020

Singapore Airlines
580 Chiswick High Road, London W4
Tel.   01-747 0007

South African Airways
251 Regent Street, London W1R 7AD
Tel.   01-734 9841

Swissair
10 Wardour Street, London W1
Tel.   01-439 4144

Thai Airways
41 Albemarle Street, London W1
Tel.   01-499 9113

TWA
214 Oxford Street, London W1N OHA
Tel. 01-636 5411

Varig Brazilian Airlines
16–17 Hanover Street, London W1R 9HG
Tel. 01-629 9408

Wardair Canada
12th Floor, Rothschild House, Whitgift Centre, Croydon, Surrey
Tel. 01-686 5255

World Airways
55 Conduit Street, London W1R 9FD
Tel. 01-439 9252

Conference production companies

The following list includes some of the companies in Britain offering conference production services. Where they are described as 'complete conference production', this means that they will arrange for the production of scripts, slides, sets, audio visual sequences and all of the hardware and technical backup needed for a conference. As a rule, they will not provide a management service covering accommodation, catering and travel.

Adanac Productions
2 Ovington Square, London SW3 1LN
Tel. 01-589 2385
(Complete conference production)

APR Ltd
The Audio Visual Studio, Weston Square, Barry, South Glamorgan
Tel. 0446 745035
(Complete conference production)

AV Creative Presentations
M.F.P. House, Harrison Road, Birmingham B24 9AB
Tel. 021-373 0450
(AV production)

AV Slide Work Ltd
42 Beak Street, London W1R 3DA
Tel. 01-439 4357
(AV production)

APR Videoscope Ltd
The Welsh Audio Visual Centre, 7 Argyle Way, Heol Trelai,
Cardiff, South Glamorgan
Tel.   0222 596146
(AV production)

Artec
117 C/D Cleveland Street, London W1P 5PN
Tel.   01-637 0237

Aspect Presentations Ltd
Silk Mill, Thorp Street, Macclesfield, Cheshire
Tel.   0625 616770
(Complete conference production)

Audio Visual Images Ltd
34 Cricklewood Broadway, London NW2 3ET
Tel.   01-450 0266
(AV Production)

Audio Visual Impact Representations Ltd
20 Bank Street, Accrington, Lancashire BB5 1HH
Tel.   0254 385409
(Complete conference production)

Audio Visual Impressions Ltd
The Willows Studio, Drayton Road, Newton Longville, Milton
Keynes MK17 0BH
Tel.   0908 641889
(AV production)

Audio Visual Seen and Heard Ltd
17 Queens Lane, Newcastle NE1 1RN
Tel.   0632 325736
(Complete conference production)

Audio Visual Services
Cherry Orchard, Nickle Farm, Chartham, Canterbury
Tel.   0227 731278
(AV production)

Audio Visual Techniques
AV House, 86 Preston Road, Brighton, East Sussex BN1 6AE
Tel.   0273 561126
(AV production)

Audio Visual Workshop Ltd
68 Dalling Road, London W6 0ZA
Tel.   01-748 8013
(AV production)

Audiovisions
61 South Street, Havant, Hants
Tel.   0705 486566
(AV production)

Audio-visual Consultants Loughborough
15 Brisco Avenue, Loughborough LE11 0HB
Tel.   0509 215105
(AV production)

Audio-visual Productions
Hocker Hill House, Chepstow, Gwent NP6 5ER
Tel.   02912 5439
(AV production)

AV Consultants Ltd
Walters Farm Road, Tonbridge, Kent TN9 1GT
Tel.   0732 365107
(AV production)

Avidata Ltd
100 Leonard Street, London EC2A 4RH
Tel.   01-739 1004
(AV production)

B Audio Visual Productions
Jennings House, Thames Avenue, Windsor, Berks SL4 1QP
Tel.   07535 56775
(AV production)

Tony Ball Associates
22 Stephenson Way, London NW1 2HD
Tel.   01-388 3525
(Complete conference production)

Bright Ideas Audiovisual Ltd
16 Tariff Street, Manchester M1 2EP
Tel.   061-236 2100
(Complete conference production)

CTI Services Ltd
James House, Welford Road, Leicester
Tel.   0533 551143
(Complete conference production)

Calton Audio Visual Ltd
32 North West Thistle St Lane, Edinburgh EH2 1EA
Tel.   031 225 8871
(AV production)

Caribiner Inc
Europe House, World Trade Centre, London E1 9AA
Tel.   01-481 4033
(Complete conference production)

Conference Machine
58 Hylton Street, Hockley, Birmingham B18 6HN
Tel.   021-551 7714
(Complete conference production)

Comcept
5 Lamps Studio, West Avenue, Derby DE1 3HR
Tel.   0332 383322
(Complete conference production)

Commercial Presentations
Commercial House, 64–66 Glenthorne Road, Hammersmith,
London W6 0LR
Tel.   01-741 8922
(Complete conference production)

Communique
102 Belsize Lane, Hampstead, London NW3 5BB
Tel.   01-794 4401
(Complete conference production)

Conference Clearway Ltd
Conference House, 9 Pavilion Parade, Brighton BN2 1RA
Tel.   0273 695811
(Complete conference production)

Connections
34 Portland Square, Bristol BS2 8RG
Tel.   0272 40785
(AV production)

Nicholas Cory Ltd
19/20 Charter House, Lord Montgomery Way, Portsmouth
PO1 SU2
Tel.   0705 861451
(Management of catering, accommodation, travel, etc.)

Creative Conferences Ltd
Broadfields House, Headstone Lane, Harrow, Middx HA2 6NZ
Tel.   01-421 2999
(Complete conference production)

Edco Reed International Productions
Broadway Chambers, 14–26 Hammersmith Broadway,
Hammersmith, London W6
Tel.   01-741 1921
(Audio visual production)

Gray Audio Visual
34–36 Bickerton Road, London N19 5JS
Tel.   01-263 9561
(Complete conference production)

Hamilton Perry Ltd
27–29 Beak Street, London W1R 3LB
Tel.   01-434 3041
(Complete conference production)

Hurlston Design Ltd
113 Griffins Brook Lane, Bournville, Birmingham B30 1QN
Tel.   021-475 3352
(AV production)

Imagination Ltd
17–19 Bedford Street, Covent Garden, London WC2
Tel.   01-379 6872
(Complete conference production)

International Conferences Ltd, Guernsey
P.O. Box 76, Suite 2, Provident House, Havilland Street,
St Peter Port, Guernsey, Channel Islands
Tel.   0481 711400
(Complete conference production)

JB Presentations
15, Brackenbury Road, Shepherd's Bush, London W6 0BE
Tel. 01-749 6036
(Complete conference production)

David Jones & Co Ltd
8 Bedford Court, Covent Garden, London WC2
Tel. 01-240 6761
(Complete conference production)

Kadek Vision Ltd
Post 21, Shepperton Studio Centre, Studios Road, Shepperton,
Middlesex
Tel. 09328 66941
(AV production)

Looking Glass Productions Ltd
93 Charlton Church Lane, London SE7 7AB
Tel. 01-858 8688
(AV production)

MMA
8–20 Shorts Gardens, Covent Garden, London WC2
Tel. 01-836 8931
(Complete conference production)

Magic Lantern Productions
139 Greenwich High Road, London SE10 8JA
Tel. 01-858 5715
(Audio visual and video production)

Maritz Communications
Thames House, Marlowe, Bucks SL7 1TE
Tel. 062 84 6011
(Complete conference production)

Multivision Audio Visual
Bolton Street, Salford, Manchester M3 5FP
Tel. 061-834 9994
(Complete conference production)

Pender Kenning and Holt
54 Spencer Street, Hockley, Birmingham B18 6DS
Tel. 021-236 3362
(Complete conference production)

Planned Presentations Ltd
21/22 Warwick Street, London W1R 5RB
Tel. 01-734 9601
(Complete conference production)

Prater Audio Visual Ltd
139 Greenwich High Road, London SE10 8JA
Tel. 01-858 5715
(Audio visual and video production)

Purchasepoint
14–16 Peterborough Road, London SW6 3BN
Tel. 01-731 1377
(Complete conference production)

QAV Presentations Ltd
7 Guildford Road, Woking, Surrey
Tel. 04862 26601
(Complete conference production)

Roundel Productions
51 Loudoun Road, London NW8 0DL
Tel. 01-624 6080
(Complete conference production)

SSK Productions
48 Berkeley Street, Glasgow G3 7DS
Tel. 041-226 4774
(Complete conference production)

Showbusiness
Chelsea Wharf, Lots Road, London SW10 0QJ
Tel. 01-351 3362
(AV production)

Spectrum Communications
191 The Vale, London W3 7QS
Tel. 01-740 4444
(Complete conference production)

Triangle Audio Visual Partnership
31 Oval Road, London NW1 7EA
Tel. 01-267 7608
(AV production)

The Visual Connection Ltd
50 Glebe Place, London SW3 5JE
Tel.   01-351 5454
(AV production)

Audio-visual and conference equipment suppliers

As with production companies, there are many suppliers of audio-visual equipment both for sale and hire. The following list is far from comprehensive and inevitably, some addresses will be out of date within a short time. Even so, this list should provide a starting point for organizers wanting to hire projectors, sound systems and lighting equipment. Those companies designated 'equipment hire' claim to be able to supply all audio-visual hardware.

Audio Visual and Video Hire
138 Cardigan Road, Leeds LS6 1LU
Tel.   0532 757731
(Equipment hire)

Audio Visual Equipment (UK) Ltd
16 Southsea Road, Kingston, Surrey KT1 2EH
Tel.   01-549 7521
(Equipment hire)

Audio Visual Leisure (Halifax) Ltd
Unit 2A, West Parade Industrial Estate, Halifax, West Yorkshire HX1 2TF
Tel.   0422 59398
(Equipment hire)

Audio Visual Services
45 Stroud Road, Gloucester GL1 5AQ
Tel.   04052 35181
(Equipment hire)

Audio-visual Centre of Dundee
61 Perth Road, Dundee
Tel.   0382 27152
(Equipment hire)

Audivis (Bournemouth) Ltd
386 Ashley Road, Parkstone, Poole, Dorset BH14 0AA
Tel.   0202 735118
(Equipment hire)

Autocue
265 Merton Road, London SW18 5SS
Tel.   01-870 0104
(Hire of teleprompting systems)

Autocue North
70 Sandown Crescent, Sandiway, Northwich, Cheshire
Tel.   0606 883427
(Hire of teleprompting systems)

Availability (Audiovisual) Ltd
2 Meeting House Lane, Balsall Common, Coventry CV7 7FX
Tel.   0676 33263
(Broking service providing hire of equipment across the UK)

Berkshire Business Machines Ltd
15A Castons Yard, off New Road, Basingstoke, Hants
Tel.   0256 23978
(Equipment hire)

Bodley Knose Ltd
47/53 Station Road, Shalford, Guildford, Surrey
Tel.   0483 504868
(Sound and video equipment hire)

Briana Electronics Ltd
White Lodge, East Hanningfield Road, Sandon, Chelmsford,
Essex CM2 7TQ
Tel.   0245 71145
(Equipment hire)

Tim Burnham Associates
31 Corsica Street, London N5 1JT
Tel.   01-359 6298
(Hire of lighting systems)

Channel Islands Audio Visual
Ruette des Cherfs, Castel, Guernsey, Channel Islands
Tel. 0481 55902
(Equipment hire)

Cine Equipments Ltd
9 Dale End, Birmingham B4 7LW
Tel. 021-236 1769
(Equipment hire)

Cinephoto Equipment Ltd
17 Crescent, Salford M5 4PF
Tel. 061-736 6221
(Equipment hire)

Compact Video Systems Ltd
15 North Avenue, London W13
Tel. 01-997 5959
(Video and audio visual equipment hire)

Comtec Ltd
51 Leslie Park Road, Croydon, Surrey CR0 6TP
Tel. 01-656 6825
(Equipment hire)

Confab Associates
105 Thornton Road, Cambridge CB3 0NH
Tel. 0223 276543
(Equipment hire)

The Creative Studio
67/71 Scrubs Lane, London NW10
Tel. 01-969 9525
(Equipment hire)

W. G. Cross and Sons Ltd
70 Mardol, Shrewsbury, Salop SY1 1QA
Tel. 0743 62209
(Projector hire)

Dats Video Ltd
80/86 Bridge Street, Warrington, Cheshire WA1 2RQ
Tel. 0925 35243 ·
(Audio visual and video hire)

Davengers Systems
25/27 May Street, Derby DE3 3UQ
Tel. 0332 371988
(Equipment hire)

Edric Audio Visual Ltd
34/36 Oak End Way, Gerrards Cross, Bucks SL9 8BR
Tel. 0753 884646
(Equipment hire)

Electronic Sound Entertainments
38 The Orchard, Market Deeping, Peterborough PE6 8JR
Tel. 0778 343491
(Sound and lighting equipment hire)

Ellis Screen Presentations Ltd
Ledsam House, Ledsam Street, Birmingham B16 8DN
Tel. 021-454 5599
(Equipment hire)

Eros Screen Presentations Ltd
51 Upper Elmers End Road, Beckenham, Kent
Tel. 01-658 5024
(Equipment hire)

Erricks of Bradford
Fotosonic House, Rawson Square, Bradford BD1 3JR
Tel. 0274 309266
(Equipment hire)

Paul Farrah Sound
Unit 7, St George's Industrial Estate, Richmond Road, Ham,
Surrey
Tel. 01-568 2313
(Video and audio equipment hire)

Brian Goodchild Ltd
63/65 Regent Street, Leamington Spa, Warwickshire
Tel. 0926 24076
(Equipment hire)

Gray Audio Visual
34/36 Bickerton Road, London N19 5JS
Tel. 01-263 9561
(Equipment hire)

Lorne Hamilton
59 Albion Road, Sutton, Surrey SM2 5TD
Tel. 01-661 0862
(Equipment hire including stages and sets)

Hargreaves Audio Visual and Video
204/206 Warbreck Moor, Aintree, Liverpool L9 0HZ
Tel. 051-525 1786
(Equipment hire)

Hewitt Photo Sales Ltd
36 St Botolph's Street, Colchester, Essex CO2 7EA
Tel. 0206 573444
(Equipment hire)

Peter Horsley and Co.
2 Poulton Street, Fleetwood, Lancashire
Tel. 03917 2765
(Equipment hire)

Istead Video & Audio Visual
60–61 Lionel Street, Birmingham B18 6HN
Tel. 021-554 2947
(Equipment hire)

KP Professional Sales
Camera House, Quayside, Bridge Street, Cambridge CB5 8AB
Tel. 0223 64915
(Equipment hire)

Kermac Electronics
112/124 Woodlands Road, Glasgow G3 6MB
Tel. 041-332 2036
(Equipment hire)

Leeds Camera Centre Ltd
Lovell House, North Street, Leeds LS2 7PM
Tel. 0532 456313
(Equipment hire)

Mediatech
Woodside Place, Alperton, Wembley, Middx HA0 1XA
Tel. 01-903 4372
(Equipment hire)
Also in Manchester and Holland.

Midland Audio Visual
Rear of 202 New Road, Rubery, Birmingham B45 9JA
Tel.   021-453 3141
(Equipment hire)

Terry More Photographic
49 George Street, Luton, Beds LH1 2AQ
Tel.   0582 23391
(Equipment hire)

Multicord
1/3 Ravensworth View, Dunston, Newcastle-on-Tyne, Tyne and
Wear NE11 9DQ
Tel.   0632 609209
(Equipment hire)

Northern Ireland Audio-visual Aids Centre Ltd
87 Rugby Avenue, Belfast BT7 3FE
Tel.   0232 233094
(Equipment hire)

PTS (Electronics) Ltd
St Alkmunds Way, Derby DE1 3GO
Tel.   0332 372345
(Equipment hire)

Pace Presentations
170 Camberwell Road, London SE5 0EE
Tel.   01-701 6145
(Equipment and crew hire)

The Photo Centre
Unit 8, Barclayhill Place, Portlethen, Aberdeen AB1 4PF
Tel.   0224 780080
(Equipment hire)

Q-TV Prompting Services
10–20 Shorts Gardens, London WC2H 9AU
Tel.   01-836 6757
(Teleprompting systems hire)

Rew Communications
52/62 Raymouth Road, London SE16
Tel.   01-231 8497
(Equipment hire)

Roche Audio Visual
St Andrew's Court, Mawdsley Street, Bolton BL1 1RR
Tel.   0204 389124
(Equipment hire)

Samuelson Communications
120 Cricklewood Lane, London NW2
Tel.   01-208 0011
also at:
Unit 60, Gravelly Industrial Park, Tyburn Road, Birmingham
Tel.   021-327 0151
(Equipment hire)

Solent Audio Visual
228 London Road, Portsmouth, Hants
Tel.   0705 662091
(Equipment hire)

Staging Post
44 Gloucester Avenue, London NW1 8JD
Tel.   01-586 5313
(Equipment hire and conference management)

TBA Lighting
(*See* Tim Burnham Associates)

Theatravisual Ltd
10/20 Shorts Gardens, London WC2
Tel.   01-836 7574
(Equipment hire)

Viewplan
Alice Owen Technology Centre, 251–279 Goswell Road, London
EC1V 7JQ
Tel.   01-734 8833
(Equipment hire)
Also at Birmingham and Heathrow.

Western Cine Services
Rutherford House, 30 Alphington Road, Exeter, Devon EX2
8HN
Tel.   0392 56651
(Equipment hire)

The Wiltshire Film Unit
138/140 County Road, Swindon, Wiltshire SN1 2DY
Tel.   0793 23430
(Equipment hire)

Interpreters

A significant number of interpreters operate on a freelance basis. Whilst some companies providing interpretation services are listed, contact can be made with qualified individual interpreters through their Association:

AIIC Interpreters — British Isles
Cunningham House, Westfield Lane, Harrow, Middx HA3 9EA
Tel.   01-907 4211

Companies specializing in providing conference interpreters
Cambridge Interpreters
59 Goldieslie Road, Sutton Coldfield, West Midlands B73 5PF
Tel.   021-355 4823

M & R Conference Communications
Acron Workshops, School Road, London NW10 6TD
Tel.   01-961 1777

Technical Translation International Ltd
Imperial House, 15/19 Kingsway, London WC2B 6UU
Tel.   01-240 5361

Conference Interpretation Equipment
There is a professional association for suppliers of equipment for simultaneous interpretation:

Simultaneous Interpretation Equipment Suppliers Association
9 Hesper Mews, London SW5 0HH
Tel.   01-373 9474

Individual members are as follows—

Ascott Sound Engineering Co Ltd
88 Old Bedford Road, Luton, Beds LU2 7PD
Tel.   0582 23739

Hayden Laboratories Ltd
Hayden House, Chiltern Hill, Chalfont St Peter,
Gerrards Cross, Bucks SL9 9UG
Tel.   0753 888447

M & R Conference Communications
7 Bell Industrial Estate, 50 Cunnington Street,
London W4 5HB
Tel.   01-995 4714

Philips Electronics
Communication and Control Division,
Cromwell Road, Cambridge CB1 3HE
Tel.   0223 245191

Sicom Conference Services Ltd
Park Mews, Park Hall Road, West Dulwich, London SE21 8EX
Tel.   01-670 9351

Westminster Audio Communications
17 Canterbury Grove, London SE27 0NT
Tel.   01-761 0022

Conference magazines

Those magazines marked with a * specialize in conferences.
Others run occasional conference features or deal with associated
subjects.

Audio Visual
P.O. Box 109, Maclaren House, Scarbrook Road, Croydon,
Surrey CR9 1QH
Tel. 01-688 7788

Campaign
22 Lancaster Gate, London W2 3LY
Tel. 01-402 4200

Conference Britain
2 Queensway, Redhill, Surrey RH1 1QS
Tel. 0737 68611

Conferences & Exhibitions International
2 Queensway, Redhill, Surrey RH1 1QS
Tel. 0737 68611

Corporate Meetings and Incentives
Harcourt Brace Jovanovich Publications, 747 Third Avenue, New
York, New York 10017 USA
Tel. 010 1 212 418 4144
(American magazine)

Marketing
22 Lancaster Gate, London W2 3LY
Tel. 01-402 4200

Marketing Week
60 Kingly Street, London W1R 5LH
Tel. 01-439 4222

Meetings and Conventions
West Heath House, 32 North End Road, London NW11 7PT
Tel. 01-458 7322
(American magazine specializing in meetings)

Promotions and Incentives
P.O. Box 109, Maclaren House, Scarbrook Road, Croydon,
Surrey CR9 1QH.
Tel. 01-688 7788

Successful Meetings
633 Third Avenue, New York, New York 10017, USA
Tel. 010 1 212 986 4800
(American magazine specializing in meetings)

Televisual
Fredrica House, 12 Oval Road, London NW1 7DH
Tel. 01-485 0975

Venue
Juniper Press Ltd, 66 Great Cumberland Place, London
W1H 7FD
Tel. 01-402 3421

Professional associations

The following list shows organizations connected with the conference industry and associated activities.

Asian Association of Convention & Visitor Bureaux (AACVB)
Asian Institute of Tourism, University of the Philippines, Don Mario Marcos Ave, Dilman, Quezon City, Metro Manila, Philippines
Tel.   010 63 2 96 90 71

Association Francaise des Professionnels du Tourisme D'affaires
Boulevard Malesherbes 9, 75008 Paris, France
Tel.   010 33 1 42 66 91 46

Association International Des Interpretes de Conference
Cunningham House, Westfield Lane, Harrow, Middlesex HA3 9EA
Tel.   01-907 4211

Association Internationale des Palais de Congres
Palais de Congres de Versailles, Rue de la Chancellerie 8–10, F 78000 Versailles, France
Tel.   010 33 39 51 46 30

Association des Villes Francophones de Congres
Siege Afal, Rue du Lille 47, 75007 Paris, France

Association for Multi-image International Inc. (AMI)
8019 N Himes Ave, Suite 401, Tampa, Fl 33614, USA
Tel.   010 1 813 932 1692

Association of British Professional Conference Organizers
100, Park Road, London NW1 4RN
Tel.   01-723 6722

Association of Conference Executives International (ACE)
Riverside House, High Street, Huntingdon, Cambs PE18 6SG
Tel.   0480 57595

Association of Yugoslav Congress Towns
Yugocongress, 41000 Zagreb, Kaptol 5, Yugoslavia
Tel.   010 1 38 41 444 529

Audio Visual and Presentation Advisory Service
P.O. Box 21, Trowbridge, Wiltshire BA14 8UB
Tel.   02214 68083

Audio Visual Association (AVA)
46 Manor View, London N3 2SR
Tel.   01-349 2429

British Association of Conference Towns (BACT)
International House, 36 Dudley Road, Royal Tunbridge Wells,
Kent TN1 1LB
Tel.   0892 33442

British Exhibition Contractors Association
Kingsmere House, Graham Road, London SW19 3SR
Tel.   01-543 3888

British Incoming Tour Operators' Association
16 Catherine Place, London SW1 6HF
Tel.   01-828 4497

British Industrial and Scientific Film Association (BISFA)
120 Long Acre, London WC2E 9PA
Tel.   01-240 1073

British Tourist Authority
Thames Tower, Blacks Road, Hammersmith, London W6 9EL
Tel.   01-846 9000

British Universities Accommodation Consortium (BUAC)
P.O. Box 287, University Park, Nottingham NG7 2RD
Tel.   0602 504571

Caribbean Tourism Association Europe
c/o Palt Public Relations, 161 Fulham Road, London SW3 6SN
Tel.   01-581 4094

Conference Managers' Association
c/o Schwarzkopf Ltd, Penn Road, Aylesbury, Bucks HP21 8HL
Tel.   0296 88101

English Tourist Board
Thames Tower, Blacks Road, Hammersmith, London W6 9EL
Tel.   01-846 9000

Euromic
c/o Spectra Travel, 12–15 Hanger Green, London W5 3EL
Tel.   01-998 1021

European Federation of Conference Towns (EFCT)
Rue Washington 40, B 1050 Brussels, Belgium
Tel.   010 32 2 64 01 808

European Society of Association Executives
Peter Houghton, c/o Birmingham Settlement, 318 Summer Lane,
Birmingham B19 3RL
Tel.   021-359 2113

Exposiciones Congresos y Convenciones de Espana (ECCE)
Juan Hurtado de Mendoza, 4 Madrid 16, Spain
Tel.   010 34 1 458 70 92

France Congres — French Association of Convention Cities
24 Avenue de l'Opera, 75001 Paris, France
Tel.   010 33 42 96 03 78

Higher Education Accommodation Consortium (HEAC)
36 Collegiate Crescent, Sheffield S10 2BP
Tel.   0742 683759

Institute of Association Executives
67 Yonge Street, 1101 Toronto, Ontario M5E 1J8, Canada
Tel.   010 1 416 367 1134

International Association of Convention & Visitor Bureaux
P.O. Box 758, Champaign, IL 61820, USA
Tel.   010 1 217 359 8881

International Association of Professional Congress Organizers
Rue Washington 40, B 1050 Brussels, Belgium
Tel.   010 32 2 640 18 08

International Congress & Convention Association (*ICCA*)
c/o Geoffrey V. Smith, 137 Sheen Road, Richmond, Surrey
TW9 1YJ
Tel.   01-940 3431

Italcongressi
Piazza della Liberta 21, 00192 Roma, Italy
Tel.   010 39 6 32 25 58

Mechanical Copyright Protection Society (*MCPS*)
Elgar House, 41 Streatham High Road, London SW16 1ER
Tel.   01-769 4400

Meeting Planners International (*MPI*)
c/o Geoffrey V. Smith, 137 Sheen Road, Richmond, Surrey
TW9 1YJ
Tel.   01-940 3431

Pacific Area Travel Association
228 Grant Avenue, San Francisco, California 94108, USA
Tel.   010 1 415 986 4646

Performing Right Society (*PRS*)
28–33 Berners Street, London W1P 4AA
Tel.   01-580 5544

Simultaneous Interpretation Equipment Suppliers' Association
9 Hesper Mews, London SW5 0HH
Tel.   01-373 9474

Union of International Associations
Rue Washington 40, B 1050 Brussels, Belgium
Tel.   010 32 2 640 41 09
Also 010 32 2 640 18 08

Entertainments, after-dinner and guest speakers

There are a number of books that list prominent people in the broadcast media and their agents. If a specific individual is required for an event, the name of their agent can probably be found in one of the following:

'Who's Who on Television' published by ITV Books in association with Michael Joseph.

'Who's Who on Radio' compiled by Sheila Tracy and published by World's Work Ltd, The Windmill Press, Kingswood, Tadworth, Surrey.

'Spotlight' published by The Spotlight. This is a vast work running to four large volumes and is probably best consulted through an advertising agent or one of the following companies that specialize in providing entertainment and speakers for conferences.

Pat Campbell Entertainments
48 Westmount Road, Eltham, London SE9 1JE
Tel.   01-850 4343
(Organize cabarets and after-dinner speakers)

Enterpol Productions
The Folly, Pinner Hill Road, Pinner, Middlesex HA5 3YQ
Tel.   01-429 3737
(Organize cabarets)

Hamilton Perry
27/29 Beak Street, London W1R 3LB
Tel. 01-434 3041
(Arrange guest speakers for conferences)

Robert Holland-Ford Associates
103 Lydyett Lane, Barnton, Northwich, Cheshire CW8 4JT
Tel. 0606 76960
(Arrange guest speakers for conferences)

London Management
235/241 Regent Street, London W1A 2JT
Tel. 01-493 1610
(Organize cabarets)

MAM
24/25 New Bond Street, London W1
Tel. 01-629 9255
(Organize cabarets)

MMA Presentations Ltd
8/20 Shorts Gardens, Covent Garden, London WC2 9DP
Tel. 01-836 8931
(Arrange guest speakers for conferences)

Personality Presentations
51 Loudoun Road, London NW8 0DL
Tel. 01-624 6080
(Arrange guest speakers for conferences)

Jo Peters Management
53 North End House, Fitzjames Avenue, London W14 0RT
Tel. 01-603 8930
(Organize cabarets and after-dinner speakers)

Prime Performers
5 Kidderpore Avenue, London NW3
Tel. 01-431 0211
(Organize cabarets and after-dinner speakers)

Private Casino Promotions
Suite 2, Whitehall House, London Road, East Grinstead, Sussex
RH19 9AP
Tel. 0342 313533
(Organize on-site casinos)

Production Plus Ltd
The Courtyard, 44 Gloucester Avenue, London NW1
Tel.   01-586 9771
(Organize cabarets)

Song and Supper Music Hall Ltd
1B Montagu Mews North, London W1H 1AJ
Tel.   01-486 7383/7314
(Organize music hall entertainment)

Conference accessories

There are obviously many hundreds of companies supplying the wide variety of goods needed by a conference organizer. This list includes a few of them. It is in two parts: suppliers listed under subject headings and an alphabetical list by company name.

Badges
De Graff/Grovemetal Manufacturing/The Incentive Group of Companies/Kenex/Nickwood Plastics/Renamel/Toye, Kenning and Spencer.

Sports and zip-up bags
Lapco (UK) Ltd/Logoplus/Mainline Promotions Ltd/Micropharm Ltd

Clothing (Including tee shirts, sweat shirts, etc.)
Mainline Promotions Ltd/TNT Printed Leisurewear/Winston Promotions Ltd

Conference folders, clipboards and wallets
Anderson Distribution/Josiah Brown/Elk and Co./Executive Products/Arnold Jessel Ltd/Juon Plastics Ltd/Philmar Trading

Leather goods
Fourteenth Century Art Studios

Matches
Josiah Brown/Kenex/Venture Matches

Pens
Berol/Hitco/The Incentive Group of Companies/Kenex/Pentel/Synapse International

Ties and scarves
ADB (London) Ltd/Brand Marketing/Cravats Ltd/The Incentive
Group of Companies/Cornelia James Contracts/KC Promotional
Gifts Ltd/Mainline Promotions Ltd

Slide charts
Slide Charts Britain Ltd

Sourcing Service
Promotion Sourcing Ltd

Alphabetical list of companies

14th Century Art Studios Ltd
6 Langledge Lane Estate, Langledge Lane, Edmonton, London
N18 2TQ
Tel.   01-884 1414
(Leather bookmarks, wine coasters, key fobs, etc.)

ADB (London) Ltd
49/57 Harrow Road, London W2 1JH
Tel.   01-402 5671
(Ties)

Anderson Distribution Ltd
Bertie House, Bearsted, Maidstone, Kent
Tel.   0622 37025
(Conference folders, clipboards, desk accessories and note pads)

Berol Ltd
Specials Business Manager, Oldmeadow Road, King's Lynn,
Norfolk PE30 4JR
Tel.   0553 61221
(Pens and pencils)

Brand Marketing Ltd
380 Boldmere Road, Sutton Coldfield, West Midlands
Tel.   021-350 0555
(Ties, promotional clothing and advertising give-aways)

Josiah Brown Ltd
West Gate, Long Eaton, Nottingham NG10 1EG
Tel.   0602 734457
(Folders, briefcases, wallets, coasters, drip mats, badges, matches,
flags, stickers, etc.)

Cravats Ltd
207 Regent Street, London W1
Tel. 01-734 3199
(Ties and scarves)

Elk & Company Ltd
Elkon Works, Down Street, West Molesey, Surrey KT8 0TT
Tel. 01-979 9921
(Leather and PVC document cases and clipboards)

Executive Products
The Showrooms, 1 Chestnut Road, London SE27 9EZ
Tel. 01-670 7416
(Conference folders)

De Graff
1 Hinde Street, London W1M 5RH
Tel. 01-486 5231
(Badges, key fobs, matches, etc.)

Grovemetal Manufacturing
216/218 Homesdale Road, Bromley, Kent BR1 2QZ
Tel. 01-464 5936
(Conference badges)

Hitco UK Ltd
19 Princess Road, London NW1 8JR
Tel. 01-586 7011
(Pens)

The Incentive Group of Companies Ltd
101/105 Plough Road, London SW11 2BJ
Tel. 01-228 7890
(Badges, keyrings, cufflinks, ties, scarves, pens and gifts)

Cornelia James Contracts Ltd
53/55 New Bond Street, London W1Y 9DG
Tel. 01-499 9423
(Scarves and ties)

Arnold Jessel Ltd
P.O. Box 12, Corporation Street, Walsall WS1 4HP
Tel.   0922 24649
(Conference folders and leather goods)

Juon Plastics Ltd
Burfield Works, Old Windsor, Berks SL4 2RB
Tel.   07535 53217
(Plastic ring binders, conference folders and wallets)

KC Promotional Gifts Ltd
21a Farncombe Street, Godalming, Surrey
Tel.   04868 29294
(Ties and scarves)

Kenex
Charter Industrial Estate, Charter Street, Leicester LE1 3UD
Tel.   0533 22795
(Button badges, keyfobs, pens, matches, etc.)

Lapco (UK) Ltd
80 Main Street, South Croxton, Leics
Tel.   0533 544424
(Sports bags)

Logoplus Ltd
Western House, 93 Adderley Road, Wilmslow, Cheshire SK9 1RD
Tel.   0625 527480
(Zip-up bags for first aid kits, travel kits, etc.)

Mainline Promotions Ltd
The Common, Cranleigh, Surrey GU6 8RZ
Tel.   0483 271171
(Tee shirts, sweat shirts, caps, scarves and bags)

Marketing Aids Ltd
64 Southwark Bridge Road, London SE1 0AW
Tel.   01-261 9311
(Business gifts)

Micropharm Ltd
61 Morshead Road, London W9 1LF
Tel.   01-289 6334
(Zip-up bags containing conference survival kit, etc.)

Nickwood Plastics
75/99 Nathan Way, Woolwich Industrial Estate, London
SE28 0BQ
Tel. 01-854 0137
(Plastic binders, clipboards and wallets)

OK Promotions
131 Salisbury Road, London NW6 6RG
Tel. 01-328 4866
(Business gifts)

Pentel Ltd
The Wyvern Estate, Beverley Way, New Malden, Surrey KT3 4PF
Tel. 01-949 5336
(Pens)

Philmar Trading
P.O. Box 10, Rochester, Kent
Tel. 0634 46455
(Conference aids)

Promotion Sourcing Ltd
Thames House, 140 Battersea Park Road, London SW11 4NB
Tel. 01-627 3250
(Sourcing service for conference accessories and business gifts)

Renamel
Cumberland Road, Stanmore, Middx HA7 1QH
Tel. 01-204 9522
(Badges)

Slide Charts Britain Ltd
13 Burcot Park, Burcot, Abingdon, Oxon OX14 3DH
(Specially designed slide charts)

Synapse International
Suite 10a, 140 Park Lane, London W1
Tel. 01-499 5401
(Pen and pencil sets, folding scissors and general business gifts)

TNT Printed Leisurewear
12/14 London Street, Reading RG1 4SG
Tel. 0734 580552
(Printed tee shirts and sweat shirts)

Toye, Kenning and Spencer Ltd
77 Warstone Lane, Birmingham 18
Tel.   021-236 3615
(Badges)

Venture Matches
Best Street, Kirkham, Preston PR4 2JD
Tel.   0772 685119
(Book matches)

Winston Promotions Ltd
9 Hatton Place, Hatton Garden, London EC1N 8RU
Tel.   01-405 0960
(Printed tee shirts)

Insurance services

The following companies specialize in providing insurance cover for conferences.

Expo-sure Limited
51 The Pantiles, Royal Tunbridge Wells, Kent TN2 5TH
Tel.   0892 39506

Exhibition & Conference Insurance Services
Millard House, Cutler Street, London E1 7DJ
Tel.   01-283 3951

Robertson Taylor Insurance Brokers Ltd
Millard House, Cutler Street, London E1 7DJ
Tel.   01-283 3951

Appendix
Sequence of events

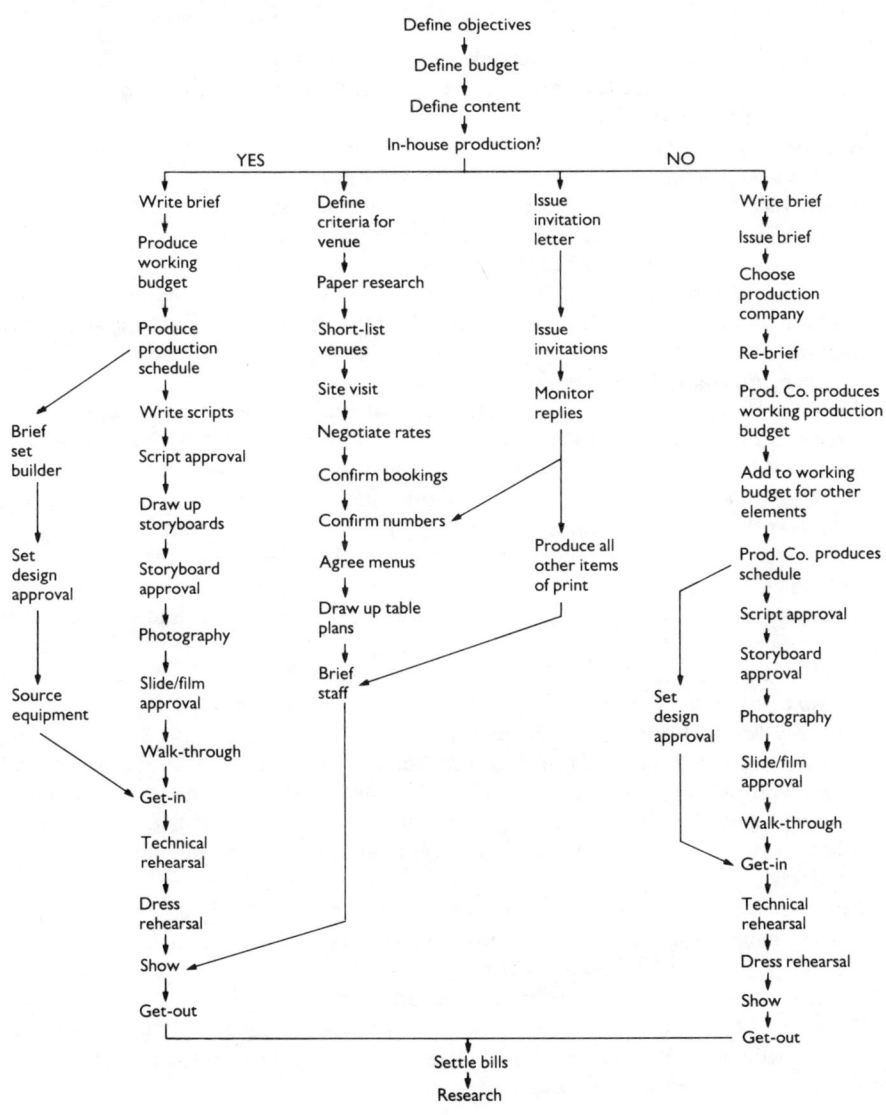

Define objectives
Define budget
Define content
In-house production?

YES   NO

Write brief

Produce
working
budget

Produce
production
schedule

Brief
set
builder

Write scripts

Script approval

Set
design
approval

Draw up
storyboards

Storyboard
approval

Photography

Source
equipment

Slide/film
approval

Walk-through

Get-in

Technical
rehearsal

Dress
rehearsal

Show

Get-out

Define
criteria for
venue

Paper research

Short-list
venues

Site visit

Negotiate rates

Confirm bookings

Confirm numbers

Agree menus

Draw up table
plans

Brief
staff

Issue
invitation
letter

Issue
invitations

Monitor
replies

Produce all
other items
of print

Write brief

Issue brief

Choose
production
company

Re-brief

Prod. Co. produces
working production
budget

Add to working
budget for other
elements

Prod. Co. produces
schedule

Script approval

Storyboard
approval

Set
design
approval

Photography

Slide/film
approval

Walk-through

Get-in

Technical
rehearsal

Dress rehearsal

Show

Get-out

Settle bills
Research

Glossary

Ad Lib Part of a speech not included in the written text.

Animation Technique for simulating movement using slides or a succession of still pictures on film or video tape.

Answer print Final version of a film combining both picture and sound; also known as a 'comopt', meaning a combined optical print.

Audio-visual Usually applied to programmes that use slides and a soundtrack which is on recording tape. The slides are changed at predetermined points in the soundtrack. Also referred to as A-V.

Autocue Electronic teleprompter that presents the speaker's script on a glass screen or television monitor in order that he can look at the audience as he speaks.

Back-projection System of projection where the projectors are placed behind the screen, out of sight of the audience.

Backstage Area behind the set out of sight of the audience. Can be extended to cover all areas of the theatre or conference-centre not accessible to the audience.

Band call Colloquial term for a rehearsal involving musicians.

Black A black is one of two things: a blank slide inserted into the projector, often to clear the screen for a film, or a length of black cloth hung to screen an area off.

Book As in 'The Book', the complete set of scripts for a conference.

Call The time at which those involved in the conference have to be in the conference room; usually used in the context of 'Your call, ladies and gentlemen, is for 9 a.m.'

Cans Headphones, often including a microphone.

Caption generator Used in video and television to provide a word caption to a picture; a form of computer-generated graphics.

Card ice Also known as 'dry ice', it is carbon dioxide in solid form. When dropped into warm water, this gives off a white, harmless vapour which can be spread on stage to give the effect of looking across the top of a cloud. It is frequently used in reveals. It is heavier than air so stays on the ground, and disperses fairly quickly.

Carnet In full, ATA Carnet. A document that is raised to guarantee that goods being temporarily imported into a foreign country will not be sold while they are there. A bond has to be lodged and this can be forfeit if the Carnet is not properly stamped or all the goods on it are not returned to the country of origin.

Carousel Refers to the Kodak projector which has become the industry standard. The carousel itself is the circular slide tray which sits on top of the projector. Now being superseded by the Kodak Ektagraphic.

336

Clunk   Single slide projector which is used without being linked to any others. Often used to superimpose text over a picture. To clunk through a show is to step through all the slide changes without a soundtrack.

Computer graphics   Used in video, film and slides to create images within a computer which can then be transferred on to the preferred medium. Capable of producing stunning effects, but, in its most advanced form, requires a computer with considerable memory and can be very expensive.

Concept   Initial idea for the conference covering theme, running order and set.

Conference   Gathering of people for the purposes of communication, usually in an auditorium or conference room.

Convention   American term sometimes used in Europe as an alternative to 'conference'. In fact, in the USA it is usually used to describe an association meeting.

Crew   Group of specialists who will operate all of the equipment in the conference.

Crossfade   Process of dissolving from one slide on screen to another without a blank in between.

Cue   Signal which a person involved in a conference takes as a signal to peform a task connected with the show.

Cut   As in 'cut to...', denotes a sudden change from one shot to another in video or film.

Cutting copy   Film which an editor cuts up in order to assemble the final version.

Cyclorama   Also known as a 'cyc' (pronounced sike); a curving backdrop which blends smoothly into the floor and so gives the illusion of immense depth to the stage.

DBO   Dead Black Out or the effect of suddenly turning off all of the stage lights.

Dead   Point at which a set of curtains should stop. 'Setting the Dead' is the process of fixing the Dead point.

Delegate   In true terms an individual who represents a group at a conference. In corporate meetings, this term is used to describe all those attending the event who are not involved in running it.

Dissolve   To progress smoothly from one on-screen image to another. This can be either in film or slide. One image fades out as the next is simultaneously faded in. If this is used in an audio-visual presentation, at least two slide projectors will be used. In film, the effect is achieved optically when the film is being prepared.

Dissolve unit   Electronic equipment that controls a group of projectors in order to achieve a dissolve.

Double head   A version of a film preceding the answer print. The picture will be carried on film. The sound will be on perforated recording tape. This type of film needs a double-head projector which has the optical system on one side and the sound system on the other.

Downstage   Area of the stage nearest to the audience.

Dry ice   See 'Card ice'.

Dupe   Copy (or duplicate) of a slide.

Edit suite   Also 'Editing suite'; the area within a video production company used for editing video tapes.

Eidophor   Type of big screen video projector.

ENG   Short for Electronic Newsgathering. Sometimes used as an alternative description for Minicam. Description of small video camera and recorder. Can be operated by two people.

Exciter lamp   Lamp in a film projector which shines through the optical sound-track to enable the projector to reproduce the sound.

Fastfold   Type of screen that is stretched across a folding aluminium frame. Since it has no supporting struts across the screen surface, a Fastfold screen can be used for back projection.

Feedback   Noise heard when a microphone is moved to a position where it can pick up the sounds that are being fed from it into a loudspeaker.

Flashpot   Pyrotechnic device which can be set off electronically to produce an intense flash on stage. Must be used with extreme care.

Flats   Large pieces of set that can be used to build a wall.

Fly   Process of raising a part of the set, an object or a person from the stage upwards. Flies are the ropes or wires used for this. A fly tower is the structure above the stage that allows sufficient room for a set to be flown high enough for it to be out of sight of the audience.

FOH   Front of House or the public areas of a theatre or conference centre.

Foldback   Part of the sound system that enables an on-stage performer to hear himself. Most commonly used for singers.

Follow spot   Spotlight which is designed to allow for the beam to be varied in width and can be swung around to follow a performer on stage. A follow spot operator is the person responsible for using the follow spot.

Forox   Type of specialized camera used for making slides with great precision. Very often computer-controlled, this type of camera is large and fixed in position, usually occupying a room to itself.

Freeze frame   To give the effect of freezing the action of a film on screen. This is achieved by repeat exposures of the appropriate frame in the finished film rather than stopping the projector.

Gaffer tape   All-purpose adhesive tape which is wide but easily torn into strips while retaining its great strength.

Gate   Part of a projector into which the film or a slide is inserted so that the projector bulb can shine through it.

Gauze   Thin fabric which can be hung in front of an object to be revealed. So long as no light is shone directly on to the object behind the gauze, the object will not be seen.

Gel   Film of coloured material which is placed in front of the lens of a stage light in order to colour the light.

Get-in   Process of moving all of the set and equipment for a conference into the venue.

Gobo   Metal screen that is placed in the light beam of a spotlight to project a pattern on to the set. These can be made up in the form of a company's logo.

Grading   Process of adjusting the colour rendition of a film in order to ensure that the colours are correct when it is projected. An ungraded print of the film will show colour variations.

Hash   Electronic interference on the sound system.

Hot spot   Area of a slide which is brighter than the rest of the slide.

Keystoning   Effect created when a projector is shone at an angle on to the screen. If the projector is positioned above the centre-line of the screen and pointed down on to it, the bottom of the image area will be wider than the top. Lenses are available to correct this effect now.

338

Landscape When using 35 mm slides, those that are shot so that they are wider than they are high are said to be in landscape format.

Launch Conference held to announce a new product.

Leader Length of tape or film which leads into the sound recording tape or picture. These are usually coloured to aid identification.

Level Usually associated with sound as in 'Can we have a few words for level please?' This involves the speaker saying something into the microphone so that the sound engineer can establish how much amplification to give.

Lightbox Large table with an opaque top surface which is lit from underneath. Slides can be laid out on the lightbox for checking as in a lightbox review.

Lighting desk Control desk used by the lighting engineer to fade lights up and down.

Line-up Many audio-visual modules use several projectors pointing at the same screen area. So that the module can be seen as apparently all emanating from the same source, all the projectors have to be adjusted so that they are all pointing at precisely the same spot on the screen. The projectionist will need a blackout in order to be able to do a line-up.

Magnetic sound track That part of a film which carries a soundtrack that is recorded on a thin strip of recording tape applied to the edge of the film. An alternative to optical sound track.

Maroon Device that is used to set off an explosion on stage by use of an electrical charge — to be used with extreme care.

Married print Final version of the film carrying both picture and sound.

Master Original soundtrack, film or video tape. To be protected at all costs.

Minicam Sometimes used as alternative description for ENG camera. Small television camera that can be carried by one man.

Mix-Down Combining all of the tracks on a master sound tape on to the number of tracks to be used on-site.

Module Section of the conference which is a self-contained combination of pictures and soundtrack.

Monitor Type of television that can take a direct feed from a video recorder or a computer. Has no ability to tune in to a broadcast television image.

Multiplexer Arrangement of slide projectors and a television camera designed to be used to transfer slides to video.

OB Outside Broadcast. A combination of television equipment that can be used outside a studio. Although described as broadcast, the term is used to describe equipment working to broadcast standards even if it is not transmitting a signal.

OP Opposite Prompt. Stage Right. The side of the stage opposite the traditional position occupied by the prompter in the theatre. In practice, OP means the right of the stage from the point of view of a person standing on stage, facing the audience.

Offline edit Early edited version of a video tape. Since editing of tape is an expensive process, some production companies now produce an early version of the tape for approval. This will reduce the time taken in the editing suite.

Optical sound track That part of a film which carries the soundtrack by means of an optical code which appears alongside the picture. Because the part of the projector which reads this is separated from the gate, the sound that matches a specific frame will be 24 frames ahead of it.

Paintbox Electronic equipment used in video to create and manipulate computer-generated effects. Used in broadcast television to produce weather maps among other things.

Per diems Payments made to the crew in addition to hotel and meal costs. The amount paid will vary depending on the cost of living in the town in which the conference takes place.

Portrait When using 35 mm slides, those that are shot so that they are higher than they are wide are said to be in portrait format.

Producer Individual within a specialist conference production company given the task of coordinating the production of the conference.

Programmer Individual responsible for creating the program for the minicomputer that controls the dissolve units in an audio-visual module.

Prompt side Stage left. The side of the stage traditionally occupied by the prompter in the theatre. In practice, this is the left side of the stage as seen by a person standing on the stage, facing the audience.

Proscenium arch Also called the Pross. or pross. Arch. The structure which borders the stage at the sides and the top when the stage is viewed from the auditorium.

QTV Electronic teleprompting system working on the same principle as autocue.

Quantel Example of the electronic equipment that can be used to manipulate a television picture. It can be used to distort the picture, spin it, zoom it in and out of frame, and many other things besides.

Racking Metal shelving on which projectors stand.

Radio mike Microphone which transmits its signal by radio to a receiver which then feeds it into the sound mixing desk instead of having a cable attached to it which is connected directly to the sound mixing desk.

Raked auditorium Auditorium which rises towards the back. Commonly found in theatres, cinemas and conference centres, it has the advantage that everyone can have a clear view of the stage.

Recce A visit to the venue to check on the facilities.

Register Usually used in the negative sense as in 'out of register', meaning that two slides do not marry up on screen. This can be caused either by a defective line-up or by the slides having been produced out of register.

Reveal Process of showing an object or person to the audience for the first time. Commonly used in new product presentations.

Revolve Turntable that is installed on-stage to enable a part of the set or an object to revolve in front of the audience. May be operated electrically or manually. Trucking revolve is a revolve mounted on wheels in order that it can move across the stage as it turns.

Rig Process of erecting the set and installing all the equipment necessary for the show. This forms part of the get-in.

Riggers Individuals whose job is to rig equipment, usually at high level.

Rostrum Platform on the stage.

Rostrum camera Specialized camera, usually having no visual resemblance to a hand-held camera which is capable of producing slides to very fine tolerances. Forox, Marron-Carrel are two of the better known makes of rostrum camera.

Roughcut The first roughly assembled version of a film. Also applied to video tape although editing video tape involves no cutting as such. The roughcut will have none of the dissolves or other optical tricks which will be incorporated at a later stage of the production.

Rushes Film which is processed quickly in order that it can be viewed the day after shooting. Because video gives an instant playback, there is no equivalent in video.

Scissor jack Mechanical device used to raise an object on stage. May be operated hydraulically or electrically.

Showcaller Person who gives audible cues to the crew during a conference session. The showcaller will call lighting changes, sound cues – in fact every cue that the crew needs to run the show.

Sightline View obtained by a member of the audience sitting in a specific part of the auditorium. Four are usually of interest: the sightlines from the centre of the front row where an individual may be able to see up into the roof above the stage; from the centre back of the auditorium where an individual may be able to see behind low parts of the set; from the extreme left and right of the auditorium where an individual may be able to see into the wings.

Slash Form of curtaining, usually of metallic finish which is cut into narrow strips.

Slash print Early copy of a film which does not yet have optical effects and has not been colour-graded. This will usually have a line running across the picture area where a dissolve is to take place which will have been put on the cutting copy with a chinagraph pencil.

Slide mount Plastic holder into which the slides are set for projection.

Smoke gun Device used to create smoke for use on stage. This hangs in the air, unlike dry ice, and can take a long time to clear. Necessary for lasers if the beam is to be visible.

Snap A sudden change from one slide to another without a dissolve.

Soft edge Device that is used where slides are designed to overlap without the join being visible on screen. This is the slide equivalent of wide-screen in the cinema. It is achieved by mounting an extra piece of film into the slide mount, which has the effect of darkening the edges of the picture.

Sound mixing desk Equipment used by the sound engineer to mix the sounds from different sources before feeding them into the amplifier and thence to the loudspeakers.

Spike Momentary disturbance of the power supply which can be disastrous in a modern conference since much of it will depend on computers which will be disrupted by a mains spike.

Stacker Equipment which allows slide projectors to be stacked one above the other and still allow room for the slide tray to be changed.

Stage Area of the conference room on which the speakers stand to deliver scripts.

Stage left Area of the stage to the left of a person standing on stage and facing the audience. Also known as 'prompt side'.

Stage manager When a complex conference is being organized with many backstage movements and speakers to be cued on, a stage manager may be employed to make sure that everything backstage happens as it should.

Stage right Area of the stage to the right of a person standing on stage and facing the audience. Also known as 'opposite prompt' (or OP) side.

Stagger through First rehearsal which staggers slowly through the conference. Can be used to describe either a walk-through or the rehearsal before a walk-through.

Storyboard Sequence of hand-drawn pictures which illustrates what will be seen on screen. Can be used for speaker support or audio-visual modules.

Stretch screen Screen which is stretched from several points rather than being attached to a frame. This type of screen can be virtually any shape that is wanted. Often used where no other set is to be installed.

Strike To remove the set from the venue.

Strobe Stage light which flashes quickly. If used with dancers on stage, this can create the effect of slow-motion movement.

Super To superimpose one image on another. Usually used to describe the superimposition of words on a picture as in 'We will super the sales figures over the product shot'.

Superslide Slide with a mount of the same external dimensions as a 35 mm slide but with an image area of 46 mm by 46 mm.

Sync Synchronization of sound and picture. Lip sync is the description of the technique of someone being seen talking on screen at the same time as his voice is heard.

TABS Curtains at the front of the stage.

Tab track Track from which the curtains or tabs are hung.

Talkback System allowing all the members of the crew to converse. This involves each of them having a set of cans (headphones and microphone) and is usually controlled by the showcaller.

Tech Technical rehearsal, organized to familiarize the crew with the content of the show.

Thrust stage Stage which projects into the auditorium, possibly with the audience sitting around it.

Tray Receptical that holds the slides and is positioned on top of a Carousel or Ektagraphic slide projector.

Tray change Since a Carousel tray holds only 80 slides (an Ektagraphic tray holds more), a long show may require that the trays be changed while some action is happening on stage.

Treatment Written description of what will happen in a conference, video tape or film.

Truck Also known as a stage truck. A platform on wheels which can be moved or trucked on to and off the stage.

Truss Metal structure at high level from which the stage lights are hung.

Upstage Area of the stage furthest from the audience.

Venue Place where the conference is to be held. Usually describes the actual building rather than the town or country.

Video projector Electronic equipment capable of projecting a video or television image on to a screen.

Voice-over Soundtrack which provides a commentary where the commentator is not seen.

VT Video tape.

Walk-in music Music soundtrack played as the audience walks into the auditorium.

Walk-in state Sound and lighting state set for the moment when the audience enters the auditorium.

Walk-out music   Music soundtrack played as the audience leaves the auditorium.

Wings   The areas at the side of the stage out of sight of the audience.

Zoom   To move in on an image. In film or video, this can be a smooth movement. In slides, it will be a stepped progression, described as a five-part zoom if the movement takes place in five parts.

Zoom lens   Lens that can be adjusted to change the size of the projected image. Commonly used in smaller shows when the exact distance from the screen to the projector is not known in advance or will change between venues.

Index